Field Theory

Curriculum Studies at Work

David P. Owen, Jr. (Ed.)

ISBN 978-1-64504-023-1 (Hardback)
ISBN 978-1-64504-022-4 (Paperback)
ISBN 978-1-64504-024-8 (E-Book)

Printed on acid-free paper

This book is part of the *Critical Pedagogies* Series
Series Editor: Shirley R. Steinberg

Acknowledgments

I would like to thank all of the teachers and theorists in my life who have shown me that each job can be more than we usually expect of it. I would like to thank John A. Weaver, in particular, for encouraging me for years now to pursue this project, and also Shirley Steinberg for believing in this book from the start. They, like Stacey T. Brown, John Cato, James Grant, and Dana Compton McCullough, are true teacher-theorists interested in asking what education can mean and be, never satisfied that we have done all we can do.

I would also like to thank Courtney and Patrick—my favorite teacher and my favorite student—for being constant reminders of why this kind of work is so important.

Table of Contents

Foreword

An Intellectual Life

An American Tragedy

John A. Weaver

Whenever a doctoral candidate successfully defends their work and earns their Ed.D. at Georgia Southern University, I like to keep up with those students to see what they do afterwards. An Ed.D., like a Ph.D. or and M.D. or J.D., is a terminal degree; therefore, the person with this title has earned the right to finally educate themselves. One of our students upon graduation ran for the Georgia state house, lost, ran for county commissioner and won. Another formed a group for women and progressive politics and helped flip a House of Representatives seat that Newt Gingrich once occupied. Another student has set a goal of visiting 50 countries before she turns 50. Her partner will retire soon, return to improvisational acting, and write plays. They have all earned this right of self-determination in a land that pays lip service to the idea but allows very few people the means to do so. The teachers assembled in this collection all graduated from Georgia Southern University's curriculum studies Ed.D. program, and all have decided they want to continue on their own intellectual journey. This is a rare occurrence, unfortunately. Most graduates of any terminal degree rarely continue on any kind of intellectual path. These five scholars have elected to stay on this path of curiosity, intellectual creativity, disciplined reading, and creative writing. The unfortunate part is not that most terminal degree graduates do not continue along an intellectual path; it is, in regards to teachers, that public schools afford little opportunity to be an intellectual and a teacher at the same time. Because of a decades-long influence of neoliberal and conservative forces, public education has been intentionally starved. The students and teachers in these institutions are intellectually emaciated, yet these five teachers have found a way to feed themselves and their

David P. Owen, Jr (ed.), *Field Theory: Curriculum Studies at Work*, ix–xiv.

students. What you will read in the chapters to follow are attempts to be a teacher and an intellectual; a practitioner of the art of teaching and a theoretician. These teachers prove one can be both. And, more importantly, they prove the United States, an intellectually dead society, desperately needs teachers to be both, but as a nation, the United States is unwilling to afford teachers the time to do either. As a result, dear reader, do not underestimate the great sacrifice these teachers have had to make in order to live the life of an intellectual. Society mocks them; their institutions erect barriers against them; anti-intellectual politicians undermine them; business leaders, the false prophets of our age, abuse them; and parents for the most part disrespect them and want to only know if their child is prepared to go to the best university with a strong return on investment. As a reader, do not join this mob. Respect and honor these teachers who have made the intellectual commitment you should aspire to as well.

Poetic Living

Most of our students, when they enter our curriculum studies program, experience a culture shock. It is not something they are used to academically. David Owen, though, lived a life of academic vigor before he started his doctoral journey. David was a poet before he entered our program and remains a poet today. His first chapter, "Field Theory: The Possibility of a *Search*," proves this point immediately when he opens with one of his own poems, "Teaching and Learning." When I read this poem I returned to a poem by Tony Hoagland (2015), "Ode to the Republic," that describes the reality of U.S. decline in the world. Poetry allows us to live a life in the real, not some fantasy of world dominance and greatness. It allows us to express how the United States is crumbling but we are too proud to admit it, and how schools have been hollowed out by low standards, greed, reductionist economics, puppet politicians, faithless Christians, and meaningless standardized tests. All of these valueless values and people are the result of policies to not allow teachers to teach students about reality. The conservative political philosopher Leo Strauss (1952) in his book, *Persecution and the Art of Writing*, noted that when society is more autocratic and dictatorial, the writers become more cryptic. Poetry is not a cryptic form, but it is a means of expressing a cryptic message about a repressive society that is intolerant of alternative ways of acting, being, and thinking. To live today poetically is to live an intellectual life as a voice of resistance against the reductionist forces of economics, religion, and politics. Life is about economics, religion, and politics, but when it is all that is allowed in society, poetry must rescue us from this death grip. David is here to help us to see our repression and light a way out.

Blessed Solitude

David has always been a light. He was the first person from his high school to enter into our program, and there are now seven of his colleagues who have either graduated from or are in our program. The second person was Stacey Brown. Stacey is interested in carving out some space for needed solitude in order to read, think, and write. I should not have to explain the difference between solitude and loneliness, but most people in the United States are lonely. Solitude is where one retreats to understand the world and self. It is an empowering and a refreshing place. It is, as Stacey writes, "fertile soil." Loneliness is where people are afraid; therefore, they seek out constant entertainment and quick, passive occupation. This is why the United States has so many smartphone users. It is sad to see so many lonely young people sitting in a crowd together mesmerized by the glow of their phones. Why are schools such crowded lonely places? Stacey provides an answer: "the soil we till in education is barren." The only way out of a barren land is through an intellectual journey, but what does it say about a nation when their intellectual institutions have been purposely hollowed out? Where do people turn for nourishment from fertile soil? Stacey turned to philosophy and literature. Still fruitful soil, too often marginalized in public schools and universities.

Ugly James

James Grant is an ugly person. I can attest to that—I served on his committee. He even admits it in a story he tells about seventh grade. Here is the rub, though: James is not referring to an ugliness often juxtaposed to beauty. James's ugliness is an aesthetically pleasing idea. We need more ugly teachers like James. Schooling has become a beautiful façade. The success of a school is reported through neat, scrubbed data; students pass well-ordered standardized tests to testify to the truthfulness of their knowledge acquisitions; curriculum is delivered in smooth, easy-going bite-size chunks; and schools pretend in a pristine world no student is addicted to drugs, abstinence sex education will prevent teen pregnancy, money does not matter, and all children are equal no matter the circumstances in which they live. It is a beautiful fantasy world adults live in. Nice and clean. We need more ugly teachers to break up this dangerous, unrealistic, delusional state. Learning is uncertain and risky. One cannot learn without taking a risk of admitting one does not know something. This risk makes one vulnerable, yet this is the only way one can learn. Teaching is messy. One student gets what you as a teacher are trying to convey, another one does not care for any number of reasons, another one just lost a parent to drug rehab, again. Still another has just been kicked out of their house because they came out to their fundamentalist parents. Hopefully you get the picture. Every student is different and approaches your class differently, yet you are judged by unqualified politicians, business people, and administrators who live the delusional fantasy of simple similarity. Schooling should be chaos in an ugly environment. Too much order from this chaos, and it creates a sanitary murder scene. The art of teaching and leading in a school system is to let meanings emerge from the chaos. Once these meanings emerge, then let the students and teachers determine how to develop them. The bitter irony of public schools today is they proclaim to be preparing young people for the "real world", yet there is nothing real about standardized tests, the reduction of learning to economics and a stagnant business model, or the idea that everyone should learn the same thing. Reality is ugly, and I am not referring to all the wars, disease, and poverty in the world. These are ugly realities. I am referring to how we create space to construct intellectual gratification. James knows what I am talking about because he is ugly. Are you?

Loafing

The first time I met Dana McCullough I asked her if she had read Rebecca Skloot's book. That was the beginning of her trek in not only understanding the life of Henrietta Lacks but also understanding how to approach teaching and learning from a very different perspective. Dana does not use the word loafing in her play, but I know she understands that term in its full Whitmanesque context. Most United States citizens find the word loafing distasteful. For them loafing means someone is lazy and unproductive, and in capitalist America those are mortal sins. What is an even more mortal sin, though, is a lack of imagination and an inability to foresee alternative ways of living in the world. Walt Whitman, the American poet whom the United States rejected, saw loafing as a form of solitude, a way of learning, and a way of being in the world. Thoreau also knew this alternative notion of loafing. Loafing is knowing your basic needs, your true passion, and working to achieve both. Whitman was a teacher, carpenter, Civil War administrator, and a newspaper editor during his lifetime, but they were not his vocations. By vocation and avocation Whitman was a poet, and he worked those other jobs in order to make enough money to take care of his basic needs. And once those needs were met, he spent the rest of the year honing his craft, poetry. Thoreau worked two months of the year for his basic needs and spent ten months doing whatever he wanted to do. U.S. citizens today are so impoverished with their wealth that they work 12 months of the year for two weeks off, if they are lucky, and weekends so some billionaire can do whatever he (usually a *he* isn't it!) wants and proclaim he amassed his wealth all by himself. How insane can people be? As a result we have become what Robert Harrison (1992) correctly describes as a nation of debtors, gossipers, property owners, and spectators. Dana is no debtor, gossiper, or spectator. She may own property, but it does not own her. She is a loafer. A biology teacher who teaches the history of science to her students and all the racism and exploitation of poor people that goes along with it. In the time she has carved out for herself, she writes plays. I hope you will become a loafer, historian of science, and playwright. When you do, make sure you say hello to Dana and me. We will be loafing in our own ways alongside you.

That Lying Cato

I am not referring to the Cato Institute, that libertarian think-tank bankrolled by the billionaire Koch brothers, who love busting unions and then proclaiming everyone should be free from need and want from the federal government. Libertarianism is a rich person's philosophy that believes if a rich person can live without government support, then all people should. How is that for a big lie? I am referring to John Cato. He admits to being a liar in his first chapter, so we should take him at his word. Not true? Well maybe not, because when he admits to lying he speaks the truth. John riffs off of the novel, *Life of Pi*, and speaks about his own intellectual biography and how he went from public school mediocrity, to West Point plebe, to physics teacher. In his journey he acknowledges that intellectual journeys are autopoietic and poietic. These are two complimentary but separate concepts. To be autopoietic means to be a self-sustaining creature, but one that depends on environments to be self-sustaining. It is a biological concept that proves the political philosophy of libertarianism false. Autopoiesis has great import for the classroom. The classroom is the environment, and the students and the teachers are self-sustaining organisms who will thrive or stagnate depending on how well each organism will sustain the others. The more intellectually vibrant the environment, the more the students and teacher will thrive. This is very different from most public school classrooms, in which the prevailing assumption is most students will only grow a little each year and the school officials have the test scores and I.Q. exams to prove their assertion. Students are limited as soon as they enter these schools and they become self-fulling prophesies, and the school officials see them graduate in 13 years and say to themselves, "See, I told you they would not amount to much." In an autopoietic classroom, students are not limited by test scores that mean nothing and adult assumptions about their intellectual abilities. They are only limited by how vibrant or not the classroom is. The more vibrant a classroom, the more students will intellectually grow. This holds true for the teacher as well.

Poiesis is different. The word is Greek and it means to produce. Poetry is a production, an invention. It is even one you can patent. Got your Americanized attention now, didn't I? Standardized tests, set curricula, and data-driven learning are not poetic at all. It is intellectual stagnation resulting in death. Poiesis, on the other hand, is a craft that must be honed by decades of practice. It is writing, reading, thinking, science, history, mathematics, the arts, and literature. All classrooms should be poetic. When this happens, it will lead to real production. Not production for someone else, for some testing service, some business owner, or politician. These forms of production are merely demands made by parasites. Real production is self-sustaining, self-satisfying in a deep manner that transforms the person and all who are around her. *Life of Pi* transformed John Cato, and Cato's story may transform you. That would be poetic.

References

Harrison, R. (1992). *Forests: The shadow of civilization*. Chicago, IL: University of Chicago Press.

Hoagland, T. (2015). *Application for the release from the dream*. Minneapolis, MN: Graywolf.

Strauss, L. (1952). *Persecution and the art of writing*. Chicago, IL: University of Chicago Press.

Preface

Field Theory

David P. Owen, Jr.

This is my third book of cultural curriculum theory, and though I have discussed it in both of the other books, I am going to say it here, again, in this one: I teach at a high school. I write curriculum theory when I can, and I teach at a high school. I think my desire to repeat this fact again and again stems from my need to acknowledge its strangeness, its wonder to me in ways both personal and professional. I still find it strange that I teach, and also that I write; neither would have seemed probable to me as a child, and both still surprise me from time to time, even though I've been working at both things for years now. I am happy to be here, in this strange teacher-theorist space, but not exactly sure by which path I arrived.

It is true, of course, that neither teaching nor curriculum theory is very strange on its own, despite the strangeness I feel at being part of them; we have long determined that our young people should be taught, and it only makes sense that some of us should think deeply about what that education should look like. It is the professional strangeness of the teacher-theorist this book will address, though, the person who both teaches and theorizes about that teaching. It is a strangeness so plain, so visible, that we do not really see it, so much at home that we do not really address it. I do what I can to contribute to the "abstract" notions of the curriculum field my colleagues often complain isn't "practical" enough, and when I do, other theorists sometimes encourage me to "get out of the classroom more," leave practical matters alone in order to see the big pictures more clearly. I don't often know exactly how to answer either group, but I do know that it is strange to be a teacher who writes theory, and I would love to play a part in making it less so. However, I have also found that it is wonder-full to be a teacher-theorist, and I would love to play a part in making it more so.

I have come to call this unsettled feeling, this hyphenated, not-quite, between-worlds, extra-disciplinary existence "liminal scholarship," and I

David P. Owen, Jr (ed.), Field Theory: Curriculum Studies at Work, xv–xix.

have encouraged others like me for years now to "make a home of our homelessness, and serve as conduits for the open transit of ideas across academy thresholds" (Owen, 2011, p. 2). I still think there is much to be done "in the windows and doorways of the academy, now at the conference table or library, now in the hallways, now in the open air of the world 'outside the field,' lest those spaces-between where the inside and outside commingle become instead impermeable walls" (p. 2). And I think a good place to begin a new "complicated conversation" (Pinar, 2007, p. 8) about curriculum is with the deconstruction of one of the many binaries our culture seems to take as conventional wisdom: the oft-repeated idea that "teachers" are practitioners, and "professors" are theorists.

Why, after all, do we maintain this particular binary structure? Is it, in fact, good for us somehow, in the way that each profession, the teacher or the theorist, might be thought to contain a kind of curricular specialist? Or do we just encourage, explicitly and implicitly, professors to be poor teachers and teachers to be poor intellectuals? Surely some of the division is pragmatic, built-in to the day-to-day realities of each job. Teachers, I am all too aware, have very little time to think—though I assert that this does seem ironic in a profession that professes to encourage thought and develop critical thinking skills. Maybe we are supposed to save our thinking for summer? It is true, though, that so many of us wonder when we might eat lunch or take a restroom break during the school day, let alone construct our lessons and assessments with the care, creativity, thoughtfulness, and reflection our young people deserve, that it is easy to see why teachers don't produce much curriculum theory. "When," I can hear teachers asking me now, "are we going to write books?" The professor's day, it is also true, is much better suited to theoretical pursuits. The schedule is more flexible, the course load and social-savior duties are lighter—and the pressure to publish (or perish, as the saying goes) is much, much greater. Teachers get paid to teach, it seems, while professors get paid to publish theory. Farmers of different fields, so to speak?

Still, though, there are exceptions in both fields. In fact, most of my best teachers were professors, as it happened, and served as excellent models of how it might be done at the university level. I was granted long, winding conversations outside of office hours; special research opportunities to match my curiosities; intellectual freedom to pursue questions outside of the established course syllabus; and lunches and dinners at which the brain was fed as much as the stomach. In fact, once a professor—Dr. Jonathan Evans, widely respected scholar of Medieval British literature—even joined my band on the blues harp for a few midnight shows in dark music venues in Athens, Georgia. These people were and are powerful theorists and teachers too, and they deserve more credit than I can give them for much of what is good about my intellectual life. And so it is in the other, "teacher" field, perhaps, where we ought to begin this conversation in earnest, because while I know many people who can name a theorist who is also a great teacher, I know very few who can name a teacher who is a theorist at all. And that, it should be noted, includes many of my own students and colleagues. Like high school teachers everywhere, I keep attendance, monitor hallways, grade tests and papers, examine data, prep for standardized tests, attend meetings—and largely keep my own intellectual pursuits, curricular though they may be, to myself and after-hours. I am as tired as we all are, and have as much trouble as the next guy trying to figure out when and how I might do the work I'm advocating in this book, let alone bring it up in a workplace conversation. Make no mistake, what I am beginning to propose here will be hard.

In fact, let's just be frank: I really don't have time to write and edit this book. I work on projects like this before my family gets up and after they go to sleep, and sometimes sleep seems like the better, or at least more necessary, option. Sure, I could carve out some Saturdays here and there, or hide away in an upstairs room for chunks of time during the summer, but that would be hard to justify to my family. After all, I expect to make roughly $0 from this work, and it would be hard to explain how my family will benefit in any direct way from this book finding its way into the world. And if I decide to attend conferences to discuss/publicize this work, *maybe* improve its use and circulation, I will have to pay for flights, hotels, and conference fees out of pocket—it will *cost* us money. Neither will it help me achieve some advancement in my career; there is hardly such a thing as "advancement" in teaching, nor workplace incentives to undertake this kind of project. This book, at least as things currently stand, occupies the space in my life where we put our "passions" or "hobbies," but that also means that an author I approach for this collection might decide to take up tennis instead, or just take it easy.

In short, this is a lot to ask of people, myself included. But it is still worth asking, and I have hope that we can find room for thinking and theorizing in public education in the future. Right now, I have time only to *do* my job; maybe we will figure out how to find time to *think about how to do* our jobs—or even to think about *why* we do our jobs. And until then, this kind of work, this teacher-theorist life, will still not be impossible, as this book attests. High school has not been much of an intellectual place for a long time now, if it ever really was, and it seems to be continually moving away from the deep and careful thinking that are the hallmarks of the theorist. But our world needs all the deep and careful thinking it can get, and maybe we in the more "practical" field are shirking part of our duty when we leave these things out of the "day-to-day." Fortunately, the people featured in these pages are not ready to give up that particular fight for the soul of who we are and what we do; they are people for whom "school spirit" might mean much more than wearing the right t-shirt to the pep rally—and I am sure there are many others out there, whose works I hope to read in future books. *Near* future. The authors of these chapters are extensively educated, highly trained theorists, doctors of curriculum studies who work in our public schools (some of them in my own school, just down the hall), and we should both celebrate their work as teacher-theorists and also follow their example.

I should note, as well, that the work collected here is quite varied; just as it is obviously true that public school teachers are not the mindless automatons state and federal governments sometimes seem to wish, or at least assume, we are, so it is obviously true that the theory these teachers produce must also vary, quite naturally, in style and content and interest and concern. For example, in addition to conventional-looking scholarship, this book also contains meaningful autobiography, poetry, scenes from a play, a chapter that comes with a soundtrack, and another chapter from John Cato that exists somewhere between forms. Is he recounting a story he once told, or is he telling it now? And as for the subjects of these particular curriculum studies, they vary widely as well. I use concepts from a novel by Walker Percy (Chapter 1) to advocate a *search* for ourselves, examine America's complex relationship with drugs (Chapter 9), and explore the band Wilco's navigation of contemporary popular art (Chapter 11). Stacey T. Brown teases out the important difference between solitude and isolation in scholarship (Chapter 2) and decries the growing monoculture of public education (Chapter 6). James Grant advocates the inclusion of the ugly in our studies (Chapter 3) and shows us what lessons might be learned from horror, even headlessness (Chapter 10). John Cato illustrates in form and argument the place of storytelling in science (Chapter 4) and tries to save us, and public education, from yet another "con"—his way of describing the latest, greatest educational push from big government/corporate America, whatever it happens to be tomorrow (Chapter 8). And Dana Compton McCullough refuses to let the story of Henrietta Lacks go untold any longer (Chapter 5); she even takes a shot at telling it herself, or at least what it might look like if the story were told in school (Chapter 7). All told, this book is full of curricular explorations of fields of many kinds and the fences that would like to keep them apart. What unites these chapters is the still lively mind of the public school teacher, and the intellectual curiosity in all of us that cannot be killed—not even by whatever federal program is on its way next.

As all of these scholars remind us, we should not let specialization and workplace burden be an excuse to do only part of our jobs; we are, *all*, to think deeply and critically about our world, and also to lead our students in learning how to do the same. It is our responsibility to ourselves and our communities and our countries to be the teacher-theorists our curriculum deserves. Let us go on a search for that version of ourselves and our curriculum, difficult though it may be. Let us go on a *search*, and start today.

References

Owen, Jr., D. P. (2011). *The need for revision: Curriculum, literature, and the 21st century.* Rotterdam, NL: Sense Publishers.

Pinar, W. F. (2007). *Intellectual advancement through disciplinarity: Veriticality and horizontality in curriculum studies.* Rotterdam, NL: Sense Publishers.

Chapter 1

The Possibility of a *Search*

David P. Owen, Jr.

Teaching and Learning

The taillights pull
and I reluctantly
pledge allegiance to the
proposition that all men are created
equally capable of choosing
the right bubble to fill
the holes in our questions before
they burst and shards of
hope that can't be held
together by soap and water
scatter on cheap tile
and wait,
fodder for the push broom
of sneering, cruel history.
(Owen, 2017)

*   *   *

David P. Owen, Jr (ed.), Field Theory: Curriculum Studies at Work, 1–18.

The Possibility of a *Search*

I am an American. I am a Christian. I am a teacher. I am David Patrick Owen, Jr., a forty-two-year-old man who needs to go on a search for the soul, the identity, of his country and his vocation and his faith and himself. I must admit that all four are sunk in what Walker Percy calls "everydayness," a kind of unthinking, unaware haze that gives us nothing but the ignorance of our own despair. And as Percy reminds us by quoting Kierkegaard in the front of his novel *The Moviegoer* (1961/1998), "the specific character of despair is precisely this: it is unaware of being despair." It seems that we are all—America, Christianity, me—trucking along in an empty race with no prize other than the end of the day, or the year, or maybe even the calendar. And we have brought this empty race into our schools.

Along the way, we are also far more often characterized by hate and fear and condescension than by the love and grace that are supposed to be our foundations. And we are too often unwilling to acknowledge this; we close our eyes to what we ought to see, drown out the voices to which we should listen, and wall off our hearts to what we ought to feel. We claim to have all the answers, though we often refuse to even ask the questions, pressing ever outward while what is inward grows more and more sick. We have forgotten what James B. Macdonald taught us in "An Image of Man" (1964/1995), that openness, not tunnel vision, is the key to reaching our personal, spiritual, and national goals: "to be open to life is the maximal condition for developing human potential" (p. 20). But I am an American. I am a Christian. I am a teacher. I am David Patrick Owen, Jr., and I say I, we, need to change our course; we need to *revise* (Owen, 2011); we need to look, and listen, and feel what it is that we are, and determine what we want to be. I want to believe in my country, and my church, and my job, and myself, but I have work to do—we have work to do. We need to search for what life can be, for what we want it to be, and be open to what we find. We need to *search*.

I Still Haven't Found What I'm Looking For

Irish band U2 wrote their 1987 album, *The Joshua Tree,* inspired by their extensive experience touring in America, and their love affair with what they found, or at least what America can mean at its best. The album is certainly no simple love letter to the United States, however; images like "bullets" and "blood" play just as prominently as "liberty" and "hope," and for every soaring, uplifting chorus or goosebump-inducing guitar line, there is a matching vocal growl or stabbing, abrasive squeal from the instruments. Sometimes the drums and bass are propulsive, and sometimes they are ominous. Also, while *The Joshua Tree* is—like America—personal, spiritual, and idealistic, it is just as frustrated in all three aspects. In short, whether the album's "I Still Haven't Found What I'm Looking For" is directly related to America or not, it works perfectly as an expression of what so many people have seen when they look at this country. We have done and tried much, but there is still much to do and try; we, too, still haven't found what we're looking for. William F. Pinar apparently has not, either, even if he is primarily concerned with the field of curriculum studies in *Intellectual Advancement Through Disciplinarity: Verticality and Horizontality in Curriculum Studies* (2007). According to Pinar, we in education today have given in to a kind of "presentism" in which we ignore those who have come before us, who have spoken in the "already-existing conversation" (p. xi) in which we are now speaking. And not only do we too often ignore our curricular forefathers and mothers, as well as our own past in education, but we also "treat our contemporaries not much better," because we are buried in the day-to-day grind of "'classroom' issues" (p. xi). The problem with this, though, is that "linking lived experience to scholarship is exactly the academic enterprise," and without the "labor of comprehension, critique, and reconceptualization," we will scarcely be able to "contribute to the field's intellectual advancement and to [our] own" (p. xii).

Pinar's recommendation for how to remedy this situation is what he calls an attention to "verticality" and "horizontality" (p. xiii). By *verticality* he means the "intellectual history of the discipline" (p. xiii), which "documents the ideas that constitute curriculum studies" (p. xiv). By *horizontality* he means "analyses of present circumstances" (p. xiv). We need to look both into our past and at the world around us in the present in order to better know who we are, how we got that way, and what we want to do next. Though Pinar reminds us that we "are participating in a conversation larger, more complex, and finally elusive than any single individual or school of thought can grasp" (p. xiv), it is a conversation we must have, and must continue to have.

Pinar is not only right about the field of curriculum studies, but he is also really onto something that resonates nearly everywhere we turn. U2 tapped into the same current on *The Joshua Tree*, looking into the personal, spiritual, and political past and also at the world they saw around them, and realizing that they still needed to keep looking for the life we have all promised ourselves. Walker Percy, almost uncannily, said some very similar things in his 1961 novel, *The Moviegoer*. Percy's protagonist,

Binx Bolling, is a man who cannot quite find his place in the world. He is reasonably smart, likable, wealthy, and good-looking, and he is also a general disappointment to all of those close to him, though none of them is sure exactly what he ought to be doing with his life. He is both unsatisfied and all too satisfied with it; for example, he is a "stock and bond broker" (p. 9) who is very good at his job and yet cares very little for it. In fact, he often paradoxically gets lost in the very "everydayness" (p. 13) that he despises, that means of living in which we simply go along with our days, oblivious to most everything about them, stuck in that hollow routine of mindless work, mindless small talk, mindless television and then sleep, which also sounds a lot like Pinar's description of the current state of public education and curriculum studies. Come to think of it, Percy's *everydayness* sounds like the current state of a lot of things. This is really no surprise, however; at their roots, curriculum questions are questions about who we are, and who we want to be, in the biggest picture we can draw. Not only does it make sense that the world inside education often parallels the world outside of it, but perhaps we should also start our curricular inquiries sometimes with the people we are outside the classroom, in order to better decide what we should bring into it. If we can do this, perhaps we will be able to help our students do it, too.

And that is where the "possibility of a search" (p. 10) comes in; as Binx says, "the search is what anyone would undertake if he were not sunk in the everydayness of his own life" (p. 13)—to find something else, something more, to see familiar things in a new way, to understand truth, and maybe to find God in the process, whatever that means to the person on the search. In short, though his terminology is different, Binx says we need a kind of personal and spiritual *"revision"* (Owen, 2011)—that is, we need "an iterative, recurrent way of seeing, of thinking, of reading and writing in a dynamic world; I mean *revision* as a positive and possibility-full way of life." In addition, U2 urges us onto it, and so does Pinar, and they both realize that the stakes are high. Binx's life is a perfect example, and he knows it: "to become aware of the possibility of the search is to be onto something. Not to be onto something is to be in despair" (p. 13). This passage echoes Aldous Huxley's assertion that "most men and women lead lives at the worst so painful, at the best so monotonous, poor and limited that the urge to escape, the longing to transcend themselves if only for a few moments, is and has always been one of the principal appetites of the soul" (1954, p. 62). For example, Binx goes to the movies to stave off the *everydayness*, just like a lot of us do, both literally and figuratively. But The Movies are only a temporary relief and will not hold off despair forever, and besides, even Binx knows that they too often "screw it up," having a hero off on the *search* who nevertheless eventually "settles down with a vengeance," and "in two weeks time" is so "sunk in everydayness that he might just as well be dead" (p. 13).

And so, Binx says, if we want to overcome the *everydayness*, the despair of our own existence, then we must go on a *search*, we must "*revise*"; we must go on it ourselves, and with open eyes, and an honest heart, and we must not ever settle down "with a vengeance" lest we slip again into despair. We must keep in mind, though, that the *search* has no set path or direction; there is no "five-step plan," no neatly-colored-and-boxed-and-buzzworded chart for a trip into the mystical and spiritual realms, or a journey into the true heart of things. There is no easy, clear-cut way to understand the concepts and emotions we find most important but cannot quantify, like *love* or *country* or *faith* or *self*. Luckily, we do not just have to take Binx's word for what a *search* is like, since Percy gives us some guidance we can use in our own lives through Binx's mostly interior-monologue descriptions of aspects of the *search* that are scattered throughout the novel. And we should not be put off by Binx's own struggles with the *search*. Rather than dismiss these ideas as the well-intentioned slacker dreams of a man who is like the friend we all have, always just on the cusp of getting his life together, we should look at them the way we look at our Declaration of Independence; things like "liberty," "equality," and "self-evident" truths might be wonderful, if we ever actually tried them. But trying them, it turns out, is hard.

Besides, Binx even has a couple of ideas about the *search* that correspond pretty neatly with Pinar's notions of *verticality* and *horizontality* in curriculum studies. As Binx says, during one "vertical search," he "stood outside the universe and sought to understand it" (p. 69); in other words, he took his mind out of its place and time and applied it to all places in all times, much like Pinar does when he listens to all the voices of the "complicated conversation" that have come before him. On the other hand, when Binx goes on a "horizontal search," he reports that "what is important is what I shall find when I leave my room and wander in the neighborhood" (p. 70). In these efforts, he studies the world around him in his particular place and time. On a *vertical search*, he might read intently and then "wander as a diversion"; on a *horizontal search*, he might "wander seriously and sit and read as a diversion" (p. 70). Just as in Pinar's ideas about curriculum, though, both are equally important.

Other aspects of the *search* are also important, and also applicable to curriculum studies both in and out of the classroom, particularly *certification, repetition, rotation, malaise,* and *wonder.* By *certification,* Binx means the curious property of those events and objects that we believe provide "one's right to exist" (p. 7) as a "person who is Somewhere and not Anywhere" (p. 63), like a driver's license, for example, or a ticket stub, or a diploma—or a teaching certificate. A *repetition* is the "re-enactment of past experience" (p. 79-80) so that the "time segment" between those events can be isolated and "savored of itself"; we can look at all the life between those two twin events in order to understand it better. A *rotation* is the best we can hope for in life, seemingly, since it is the "experiencing of the new beyond the expectation of the experiencing of the new" (p. 144), or those blessed moments when we discover the future held more than we thought it might. The *malaise* is the opposite *search* experience, when the *search* is frustrated, and the "world is lost" (p. 120) to us to the extent that we are "no more able to be in the world than Banquo's ghost."

Malaise often kills a *search*, but the *wonder* can start it anew. The *wonder*, which we are often distracted from, is like the moment when we realize there is in each tiny instant more to the world than we thought, in detail and possibility, and it can come from something as simple as finally seeing what we have looked at countless times. It is like the awe, the wordless appreciation of the beauty of life as it might be, if we just looked hard enough. As Binx puts it, "a man can look at this little pile on his bureau for thirty years and never once see it" (p. 11). But Binx finally does see it, and it looks both "unfamiliar" and "full of clues" (p. 11). And this is how our world must look to us, too, if we are to have "the possibility of a search," if we are to "*revise*" (Owen, 2011). We must look in familiar places and see things we have not seen if we want to find what we're looking for.

Certification

One familiar thing we must look at in a fresh way is *certification*. Binx Bolling admits that he loves *certification*, and it is easy to understand why, since it does in some ways give us a "right to exist" (Percy, 1961/1998, p. 7), and can often help relieve *everydayness*. We all have felt, at one time or another, Binx's joy at obtaining a "receipt" of some kind that recognizes the things we have done, or a "neat styrene card with one's name on it," even if few of us would go so far as to exclaim "what satisfaction I take in appearing the first day to get my auto tag and brake sticker!" (p. 7). Even if I do not get so excited about renewing my tag, I have to admit that the very first time I did so was one of the most exciting times of my life. I see dozens of students every year fall under that same joyous spell when they finally get their driver's license and spend the next few weeks showing anyone who will look and feign interest. We have also no doubt felt the warm sense of pride of a man who "sees a movie which shows his very neighborhood" (p. 63), and feels, maybe for the first time, like his hometown actually exists in a way it did not before. I have felt this sensation, too, any time my college campus made the broadcast of *College GameDay* on ESPN, especially if I saw someone I knew or a building where I met for class.

There is something hopeful, and vindicating, about *certification* as Percy describes it. We get diplomas and degrees when we graduate from educational programs as an important and recognizable sign of our growth and accomplishments—we even hang these on the walls of our homes and offices long after they have served most of their usefulness. On a smaller scale, we have grades and test scores and award letters and trophies, which mean so much when we are young that our parents often "publish" them on the refrigerator or mantle. I personally even go so far as to keep—well-organized, no less—souvenir t-shirts I can no longer wear and ticket stubs of all kinds, for movies and concerts and big sporting events that have mattered to me. We keep all of these things as reminders of important moments or steps in our lives, and hope that their physicality will somehow quantify, *certify* those ineffable aspects of our lives that we worry may otherwise be fleeting and inconsequential. I am surprised, actually, that Binx Bolling was not a photographer, come to think of it.

However, too much *certification* can have plenty of negative consequences as well, and can contribute to *everydayness*, and even *malaise*. Our various forms of *certification*, then, can be good places to begin a *vertical* or *horizontal* search. For example, when grades and test scores are emphasized too much it is easier to recognize how hollow they can be; anyone who wants to can make himself a trophy at the store, print a "certificate" on his computer, or cheat for a grade. Sometimes the "certificate" is a letdown, or a reduction of sorts; one of the most disappointing *certification* experiences of my life came during the ceremony for my completion of the Honors Program at the University of Georgia. I invited my parents to the ceremony, dressed up as best I could, climbed the enormous staircase, shook the president's hand, and received…a sheet of thin paper, poorly inked with vague, meaningless, scripted text. In an instant, the ineffable was lost to me; it could not be caught and held this time, and my experience was reduced to the faded and spotty words "High Honors," and my pride reduced to an uneasy awkwardness.

Countless students have complained of the same sort of *reduction* by colleges and state education departments, who take real, live people and turn them into numbers and GPAs. "For this?" they ask, looking to me for validation of *all* of them, of their wholeness, rather than the parts of them that can be located on a transcript. We also run the risk sometimes of *certifying* only one thing at the expense of others (teachers but not theorists, for example), of saying too much that *this* is it and *that* is not, and ending up with a certificate or label that does not fit, a signifier that does not correspond to the signified. In politics we have the ever-present American flag, for example, which has been spread so thin among all political parties, car lots, bikinis, etc., that it is hard to tell what it means anymore—a quick examination of the various positions in the NFL national anthem controversy will be plenty of evidence here. But if we go without it, we might be considered "un-American." This kind of co-opting of America and its symbols to serve specific and narrow and sometimes selfish purposes is pretty widespread today; for example, Naomi Klein offers 500 pages of economic examples in *The Shock Doctrine* of our insisting to countries around the world that "Washington Consensus policies were the only recipe for stability, and therefore democracy" (2007, p. 165) despite plenty of evidence otherwise, and Donald Trump's "Make American Great Again" campaign slogan has certainly ignited debate about the meaning(s) of all four of those words.

　　We must be careful, too, with religious *certification*; I was baptized, proudly, as a Christian at ten years old, and could not have been happier about it. However, as the years passed, many churches with the "Christian" label seemed to become more and more the kinds of places where I could hear "exultant sermons that mingle Christianity, self-help, and right-wing politics" (Goldberg, 2007, p. 53). By the time I heard a minister say from the pulpit that "no Christian in good conscience could vote for the Democratic Party," I knew that being a "Christian" was a far more complicated *certification* experience than ten-year-old me could have imagined, though I still did not know exactly what to do about it.

Everydayness and Malaise

Unfortunately, the kind of experience I had at that church long ago passed into *everydayness*. I am used to a religious climate in which we seem primarily interested in what Eugene H. Peterson calls "domesticating God," and reducing Him to a "size that conveniently fits our plans and ambitions and tastes" (2003, p. xii). As Peterson further laments, in "every age, religion has served as a convenient cover among an astonishing number of people for cozy self-righteousness and a judgmental rejection of suffering sinners" (p. xiv), but this seems especially common today. When I read Michelle Goldberg's account of the "domesticating of God" for all kinds of purposes in *Kingdom Coming: The Rise of Christian Nationalism* (2007), I am no longer surprised at the way my faith looks to her, since I hardly recognize it as my faith anymore. When I hear about Jerry Falwell and Pat Robertson attributing 9/11 to "abortionists," "feminists," "gays," and the "ACLU" (p. 8), or hear that when James Dobson advocates a "Focus on the Family," he also means encouraging discrimination against homosexuals (p. 15), I cannot understand how we are supposed to share a religion. Despite their claims that "the Bible is absolutely and literally true" (p. 6), and their insistence on making everything about "good and evil" (p. 4), I just disagree. Was Jesus not a master of the parable, and the metaphor? Do these people really think, for example, that he was talking about vines and branches and fruit in the literal sense? And did he not say that the greatest commandment was to love everyone—enemies too? The Bible may indeed be printed in black and white, but its message seems much more complex than that to me.

As writers like Goldberg and Klein and Kevin Phillips (2006) have noticed, politics and religion have become tightly intertwined lately, and that means religion feels increasingly political and politics feels increasingly religious as well. In fact, Michael Gerson, in an article for *The Atlantic*, called "The Last Temptation," argues that "the moral convictions of many evangelical leaders have become a function of their partisan identification" (2018, p. 45). He asserts, as well, that since they are "blinded by political tribalism and hatred for their opponents," they do not recognize that "they are undermining the causes to which they once dedicated their lives," and concludes that despite these leaders' attraction to a very public stage, "little remains of a distinctly Christian public witness." I do not mean, though, that we are suddenly electing ministers to diplomatic posts; I mean that we treat our political positions as if they are a matter of inarguable, irrational faith, and this may be just as big a problem as the politicization of the pulpit. Michel Foucault deals with exactly the type of government we see today in *Security, Territory, Population* (2007). Our current political climate is dominated by our obsession with "security," which Foucault says is dealing with a "series of possible events" (p. 20), and it is easy to see right away what is so dangerous about this obsession. We promise as a government and demand as a people protection from things that *might* happen; we are like the city dweller who says "promise me I'll never get mugged," even though we know that no such promise can be kept and that we might *not* get mugged, regardless of what our government does. What the government gives us instead is the *illusion* of security by the only means available to it: "disciplinary normalization" (p. 57). In other words, the government insists that we will be safe if only we will conform to an "optimal model" (p. 57), which in this case consists of complete obedience to leadership, obvious shows of patriotism, and the spending of whatever cash we have available, or credit if we can get it, since little matters to us as much as the economy. As Susan Faludi notes in *The Terror Dream* (2007), we were told after 9/11 to effectively "max out our credit cards for the cause" (p. 3). Anything short of this optimal model, we are often told, "helps the terrorists."

All of this has produced in me a serious *malaise*. I simply have reached a point where I do not understand how my country, and my faith, can say and do the things that I am witness to daily. I have almost accepted that in my government, "the end of sovereignty is circular" (Foucault, 2007, p. 98), that the purpose of their power is to keep it. I have accepted from exhaustion that none of these things is a safe topic in the public school system (if I want to continue to work in it), despite it being the ideal place to talk through formative and delicate matters with young people who will one day soon be expected to act on positions they have hardly considered. I also find myself ignoring many of the most public voices of the faith to which I am supposed to belong—maybe I hope that they will all go away? I have for some time now just been going through the spiritual and patriotic and curricular motions, treading water in a sea of *everydayness* until I drown in the *malaise*. I do not wear the flag pins, catchy-religious-slogan t-shirts, or any of the variety of bumper stickers that are supposed to be *certificates* of my twenty-first century American citizenship, but I do not fight them much either; rather, I find myself turning off the television, avoiding social media, tuning out the preacher of *that*-church-over-there, and hoping no one asks me any pointed questions. I also carry some of this *malaise* into work with me, and unfortunately into my classes; I say the pledge, observe the "moment of silence," prepare students for all of those standardized tests, and discuss scores and statistics and charts *ad nauseum*, and do all of that without nearly enough critical thought—let alone the voicing of such critical thought. I get up, go to work, daydream through meetings, and know that the world is lost to me.

Disaster and the *Search*

Oddly, perhaps, the first time a *search* occurred to Binx Bolling was a time of disaster. He had just been injured in warfare, and he awoke "under a chindolea bush" (p. 10) to see a beetle scratching around in the leaves. As he says, "there awoke in me an immense curiosity. I was onto something" (p. 11). Jolted out of *everydayness* by his injury, he vowed then to pursue the *search* for something more, to *revise*, to see the things he had not seen, and to live according to what he found.

I had a similar experience (war and injury aside) on a sidewalk in New Orleans—coincidentally (?) the setting of Percy's novel—during Mardi Gras when I was nineteen. Separated pre-mobile phones from the only people I knew in the city, broke, and exhausted, I suddenly saw myself in a new light. My life was headed nowhere near where I wanted it to, and I was suddenly worried that if I did not right the course then, I might not ever. I was not even sure I would find my way home. I did, fortunately, and I sat later that night, reunited with my friends on the banks of the Mississippi, and saw in that dark water and the bright lights around it shades and traces of things I had never noticed before, and promised myself I would not go back from my new, perceptive, purposeful self. Like Binx, though, I made progress but was eventually swept away again by *everydayness*, for which even the mighty Mississippi is no match.

Today, though, we seem to have no shortage of disasters, whether they are personal, national, spiritual, economic, political, military, etc., to shake us; the news, in short, is like an endless tape-loop of disasters which ought to prompt *searches*. School shootings plague us, climate warnings seem to come daily, and privacy and other worries about technology are constant headlines. But rather than see these as causes for "*revision*" (Owen, 2011), rather than question who we are and what kind of world we live in when we encounter a crisis, we seem today to hold ever tighter to the party line—we "stay the course," even if we do not know much what it is, and we learn just as little from the disasters around us as we do from the ones we have already experienced. We refuse to "*revise*," despite disaster. Christian leaders like Falwell, Robertson, and Dobson blame "sin" everywhere they see it, big businesses seemingly always manage to acquire a taxpayer-funded bailout or law change for whatever troubles they create, and politicians have actually figured out how to profit from these situations.

Klein has even found a name for this approach we have to crisis, calling her depressing detailing of these kinds of events in our history *The Shock Doctrine: The Rise of Disaster Capitalism* (2007). The personalities and characterizations of our political and religious leaders in the public eye do change during these times, but not in good ways; rather than become the honest, humble, serious men and women we need, they often become ridiculous caricatures. For example, Faludi says that after 9/11, the disaster that shook America like no other has, Washington began to look and sound like a "Wild West stage set" (p. 5), and notes that the more "cartoonish" (p. 47) President Bush—our most outwardly religious president in recent memory—acted, the more popular he became. And for all our talk about the schools and students in "crisis," we have really done little more in the face of that crisis than help the testing industry make more money, and send enough "thoughts and prayers" to suffering people that sympathy and spiritual striving have been reduced to fodder for Internet memes.

And this is where I get off. This is *my* disaster, this turning of America, and Christianity—and education—from something hopeful and beautiful into something ridiculous, greedy, macho, self-righteous, and disgusting. I will not make money or gain power, or support my leaders in their attempts to make money or gain power, from the misery and suffering of others. I will search for an America, and a Christianity, and a public education, and a David Owen that can be something more than that.

Repetition

One of the great blessings and powerful tools of the *search*, especially the *vertical search*, is *repetition*, and I am perhaps blessed more than most in this regard. I love the *repetition* of my job as a teacher. I am certainly not talking about the third or fourth time that I repeat instructions to inattentive students, or the lesson I am teaching in the course of the day, though those instances can also offer valuable insights; rather, I am talking about the way my job *begins* and *ends* each year. I do not have to simply toil on into retirement at the same desk every day. Instead, if I want them or take advantage of them, I get numerous chances to "*revise*" (Owen, 2011), to reflect on what I do and why I do it. For example, every time I explain to my writing classes the beauty and freedom of expression offered by poetry, I am able to extract the segment of time since I taught the same thing last year, and measure the world I find between those moments. I see how I have grown, and changed, and learned, and while I am certainly able to improve the way I teach poetry each time, I am equally reminded why it matters so much. My teaching of poetry, as one example among many, becomes the iterative site of one of Benoit Mandlebrot's (1983) feedback loops, through which my teaching, and living, undergo "*revision*"; take the output of last year, run it back through the complex problem that is the next school year, and hope that maybe what I get out next time is beautiful. Whatever I do get out next time, I feed it back in, and begin again. It is literally a "refreshing" experience, and renews my passion for my work. And every time I see an old student, and think about what we have both become since I saw him or her last, I know why my job is worth the kind of careful attention *repetition* can prompt.

In my spiritual life, *repetition* most often occurs when I encounter songs that carry nostalgic weight, or passages from the Bible in sermons that are also attached to some other point in my life. Like I often tell my students in the case of good poetry, hymns and Bible verses mean something a little different each time we hear them, which is why they are so often repeated and read and sung. The words and songs are nourishment for my life, and my life has changed, and so the words and songs need to be revisited, and I need to be reminded of them from a new vantage point. This means *repetition* is not a force for stasis, but rather a way to measure and facilitate change. For example, one of the few clear-positives of social media is that I occasionally regain contact with old friends, sometimes as far back as elementary school, and this often produces a profound *repetition* experience. In composing the messages and letters I write these old friends, I have to take serious stock of the man I have become as I decide what to say about myself, and about the direction of my life since I have seen them last. No official "revival" experience at church could make more of an impact.

Unfortunately, though, our national leaders in politics and religion—and education—too often pretend like history has been abolished, or at least has been given a good whitewashing, and so are deprived of the *repetition* experience. Our national Christian voices are often talking about America's Christian roots, ignoring, apparently, the slavery that propped up our economy, the theft of the Native Americans' land, or (more positively) the promise of our founding fathers to protect, as Thomas Jefferson says, "the Jew and the Gentile, the Christian and Mohammedan, the Hindoo and Infidel of every denomination" (Goldberg, 2007, p. 32). As for America and its general greatness and power today, we seem to be insistent that we will be the first country to sail off into eternity with no loss of power or wealth or prestige, only moving forever outward and onward with no end in sight and regardless of what we do or how we treat other nations—as Klein's book painfully describes at length. We too easily forget that "few contemplate Madrid, the Dutch Atlas has put down his lonely burden, and the sun has set on the British Empire" (Phillips, 2006, p. 299); in other words, we are not the first "superpower"—some would say empire—the world has seen, and it is folly to think that we will be the last. It is worth noting here that we are, ironically, *built* to have the kind of *repetition* experiences we refuse: just as our school years begin and end, so do the terms of our leaders. We elect our officials every few years, and could conceivably make dramatic changes if we wanted to. We just do not seem to want to.

Rotation

All is certainly not hopeless, though. We could, in fact, begin to *search* for our soul as a nation and as a faith (and as teachers), and we could start to seek both *vertically* into our past and *horizontally* into our surrounding present for the things we so far have not seen. And sometimes, too, we are lucky enough to get what we do not even quite deserve, if we merely put ourselves a few steps down the right path. Percy calls this a *rotation*, an experience beyond what is expected, and Binx Bolling can hardly contain himself when one occurs; as he puts it on one occasion, "my heart sings like Octavian and there is great happiness between me and Lonnie and this noble girl and they both know it and have the sense to say nothing" (p. 144). I have felt this way in a number of instances, even in our time of soul-crisis. As dark as things look for our current education system, I have found to my surprise that there is still the field of curriculum studies, which is to me like the *search* as an academic discipline. Also, in high school I was once assigned at random, in a class I hated, a research project on William Blake. What I found set me on fire intellectually, so much so that I not only majored in English literature later (and teach it now), but I also focused on Blake and the Romantic poets for an MA degree. And as for *rotations* within Christianity, in college I got the chance to serve as the Music Minister (band leader) one year for an alternate service of a Methodist church. I was a Baptist playing spiritual rock music (the real kind U2 might like, not so much the watered-down, cliché-ridden "Christian" kind) in a Methodist service with a female preacher for which our t-shirts read "love god. love others. nothing else matters." Every Sunday was inspirational, but it was also the most fun I'd ever had in church (I hardly knew that was allowed).

My greatest spiritual *rotation*, though, was a trip to Monterrey, Mexico. We were a group of twenty-something students going to help a small, poor community build a church. However, I was blessed, and humbled, and educated by my work for those people in such a way that I cannot imagine that my contributions to their community balanced things out. I saw happy, loving, hard-working people, who I thought had far less than me to be happy about, love, or work hard for. I learned many new things about what the Christian faith could really mean in that experience, which came as a shock to someone who had been raised in the church since his infancy. There are apparently still things to discover about a faith thousands of years old, even for an American.

The same sort of thing could be said for my experience in teaching. I had a pretty negative view of public education after my own high school experience, and I certainly never planned to teach. I took my current job really as something I just thought I would try, until I figured out what else to do. However, little did I know that every now and then I would find, especially in my AP Literature and IB Language and Literature classes, everything that America can be. For one, my class is often as "multicultural" as any public school course I can imagine; most years, I have numerous nationalities represented—first and second generation Americans—as well as most major world religions. Some years, for example, not only do I have Muslims, but I have Shiites and Sunnis in the same room. Everything we discuss, every work we read, every idea we put forth can be examined from a variety of viewpoints, many of them held by people actually sitting in the room. I have found little else that felt so American, at least as the founders promised. It is not surprising to me, based on what I have been taught about the idea of America, that the United Nations meets here. I feel sometimes like it meets in my classroom.

There are signs of hope, even if we have to *search* for them, or "*revise*" (Owen, 2011) the way we look at familiar things in order to see how they are hopeful. As depressing as the books by people like Faludi, Phillips, Klein, and Goldberg are, at least they exist. And whatever comes of the various movements of the last few years, and all of their respective marches and demonstrations and social media campaigns, at least there are people who notice what is wrong with the directions we are headed as people and as a nation, and who speak out about the trouble they see around us and up ahead because they know we can still change course.

The Wonder

Ultimately, I cannot send America, or Christianity, or our education system, on a *search* for its soul. And I cannot decide for any of them what it is supposed to be. I do not have any secret knowledge, or any magic bullets to stop war, or perfect the economy, or rid us of greed or hate, or explain with complete authority exactly what the Bible says we should do. But I can start the *search* for those things with me, pledge my life and my efforts now to try "to see a World in a Grain of Sand," as Blake

(1863/1988) prompts me to in "Auguries of Innocence," to be as "open to life" as James B. Macdonald (1964/1995, p. 20) says I should, to never stop looking for all of the things I have not seen before, both near and far. And I can do so with an open mind and heart, and with honesty and integrity and responsibility. I can *search*, *horizontally* and *vertically* like Pinar and Percy say I should, mining my past and my present and aiming to become a man of my time and of all times. I can try to be like the biblical David, my namesake, of whom poet Robert Pinsky says, "in his faults and attainments, his losses and victories, embodies on a scale almost beyond imagining the action of *living a life*" (2005, p. 178). In many ways, David's story is the story of all of us, because it involves "the mysteries of how a person belongs or does not belong with another, or with a family or a tribe or a people" (p. 9). And mysterious this life is; in fact, as Huston Smith notes in *Why Religion Matters* (2001), "every day we discover anew that the world is more strange, more complicated, and more mysterious than we had suspected" (p. 185). The same could easily be said of America, or Christianity, or our classroom experiences.

And so what I, what we, must do is *search*, seek, question, reconsider, *repeat, rotate*, and never stop. And this is what we must help our students learn to do as well. I believe that America, and Christianity, and I can all try to live beautiful, empowering, benevolent lives in the world, and let those lives inform our curriculum; we are a country founded on possibilities, and a faith that aims for loving perfection of the heart and mind, and it is a betrayal of both to fail to hope and to work towards those ends—not to fall short, and not to admit that we have fallen short, but to quit the *search*, to stop trying to find new and better ways to live. Foucault said of government that it is "the continuous act of creation of the republic" (2007, p. 259), and it is certainly easy to see how the framers of our country had the same thing in mind. But what will we create next? What will we make of all that we have been, and all that we want to be, and that we can be? What might America be, with *"revision"* (Owen, 2011)? What might our schools be? I do not know either, but I hope Blake was right; I hope there is still time to find out. And I hope that I will never again succumb to *everydayness*; I hope that "not for five minutes will I be distracted from the wonder" of all that is and can be (Percy, 1961/1998, p.42).

                    *   *   *

To look up

The slow walk up the driveway.

Night darkness and

tree root cracks hidden

until *here* and then

the next *here* and the

ones that reach up jagged

crumbling to catch my

toe *here* and what I

want is to look up

instead of down to see

what runes of constellation

tonight are framed by

old pine tree sentinel sway

and the south roof line,

what messages are written for

me in wispy cloud wandering

and whispering stray wind,

what notes are dropped here and

there drifting on breezes

I too often fail to catch.

                    (Owen, 2017)

*"Teaching and Learning" and "To look up" are reprinted with permission from Brill | Sense.

References

Blake, W. (1988). Auguries of innocence. In D. V. Erdman (Ed.), *The complete poetry & prose of William Blake* (p. 490-493). New York, NY: Doubleday. (Original work published 1863)

Faludi, S. (2007). *The terror dream: Fear and fantasy in post-9/11 America.* New York, NY: Metropolitan Books.

Foucault, M. (2007). *Security, territory, population: Lectures at the College de France, 1977-78* (G. Burchell, Trans.). New York, NY: Palgrave Macmillan. (Original work published 2004)

Gerson, M. (2018, April). The last temptation. *The Atlantic*, 38-40.

Goldberg, M. (2007). *Kingdom coming: the rise of Christian nationalism*. New York, NY: W.W. Norton & Company.

Huxley, A. (1954). *The doors of perception and heaven and hell*. New York, NY: HarperCollins Publishers Inc.

Klein, N. (2007). *The shock doctrine: The rise of disaster capitalism*. New York, NY: Metropolitan Books.

Macdonald, J. B. (1995). An image of man: The learner himself. In *Theory as a prayerful act: The collected essays of James B.Macdonald* (B. J. Macdonald, Ed.). New York, NY: Peter Lang. (Original work published 1964)

Mandlebrot, B. B. (1983). *The fractal geometry of nature*. New York, NY: W. H. Freeman and Company.

Owen, Jr., D. P. (2011). *The need for revision: Curriculum, literature, and the 21st century*. Rotterdam, NL: Sense Publishers.

Owen, Jr., D. P. (2017). Teaching and learning. In *Fireflies: Memory, identity, and poetry*. Rotterdam, NL: Sense Publishers.

Owen, Jr., D. P. (2017). To look up. In *Fireflies: Memory, identity, and poetry*. Rotterdam, NL: Sense Publishers.

Percy, W. (1998). *The moviegoer*. New York, NY: Vintage Books. (Original work published 1961)

Peterson, E. H. (2003). Foreword. In R. J. Whiteley & B. Maynard (Eds.), *Get up off your knees: Preaching the U2 catalog* (pp. xi-xiv). Cambridge, MA: Cowley Publications.

Phillips, K. (2006). *American theocracy: The peril and politics of radical religion, oil, and borrowed money in the 21st century*. New York, NY: Penguin Group.

Pinar, W. F. (2007). *Intellectual advancement through disciplinarity: Veriticality and horizontality in curriculum studies*. Rotterdam, NL: Sense Publishers.

Pinsky, R. (2005). *The life of David*. New York, NY: Random House, Inc.

Smith, H. (2001). *Why religion matters: The fate of the human spirit in an age of disbelief*. New York, NY HarperCollins.

U2. (1987). *The Joshua tree* [CD]. New York, NY: Island Records.

Chapter 2

Solitude and Isolation

Splintering Synonyms

Stacey T. Brown

The lack of attention to and respect for actual scholarship and original thought should be a major concern in education. In order to truly think and create, we need time and space to let the mind wander and be idle. Our current educational system offers neither opportunity, for students or for teachers. Our bodies, minds, and souls, suffer greatly as a result of this lack of time and space and many of us find ourselves slipping into isolation. We become prisoners in our own classrooms, and even in our own minds, because the solitude that we need to read, write, and think is non-existent. Creativity is stifled and, as a result, we take no pride in our work and we have no zeal for it. Without time and space to further our scholarship, we no longer feel like scholars and our identities are compromised.

While seemingly synonymous, there is a profound difference between solitude and isolation. In the face of standardization and commodification of the human body and brain, teachers and students need solitude, which can be defined as the time and space to just "be" and, in being, the body, mind, and soul heal and rejuvenate. In this state, thinking and creativity take place. Whitehead supports this idea: "The combination of imagination and learning normally requires some leisure, freedom from restraint, freedom from harassing worry, some variety of experiences, and the stimulation of other minds diverse in opinion and diverse in equipment" (1929, p. 91). In solitude, we reset ourselves, we enlighten ourselves, and then share that energy and enlightenment with others, through teaching and learning and reading and writing. In the act of solitude, doing nothing is something. Being still, wandering, and loafing are all acceptable and

David P. Owen, Jr (ed.), Field Theory: Curriculum Studies at Work, 19–37.
© 2020 DIO Press. All rights reserved.

encouraged. We need to interrupt the curriculum in order to make "room" for solitude.

Arendt writes, "For if no other test but the experience of being active, no other measure but the extent of sheer activity were to be applied to the various activities within the vita active, it might well be that thinking as such would surpass them all" (1958, p. 325). Clearly, Arendt supports that thinking *looks* like an inactive process, but that it is not. We need to allow our students to sit and be idle; to think, question, and create their own wisdom in their minds. We should encourage them to take the time to think about what they are reading, studying, and experiencing. We wonder why we have a culture of non-readers, but we do not give teachers or students the solitude they need to read. Standardization requires that the teacher constantly observe action and production in her students, giving neither the teacher nor student the time to be idle, in solitude. Arendt says, "Whoever has any experience in this matter will know how right Cato was when he said: 'Never is he more active than when he does nothing, never is he less alone than when he is by himself'" (1958, p. 325). We must interrupt the standardized curriculum by creating spaces of solitude that will grant teachers and students intellectual freedom.

Solitude is the fertile soil where knowledge is planted and humanity is harvested; but the soil we till in education is barren. When starving souls remain without the nourishment provided by solitude, they mistakenly seek shelter in the dangerous wasteland of isolation, where there is no healing or rejuvenation, only deafening silence and decay. Nietzsche says:

> Out of damp and gloomy days, out of solitude, out of loveless words directed at us, conclusions grow up in us like fungus; one morning they are there, we know not how, and they gaze upon us, morose and gray. Woe to the thinker who is not the gardener, but only the soil of the plants that grow in him. (1997, p. 171)

We must tend to our gardens in solitude and not leave the vegetation of our learning in isolation, where they will surely die. The confines and confusion created by isolation often lead to behaviors and conditions that damage and destroy the body, mind, and soul. Arendt says:

> In isolation, man remains in contact with the world as the human artifice; only when the most elementary form of human creativity, which is the capacity to add something of one's own to the common world, is destroyed, isolation becomes altogether unbearable. (1968, p. 475)

The need for solitude is a concern for education, but also for social justice if we want education to occur in ways that do not isolate teachers and students. Dewey says:

> If a man's actions are not guided by thoughtful conclusions, then they are guided by inconsiderate impulse, unbalanced appetite, caprice, or the circumstances of the moment. To cultivate unhindered, unreflective external activity is to foster enslavement, for it leaves the person at the mercy of appetite, sense, and circumstance. (2012, p. 60-61)

If we do not foster solitude in education, we are at risk of becoming isolated and enslaved, unable to act, imagine, create, react, or even make sense of what is happening in our lives.

Isolation is where we find ourselves when we do not get the solitude we need. It is a desolate vacuum, where we become dehydrated and malnourished, where our souls and minds become shriveled and we feel exposed and lost and hopeless. Arendt says that isolation is "the fundamental inability to act at all" (1968, p. 474). Teachers and students suffer this isolation on a daily basis because they are not able to find the solitude they need to operate in these insufferable conditions of standardization. Isolation "is called loneliness in the sphere of social intercourse. Isolation and loneliness are not the same" (1968, p. 474). Indeed, solitude and isolation do not always imply being alone, although we are most likely to experience them when we are solitary.

It is absolutely possible to endure isolation in a crowd or to experience solitude among others, but the latter is difficult to do. Heidegger refers to this as "attunement," (1995, p. 63) when we are there, but not there. Many argue that it is impossible to be in solitude in a crowd, but, "How often it happens, in a conversation among a group of people, that we are 'not there,' how often we find that we were absent, albeit without having fallen asleep" (1995, p. 63). We call this daydreaming, but daydreamers know how to find solitude. They hear the hum in the background but are beating their own drum in their minds, keeping rhythm. This:

> ...not-being-there, this being-away, has nothing at all to do with consciousness or unconsciousness in the usual sense. On the contrary this non-being-there can be highly conscious. In such being absent we are precisely concerned with ourselves, or with something else. Yet this not-being-there is nonetheless a being-away (1995, p. 63).

It is this being away, this attunement, this solitude that we must fight for. We must find ways to create the time and space of solitude to allow teachers and students to work towards self-actualization and wisdom of the world.

Solitude involves finding harmony with the world and with one's self, even when life is not harmonious. It involves a rhythm produced by the wandering of the mind, which generates creativity. Solitude is where *currere* can take place, "a kind of free associative 'futuring' during which one seeks the revelation of one's fantasies of what one might be" (Pinar, 2004, p. 55). Solitude is not necessarily spending time *by* oneself, but spending time *with* oneself. It involves inner dialogue. Many people admit they like to talk to themselves when they are alone and working. This is an example of solitude, where there is rhythm and meter to the work of creativity and something sublime and/or profound is taking place in that rhythm and words of wisdom are being written to the music of solitude. It's a symphony. But solitude is not always the most positive experience. The rhythm can be discordant. Reading, writing, thinking, creating...we love it, and it can be inspiring and uplifting and the best sensory experience you can possibly imagine, but it can also be serious, difficult, maddening, and *messy*. Solitude is like the "zone" that athletes describe. It takes a lot of work to get there, a lot of endurance and sweat and sacrifice, but when you get in the "zone," there is nothing like it. In the "zone," in solitude, you can transcend. Heidegger says:

> We must be-there in order to be able to be away. Only as long as we are-there can we be away at all, and vice-versa. Hence being away, or this 'there and not there,' is something peculiar, and attunement is connected in some as yet obscure way with this peculiar manner of being. (1995, p. 65)

This is how solitude is sustained.

King says, "It starts with this: put your desk in the corner, and every time you sit down there to write, remind yourself why it isn't in the middle of the room. Life isn't a support system for art. It's the other way around" (2000, p. 101). People who struggle to find solitude look for perfect conditions and become frustrated when they cannot write or get anything accomplished. They want life to support their art (wouldn't that be nice?), but then they find themselves in isolation. Those who can only work in large blocks of time will never fulfill their goals as scholars, especially if they truly live in the world, in a house, with pets, other family members and loved ones, have jobs, social lives, and so on; certainly, not as teachers. Education no longer values the time and space of solitude needed for scholarship. We cannot live like hermits, as much as we might like to, and even if we could, it would be dangerous to do so. Solitude is not and cannot be a fixed state of time and space, although I use the words "time" and "space" to describe it. It must be fluid and mobile. Some people find solitude in an office or a special room or study in their homes. That is ideal and if they can find that, then they are on the right path, but even outside of that fixed time and space of that special place, we should seek solitude and strive to find it anywhere at any time, even in a crowd and especially in nature.

King aptly describes the emotional, "zone"-like aspect of solitude: "You can approach the act of writing with nervousness, excitement, hopefulness, or even despair—the sense that you can never completely put on the page what's in your mind and heart" (2000, p. 106), but if we do not face the blank page and confront our fears, we will not find solitude. We will find isolation. I have definitely experienced periods of isolation while facing the blank pages of this chapter. There were days when I believed I would never finish, that I didn't have enough grit and tenacity to do the work, the very difficult work of writing. When I literally made myself face the blank page, I found periods of solitude, many of them short and fleeting, many of them long and prolific, but ignoring the blank page is the shortest route to isolation. Even if I only sit down for an hour in the morning and an hour at night and accomplish "nothing," meaning I wrote nothing, *something* happened during that hour. I figured out what *not* to write, what *won't* work.

I might have an epiphany and completely change my opinion about an idea that I have held onto for years because I read *one sentence* in a book that someone suggested. Life-changing moments happen in solitude. Sometimes arriving upon the realization that I was wrong, misinformed, having formulated opinions without all of the information, *feels* like isolation, because it can be somewhat of a negative and frustrating experience to confront an error in judgment, but it is in fact in solitude that those realizations, those epiphanies, take place. Dewey says:

> While all thinking results in knowledge, ultimately the value of knowledge is subordinate to its use in thinking. For we live not in a settled and finished world, but in one which is going on, and where our main task is prospective, and where retrospect—and all knowledge as distinct from thought is retrospect—is of value in the solidity, security, and fertility it affords our dealings with the future." (1944, p. 151)

Prospective retrospection occurs in solitude. Again, solitude is not always listening to opera music while sipping on chai tea at an antique desk on an oriental rug. King says:

You can come to the act with your fists clenched and your eyes narrowed, ready to kick ass and take down names. You can come to it because you want a girl to marry or because you want to change the world. Come to it any way but lightly. Let me say it again: *you must not come lightly to the blank page.* (2000, p. 106)

Writing is serious. Writing is life. I am writing my life. Writing is my life.

Part of the excitement of writing comes from the unexpected. No matter what you think you know and no matter what you think you will write, no matter how much planning goes into the process, sparks fly and connections are created. Surprises! Eisner says:

In the arts, as in many other fields, surprise is a friend, not a foe. During the course of their work, students and teachers alike encounter the unexpected, students in images and qualities that they could not have foreseen but that beckon in one direction rather than another, and teachers in surprises that unscripted students create. (2002, p. 164)

Eisner explores the beauty of surprise in the process of creation, for teacher and for student, as a result of creating in solitude.

Solitude also requires a sense of vulnerability. Morris says:

Traditional scholarship is not about vulnerability. It is about the argument, the position statement, the date and the research. But who made up these rules? If scholarship is to reflect one's curriculum vita, one's lived experience, then vulnerability is certainly a part of it. (2008, p. 37)

In order to read, write, think, and create, we must cast aside many constructs about our own identity and our own way of viewing the world. We must be willing to look into our own souls, but we must be able to "take it" when honesty looks us in the eye. That requires humility and even a sense of humor. In order to face the blank page in solitude, King says:

I'm not asking you to come reverently or unquestioningly; I'm not asking you to be politically correct or cast aside your sense of humor (please God you have one). This isn't a popularity contest, it's not the moral Olympics, and it's not church. But it's writing, damn it, not washing your car or putting on eyeliner. If you can take it seriously, we can do business. If you can't or won't, it's time for you to close the book and do something else. Wash the car, maybe. (2000, p. 107)

It's these kind of conversations we must have with ourselves when we are too stubborn, or too scared, to stop the insanity of our everyday lives and push away from the madness, to retreat to the chair, the desk, the woods, the beach, to get away, to close the door in order to open up the world of solitude. We want it, but we don't always want to do what is necessary to get it. Why? Because it's messy. There is no fixed method, but that's a good thing! Dewey says, "The assumption that method is something separate is connected with the notion of the isolation of the mind and self from the world of things. It makes instruction and learning formal, mechanical, constrained" (1944, p. 179). Method should be individualized. Developing a method for finding solitude is difficult, but essential. Dewey continues: "Expressed in terms of the attitude of the individual the traits of good method are straight-forwardness, flexible intellectual interest or open-minded will to learn, integrity of purpose, and acceptance of responsibility for the consequences of one's activity including thought" (1944, p. 179). Clearly, it is important and only possible to truly enter solitude under these conditions and ways of being, further explaining how the conditions of isolation are almost exactly the opposite.

I have a huge obsessive-compulsive streak. I was actually diagnosed with OCD when my younger son was only two months old. I am very abstract in my thinking, but I must have a method for doing things and completing tasks. Writing for me is like having ten tabs open on the Internet and I am using all of them at the same time. It's maddening and absolutely thrilling, but it messes with my OCD. *It is messy.* I don't like messy. When I was a kid, I ate popcorn with a spoon. I would go inside to wash my hands while I was playing in the sandbox. But in the end, the mess is neat. Something is created. The mess is cleaned up. It's organized and it works really well. I love to cook as well, which is also messy. I have to push through the messy part, but in the end, it's a perfect, healthy meal. The presentation is beautiful. There is color and texture and layers of flavor, much like good writing. There is also the metaphor of birth. That an idea is conceived and then we gestate, three trimesters as the "child" develops and grows. Then it is time for birth. The labor is intense and painful. It is *messy*, but it produces the "child" that is the creation of being, the final product.

For me, writing is weaving. It is threading and sewing, suturing and tying, and making knots. My mother used to sew. The sewing machine was in her bedroom, and when she would sew, the work would take over the room. She was in a state of tension and stasis, creating, adding, cutting, completing. She did amazing work and was very creative. She did her work in solitude. I remember her cutting thread with her teeth when she was too impatient to find the scissors. I remember her groaning and grunting and pulling on her hair. I remember her throwing things and yelling! This was the labor. And the product was always amazing. Nobody could sew like she could. She created her own patterns and matched them with fabric and beautiful detail. She made a statement. It was art. *But, it was messy*, just like creating and writing. Doll describes her writing process and environment:

> Writing is messy. I look around the room scattered with books, papers, opened boxes, unpaid bills. I run downstairs to pick up a book for a point; it goes next to the writing table, on the floor already piled with books. Other books for other projects tumble from another table. (1999, p. 8)

These are the conditions many of us experience while reading, writing, thinking, and creating.

The cup of tea is the Starbucks I bought while waiting for my prescription for a bacterial infection that has my throat almost completely closed up, making every attempt to swallow like ingesting broken glass. Yet, I work. There is no Oriental rug; just a dusty hardwood floor that has two dead bugs on it that I don't bother to pick up. They're dead. They aren't hurting anyone. I might end up talking to them, even naming them at some point. There is laundry (it's clean) all over the living room that needs to be put away. I'll do it later. Plus, I just spilled coffee on my shirt. I can just grab another one from the sofa. But, what's a little coffee stain? It's an outward, visible sign of my labor. I wear it like a badge of honor. There are books everywhere and sticky notes, highlighters, stacks of paper, folders, and files, an explosion of office supplies meant to make the task more "fun." The opera music is a *PS3* game, namely *WWE*, the game my kids play *non-stop*. It's a *wrestling game*! So, there is a lot of male drama going on, epic theme songs, antagonistic diatribes, clever commentating, all going on in the background, just another open tab to add to the crazy chaos of my solitude. It's an oxymoron. It's crazy, but I've learned to tune out the noise and, sometimes, to make use of it. And it *works*! My children are entertained and happy and they are close by. I enjoy hearing their play. It inspires me and heightens my sensory experience. The point is that in solitude, one controls, or doesn't control, the environment and the sensory experience. It is all up to the individual, according to what creates that time and space of solitude that works.

Doll shares the experience in her strikingly similar description:

> Clothes are discarded on the sofa, along with shoes, hats, and earring…The room oozes. It will take me an hour to put everything back into place. But for now, I let it all swirl around me, since I am not yet ready to nose my way up through the ooze. Am I turtle or spider? I am both hard-shelled and filament-soft. That is the writing I do. (1999, p. 8)

Doll resonates with me because she writes so beautifully and poetically about her own craft and sees the complexity of writing and the writer and she understands the weaving process and the spinning of webs and the filament-soft vulnerability of the spider in solitude, as well as the durable work-ethic, the hard-shelled, disciplined, slow-but-steady pace of the turtle.

There are times when I need utter peace and quiet and the wrestling "just ain't gonna work." So I go hide in the laundry room and shut the door, allowing myself to be soothed by the quiet hum of the dryer as I slip into solitude. Like King, I can:

> read anywhere, almost, but when it comes to writing, library carrels, park benches, and rented flats should be courts of last resort—most of us do our best in a place of our own. Until you get one, you'll find your new resolution to write a lot harder to take seriously. (2000, p. 155)

I write in the kitchen. Half of the dining room table houses all of my "materials," and I move them back and forth from the kitchen to the dining room. It isn't ideal, but the kitchen is my favorite room in the house. It is my space and no one else's. Once I finish this chapter, ironically, we plan to find a house that has the space we all need. Solitude for everyone will be a priority. We have all learned that from my writing experience. I will have a room with a door. Right now, there aren't many doors that cannot be opened by anyone else in the house, even the laundry room. King says,

> The space can be humble (probably should be, as I think I have already suggested), and it really needs one thing: a door which you are willing to shut. The closed door is your way of telling the world and yourself that you mean business; you have made a serious commitment to write and intend to walk the walk as well as talk the talk. (2000, p. 155)

Someone told me recently that she worked in the bathroom, sitting cross-legged on the floor, using the toilet (again, it's clean) as a desk! What we won't do for our solitude.

Thinking is important, in a realm of time and space that is suspended above, but is still a part of the drudgery of everyday life. There must be time for slowness in scholarship and intellectual activity, time for the mind to wander and mull over. The average person's life is full of clutter. We economize our time and lives with technological trash. We hoard our brains with uselessness. We devour and digest what is toxic to our brains, rather than nurturing them with reading and writing and creative and critical thinking. Harvey says:

The fierce spatiotemporalities of daily life—driven by technologies that emphasize speed and rapid reductions in the friction of distance and of turnover times—preclude time to imagine or construct alternatives other than those forced unthinkingly upon us as we rush to perform our respective professional roles in the name of technological progress and endless capital accumulation. (2000, p. 237)

Teachers, scholars, and students live in this society, this fast-paced culture of high-speed Internet, instant video, Wikipedia, apps, and answers at your fingertips. We don't have to *look* for anything. We don't have to study or search or dig, if we don't want to…but what about those of us who *want* to do that? We want to further our scholarship, our lived experience. We want to broaden our horizons and deepen our understanding of ourselves and the world we live in. We don't want the instant answers. We want to wait and wonder and figure it out on our own, in solitude!

What do you do when you can't have it the way you want it? When you are forced to go with the instant answers, to make a test with only an A, B, C, or D answer, to choose only *one* of the A, B, C, or D answers, when either none of them are right, or maybe more than one of them is right, but I can't explain my reasoning because I can only click on one of them…This leads to isolation. These conditions, this way of teaching and "learning" is toxic and it is not sustainable; therefore, it does not quench the thirst we have for knowledge that we graft and create for ourselves from the knowledge we receive and the experience we have with it. Many of us are aware that we are working under these insufferable conditions, and we cleave to our innocent, yet precocious, curiosity about the world. Dewey reminds us of:

the open minded and flexible wonder of childhood and of the ease with which this endowment is lost. Some lose it in indifference or carelessness; others in a frivolous flippancy; many escape these evils only to become incased in a hard dogmatism, which is equally fatal to the spirit of wonder. Some are so taken up with routine as to be in accessible to new facts and problems. (2012, p. 30-31)

This is what happens to so many teachers and students. This is why solitude is so important. We must provide time and space for teachers and students to wander and be idle in their minds, to turn things over, to pick them apart and put them back together, to create something new, or to deconstruct something and create something fresh while paying homage to the original.

In the spirit of Dewey, teachers should insist on solitude for themselves and for their students. Resist standardization and dogmatism and draw on what is within. Stir our own souls and the souls of our students:

> With respect then to curiosity, the teacher usually has more to learn than to teach. Rarely can he aspire to the office of kindling or even increasing it. His task is rather to keep alive the sacred spark of wonder and to fan the flame that already glows. His problem is to protect the spirit of inquiry, to keep it from becoming blasé from overexcitement, wooden from routine, fossilized through dogmatic instruction, or dissipated by random exercise upon trivial things. (Dewey 2012, pp. 30-31)

We have to protect our jobs and our professions, so we must find a way to teach the standards in ways that allow for solitude. We can teach students to extract the fragmented, isolated standards and create wholeness and new knowledge in solitude. We must teach students to tap into the sociological imagination, which Mills describes as:

> a quality of mind that will help them to use information and to develop reason in order to achieve lucid summations of what is going on in the world and of what may be happening within themselves. It is this quality, I am going to contend, that journalists and scholars, artists and publics, scientists and editors are coming to expect. (2000, p. 5)

If we can do this for ourselves in solitude, we can teach our students to do the same.

People seek solitude because it is a way to escape, just as reading and writing are methods for escape. In a classroom, and even in a school, you cannot just simply shut the door. Even if you can lock the door, there is at least one person with a key who will not knock. They will just enter. The window on the door allows others to peer inside. I placed my desk in the corner of the room, where anyone who peers through the window cannot see. I can "pretend" not to be there and work in solitude. I turn out the lights and use a dim lamp. I do not like bright lights while I work. They overstimulate me. I prefer natural light, or a soft lamp. There are a *lot* of people in a school building who do not seek solitude. They crave the constant interaction of others, usually in order to complain about the current state of affairs in the building or to gossip about other teachers who seek solitude and are doing scholarly work and scholarly teaching. This is isolating. Sometimes we have to send a different message to those people because the closed doors don't speak to them. Students don't *have* doors in school. They are placed in a sea of desks with one door that they have very little control over. Many sit where they can see the door to make sure they can navigate their way into or out of any given situation that may arise.

In the absence of a door, we can find another representation of the door: music. King says:

> I work to loud music—hard rock stuff like AC/DC, Guns 'n Roses, and Metallica have always been particular favorites—but for me the music is just another way of shutting the door. It surrounds me, keeps the mundane world out. When you write, you want to get rid of the world, do you not? Of course you do. When you're writing, you're creating your own worlds. (2000, p. 157)

Music is a door that we can go through in order to create or a door that we can close in order to shut others out in search of solitude. The metaphorical door is revolving. It works exactly the way we want it to. Opera is your thing? Go for it. It seems so sophisticated and scholarly. I love all kinds of music, so it just depends on my mood. Maybe I want to hear jazz in the morning, R&B in the afternoon, and rap at night when the kids have gone to bed. They all create different rhythms and moods for my solitude and they create a bubble around the time and space I need to read, write, think, and create. Some need silence, but we have to learn to work among the noise. There is noise in nature, on the street, from a hotel window, in a restaurant. If we let it, it can be white noise that settles us, builds a rhythm. I personally cannot stand a silent classroom, which sounds entirely contrary to the idea of solitude, but the bubble we build in my classroom often encapsulates many of us, if not all of us. Some students learn to work in solitude, in a solitary manner, with themselves, by themselves, while others work in symphony with others, and they inhabit the bubble together, creating and building knowledge and wisdom that is shared and meaningful to all members. If we are willing to surrender to solitude, which is not an easy sacrifice for many of us, we can reap the benefits.

Writing helps me make sense of the world I live in, sense of who I am and what I am going through in my life, but it is only easy to surrender to it when I know the writing is only for me. When I know others will read it, I walk the fine line between solitude and isolation. I believe I will be judged and that those who read my work will see me for what I really am. They will know who I really am. My weaknesses will be uncovered. This makes me feel vulnerable. Taylor asserts that:

> Embracing rather than fleeing vulnerability exposes knowledge as ignorance and serious considerations as petty preoccupations. This acceptance sets

you free to say what you have long left unsaid and to write what you have been withholding for too long. If others don't like it, so be it. (2009, p. 271)

We must be willing to surrender completely and look in the mirror and then reveal to others in our writing what is in the mirror.

Even in fiction, the truth must be revealed. If the author is not authoring from the self, even her fiction will be a lie, a story no one believes. Lies, secrets, what we hide in the closet, these things lead to isolation. Extreme surrender means all of it, the good, bad, and the ugly. We have to exorcise our demons, admit our flaws, and reveal them. Solitude allows us the time and space to do this, to surrender, to become comfortable with being vulnerable and authentic. Davis says:

> Such is the scene of writing, which necessarily involves extreme surrender, an abandonment to one's own abandonment. According to Ronell, this is also the scene of reading: inasmuch as the reader accompanies the writer to the 'nonplace of writing' he or she experiences the 'infiniteness' of his or her own abandonment. (2007, p. 91)

Writing is an experience of enlightenment and freedom. The process involves the entire body. When I finish writing, I feel like I have purged and cleansed my entire body to the point of contented exhaustion, yet I find it hard to unwind because I feel liberated and restless over the epiphanies and discoveries I have experienced while writing. This is the result of solitude. I also experience a sort of mourning when finishing a paper, because the experience is over. It is a post-partum depression. I am so glad the paper is done, the child is born, but I don't want the experience to end.

I do not always write in solitude. Sometimes, I can't find solitude because I am in a state of isolation. When I write in this state, the paper is fake. It's a lie. It's too perfect. When I go back and read those papers, I think, "This is total garbage." This is not 'me.'" It makes me feel like a fraud. The isolation I experience when I write like that is due to personal conflicts in my life that I don't want to reveal in my writing. Not that I need to write about the specific conflict, but I need to surrender to the emotion surrounding the conflict and let that flow into my writing. This is a way to avoid or reject or free oneself from isolation. Write into contradictions. Use the messy ugliness of life to resist isolation and find solitude. Make a mess and then clean it up in the writing. It doesn't mean you will find resolution, but it's a way to theorize your life and share your own experience with others. Perfect is boring. Heroes are not perfect. What we love about them is they are like us. They are flawed. They are vulnerable. They make us believe we can be like them. Solitude allows us to surrender and to practice authenticity, to become okay with who we are and to *work* on who we are. Isolation is where we feel there is no hope. We are stuck being who we are. We are stuck being where we are. There is nothing we can do to change it. It is hopeless. No one can help. We are powerless to ask for help even if someone could help.

There are countless artists, writers, and musicians that create their way out of agony. They make beauty from their pain, but they do it in solitude, even if they climb out of or hover over the black hole of isolation. Solitude and isolation are a continuum. You cannot talk about one without talking about the other. They are yin and yang. It is parallel to experiencing joy and sadness at the same time, being able to fully appreciate one because you have experienced the other. We risk straddling both spheres when in intense thought, particularly when philosophizing, because of the uncomfortable uncertainty we may possibly encounter. Heidegger says, "Precisely because the truth of this comprehension is something ultimate and extreme, it constantly remains in the perilous neighborhood of supreme uncertainty. No knower necessarily stands so close to the verge of error at every moment as the one who philosophizes" (1995, p. 19). The tension of this state of being is exhausting, yet thrilling. Heidegger continues: "what is ultimate and extreme is what is most perilous and insecure, and this becomes more grave through the fact that it is proper and self-evident that what is ultimate and extreme must be what is most certain for everyone" (1995 p. 19). This paradox is at the crux of what education should be, and would serve us well in society.

I am not even sure one can fully experience solitude without having been in the frozen tundra of isolation. I appreciate solitude because I know what isolation is like. Knowing solitude and isolation is like relishing the experience of sitting on the couch, curled up with a blanket and a good book in front of the fire, while knowing that it is freezing cold outside, while hearing the wind whip through the air, while watching the leafless trees bend helplessly against the wind. The colors are warm and soothing inside, reds, browns, and greens, the colors of nature when it is fall, when nature is a retreat. The colors outside are dark and light. The white landscape is icy and barren. The darkness is foreboding. Creatures lurk in the darkness, the creatures that thrive in this wasteland of isolation. Step outside for long enough to allow the senses to experience this desolation and you will more fully appreciate the solitude inside. But the two are inextricably linked. Heidegger says:

We are questioning concerning an emptiness as a whole, concerning a need, therefore, which cannot possibly have the character of those needs we have enumerated. Not this social misery, not that political confusion, not this powerlessness of science, not that erosion of art, not this groundlessness of philosophy, not that impotence of religion—the need in question is not the fact that this or that need oppresses in such or such a way. Rather what oppresses us most profoundly and in a concealed manner is the very absence of any essential oppressiveness in our Dasein as whole. (1995, p. 163)

Heidegger is describing the continuum of solitude and isolation, and how oppression, some pressing need, some desire, some sense or fear of emptiness is exactly what keeps us reading, writing, thinking, and creating. He continues, explaining how the emptiness results in isolation: "The absence of an essential oppressiveness in Dasein is the emptiness as a whole, so that no one stands with anyone else and no community stands with any other in the rooted unity of essential action" (1995, p. 163). Heidegger is describing the desolate wasteland of isolation, where there is no point, no hope, no reason. Isolation is a prison of the soul.

Being a teacher and a writer is a conundrum. Teaching exhausts me completely as well, so when do I find the energy, much less the time, to write? Even King thought teaching would be a good profession that would allow him to write. He found no solitude there. He says, "The problem was the teaching. I liked my co-workers and loved the kids—even the Beavis and Butt-Head types could be interesting—but by most Friday afternoons I felt as if I'd spent the week with jumper cables clamped to my brain. If I ever came close to despairing about my future as a writer, it was then" (2000, p. 73). I find myself in the same predicament. I love teaching and I love writing and I am not willing to give up either, so I seek solitude to pursue both and push myself to be successful in both arenas. For me, the two are tied up in each other. Teaching is now driving my writing more than ever. Teaching is a part of my identity and I want to write about it, especially since I have realized that teaching is political; that everything is political. Writing is therapy. If I don't write about my experiences, I begin to feel isolated. The same happens to our students. They need to think about what they are learning in relation to what they are living. Teaching fragmented knowledge and neglecting the search for wisdom is an isolating practice that is damaging to our students.

Pinar says, "Why are teachers not permitted, indeed, encouraged, to show students that academic knowledge is not self-contained, that it often reaches out toward and back from life as human beings live it?" (2004, p. 186). Truthfully, if we do not share our scholarship with our students and with each other, we are isolating our students and ourselves, and we are isolating others from what we create. The biggest problem is balance. Teaching becomes about paying the bills. It is our job, even if it is also part of our identity. We tend to concentrate only on that and the writing and creating falls to the wayside. At the same time, so does our solitude. We look around and there we are in the desolate wasteland of isolation. How did this happen? I liken it to my two sons. It is a law of life and an unwritten rule in our household that only one of them can have a major problem at any time. They have to take turns. We cannot handle two of them having major problems at the same time. We need to be able to look at least one of them and say, "You're good! We are doing a good job with you!" while we deal with the one that is having a problem. That's the way it *should be*, and that is the way we *think it is*, but what actually happens is we devote all of our time trying to resolve the problem the other child is having and the next thing we know, the problem-free child is in a mess because we have not balanced our time between the two of them, problems or not.

This is what happens when trying to maintain a balance between teaching and scholarship, mainly writing. We are so worried about teaching and all of its problems, the paperwork, our students, the standardized tests, and then the scholarship, the solitude, is like, "Hey! Remember me? I am kind of dying here…I need you to come take care of me, spend time with me." And bam. The metaphorical door of solitude is slammed in your face and there is a lock box on it for which you have no key. Good luck getting back in. When you sit down and face the blank page it takes a lot of surrender and grit to pick that lock. You can't get inside the warm and cozy living room. You're stuck outside in frozen isolation. The scholarship and the writing are the therapy for teaching. It is that simple. There can be a symbiotic relationship between the two that works beautifully, even seamlessly. The key is to *find the time. Make* the time. People say, "I just don't have the time to write right now. There is too much going on in my life." I am one of those people. I tell that lie all the time. I think it is true. I believe it. But how much time did I spend texting or looking at Facebook or talking to co-workers on the phone about what happened at work that day? We make time to eat. We make time for our families, friends, pets, exercise, church, hair, nails, vacation…why not writing? Why not solitude? Invoke the muse. Name it. Create a Patronus. Make the magic happen. The reason we don't make the time is because there is an element of the Other to solitude. We don't really know what will happen there. I might say I am going to read *One Hundred Years of Solitude* (Garcia Marquez, 1970) for an hour every day this week, but when I go to a chair in the corner of the dimly lit living room window at dusk, I might conceive an idea about a paper or a short story. Or maybe the novel will bring back a memory that is not pleasant so I start thinking about my Daddy issues and I don't read the book. Instead I face the Daddy demons. It's not what I planned. It isn't pleasant, but it leads me to a better place.

If we do not find solitude, we keep the demons in the closet, but we don't forget them. We hear them beating on the door. We hear the door rattling. We hear the moaning and cackling and the scraping and the pain. It is behind the door, but it's there. Either we open the door and invite them in or they beat down the door and push us into isolation. Solitude allows us to surrender to it and deal with it, even use it. But, sometimes we might be pleasantly surprised by what happens in solitude, when we have a plan to read One Hundred Years of Solitude (Garcia Marquez, 1970), but instead we come up with a seemingly endless list of hilarious puns about cats that we want to share with our students tomorrow, or a project idea where students create a reality show for Shakespeare and his contemporaries, writing and performing the dialogue that might have existed among fellow writers and in their daily lives as they created stunning and timeless work. This often happens on the drive home, or at the gym, or in the shower, or while you are cooking a meal, and that's great, but how much of it do you carry with you and turn into reality? If you are not truly in solitude where you can flesh these ideas out, they will not materialize to their fullest potential.

We must compose a life for ourselves that is inclusive of all that we are and all that we experience, whether it be good, bad, or ugly. Bateson says, "Nevertheless, when there is a rent in the canvas, a discord in the harmony, a betrayal, it is important not only to recover but to discover a new and inclusive pattern of meaning. Part of the task of composing a life is the artist's need to deny it, to use it in the broader design" (1989, p. 211). Paradox? Maybe. We need to deny the demons, deny their control over us, but we can face them in solitude and channel the emotion of that confrontation, of that conflict into something we create that has meaning and purpose, not just for ourselves, but for others. Bateson says:

> Impersonal writing often claims a timeless authority: this is so. Personal writing affirms relationship, for it includes these implied warnings: this is what I think at this moment, this is what I remember now, continuing to grow and change. This finally is contingent on being understood and responded to. (1994, p. 76)

Our lives are fluid. Our scholarship should be fluid also. I wrote a paper four years ago that I absolutely loved. I believed every word of it. I considered it a perfect, permanent piece of my work that I would never change. When I read it the other day, I completely disagreed with one important piece of it. I had just finished reading a book that my professors suggested and had a realization. I didn't want to read her work because I knew it conflicted with mine, but I read it…and agreed with it…and changed the permanent paper to reflect a relationship between my ideas and hers that worked beautifully without fully compromising the original premise of the paper and, in fact, strengthening the premise. Holding on to that paper as a permanent piece of my work was dogmatic. Dogma is isolating.

Whitehead says, "You must be free to think rightly and wrongly, and free to appreciate the variousness of the universe undisturbed by its perils" (1929, p. 93). It was difficult to go back into the tapestry and undo the knots that were tied too tightly by dogma and weave those fresh threads together with something previously foreign and uncomfortable. I was personally suturing my "self" into that tapestry and it didn't feel good. But once I created the pattern and sewed the pieces together, it felt right and it felt comfortable and it felt just as much like a piece of conceptual and stylistic writing as it did before. Without trying it on for myself and tailoring it to fit me, it would be a lie. That was my greatest fear, that a paper that felt so much like me, a piece of writing that I could boldly share with others while feeling bulletproof, would become a lie, but it already was. More accurately, my knowledge, or at least my understanding of what I was reading and writing had changed. Pinar says:

> As soon as we take hold of the curriculum as an opportunity for ourselves and our students, as citizens, as ethical and spiritual persons, we realize that curriculum changes as we engage it, reflect on it, and act in response to it, toward the realization of our private-and-public ideals and dreams. (2004, p. 187)

The experience of editing that paper to better reflect what I continue to learn, know, and understand made me feel vulnerable, but I was reminded, in solitude, that I am not bulletproof, nor do I want to be. I don't want my experience with learning to be finite. I want it to be fluid. To be an important writer, to be a respectable scholar, I have to remove the bulletproof vest and put "CS" on my chest, Curriculum Studies. I have to be brave enough to be vulnerable and to share that with others. I have to face the good and the bad, in the time and space of solitude, in order to create and in order to avoid isolation. Dewey says:

Genuine freedom, in short, is intellectual; it rests in the trained power of thought, in ability to 'turn things over,' to look at matters deliberately, to judge whether the amount and kind of evidence requisite for decision is at hand, and if not, to tell where and how to seek such evidence. (2012, p. 60)

In fighting for solitude, we are fighting for intellectual freedom.

References

Arendt, H. (1958). *The human condition*. Chicago, IL: The University of Chicago Press.

Arendt, H. (1968). *The origins of totalitarianism*. New York, NY: Harcourt, Inc.

Bateson, M. (1989). *Composing a life*. New York, NY: Grove Press.

Bateson, M. (1994). *Peripheral visions: Learning along the way*. New York, NY: Harper.

Davis, D. (2007). Confessions on an anacoluthon: Avital Ronell on writing, technology,   pedagogy politics. In *The Politics of Possibility: Encountering the imagination* (pp. 89-126). Boulder, CO: Paradigm.

Dewey, J. (1944). *Democracy and education: An introduction to the philosophy of education*.   New   York, NY: Free Press.

Dewey, J. (2012). *How we think*. United States: Renaissance Classics.

Doll, M. (1999). The web and the work. In M. Morris & M. Doll, *How we work* (pp. 1-10). New York, NY: Peter Lang Publishing.

Eisner, E. (2002). *The arts and the creation of the mind*. New Haven, CT: Yale University Press.

Garcia Marquez, G. (1970). *One hundred years of solitude*. New York, NY: Harper & Row.

Harvey, D. (2000). *Spaces of hope*. Berkeley, CA: University of California Press.

Heidegger, M. (1995). *The fundamental concepts of metaphysics: World, finitude, solitude*. Bloomington. IN: Indiana University Press

King, S. (2000). *On writing: A memoir on craft*. New York, NY: Scribner.

Mills, C. W. (2000). *The sociological imagination*. Oxford, England: Oxford University Press.

Morris, M. (2008). *Teaching through the ill body: A spiritual and aesthetic approach to pedagogy and illness*. Rotterdam, NY: Sense Publishers.

Nietzsche, F. (1997). *Daybreak: Thoughts on the prejudices of morality*. Cambridge, MA: Cambridge University Press.

Pinar, W. P. (2004). *What is curriculum theory?* Mahwah, NJ: Lawrence Erlbaum Associates, Inc.

Taylor, M. C. (2009). *Field notes from elsewhere*. New York, NY: Columbia University Press.

Whitehead, A. N. (1929). *The aims of education and other essays*. New York, NY: The Free Press.

Chapter 3

Layers of Rotting Wood

A Meditation on the Curricular Value of the Ugly

James Grant

Introduction[i]

When I was in the 7th grade I had a crush on a girl. Honestly, I had several crushes that year, and I had something to learn from each of them, but this crush has always stood out in a very particular way. Here's the scene: I'm in 7th grade and kind of awkward, particularly with girls. It's the early 90s, so three-way calling is a thing, but I don't have it. My buddy CJ does, though. The plan was that I would call him, then he would call this girl—let's call her Cheryl to cut down on reducing her to an extension of her gender—through his three-way and ask her if she was interested in being my girlfriend. If she said yes, I would chime in and things would go from there (a sneaky tactic, perhaps, but not uncommon among the kids I knew, male and female alike). If she said no, I would stay hushed and that would be that for a few awkward minutes or just hang up. When CJ popped the question, however, things took a turn that I was not prepared for. "James?!" she asked, flabbergasted at the suggestion. "No! He's ugly!" I was crushed. Not because she said "no," but because she used that word: ugly. What could have been worse, more debilitating to any developing sense of ego? While I have no recollection of ever thinking myself the handsomest of my peers, I certainly had never considered myself *ugly*. Having cobbled together my own understanding of what ugliness was from fairy tales, exaggerations of the human form in horror and comedy films, and the gross creations of my own imagination, I had to wonder: did she really think I was *that*? The fact is that she couldn't have, because mine, as is often the case, was a very private conception, and this is the issue: while

David P. Owen, Jr (ed.), Field Theory: Curriculum Studies at Work, 39–59.

the notions of beauty and ugliness are both relative and often deeply personal, there are still general consensuses for what beauty is at any given time and in any given place. When we talk of aesthetics, what we tend to talk about is what is beautiful and what makes it so. What we do not talk about, however, is what is ugly, what makes that thing ugly, or whether the fact of its ugliness renders it meaningless, valueless. Just as ugly people, ugly feelings, and ugly thoughts are overlooked and pushed toward the edges of what we are willing to consider, so too, very often, is the very *concept* of ugliness. Further, just as there is a cultural curriculum of beauty that instructs us through such course materials as advertisements, television programs, and films that idealize beauty for us, as well as trashy magazines that do the same, each of which would have us striving to reach and maintain very particular body images, there is also a curriculum of the ugly. However, whereas so-called beauty teaches us through constant bombardment with images and lulling sounds, ugliness often teaches us by presenting to us that which we would rather not talk about, leaving us with thoughts unspoken yet not unspeakable. Due to its marginalized status in the field of aesthetics and everyday conversation and its pedagogical potential, ugliness deserves a voice in the curriculum conversation. Not only can it be tacitly instructive as to what we value culturally, but also as to why we keep silent about certain subjects, as well as actively creating silence about others.

Schubert (1991) wonders how it is that "educators unwittingly can be so certain about solutions to curriculum problems, when those very problems are embedded within a context of uncertainty amid the most profound questions that beset humankind" (p. 67). With this in mind, I must say that if we are to meditate sincerely on the instructional value of ugliness (or the problem that ugliness proposes for curriculum), we must consider it for its own sake. That is, instead of exploring ugliness toward the end of finding some beauty within it or that it may reveal to us—as Esch (2010) does consistently in her essay extolling the virtues of the show *Ugly Betty*, inadvertently undercutting the value of the ugly as such—we must explore ugliness toward better understanding ugliness *as* ugliness, without pussyfooting the disquieting task and replacing it with something that is altogether more pleasant; such a displacement would be falling right into the trap that I am seeking to unhinge: allowing the ugly to silence honest conversation through the belief that we've *solved* a deep-seated issue while ignoring the context from which it arises.

Elizabeth Vallance (1991) tells us that aesthetic inquiry "demands that the researcher have *both the large perspective of the big picture and a sensitivity to the telling detail*" (pp. 168-169). With regard to this, I argue that the "big picture" extends beyond any given aesthetic moment, any singular work of art and into the myriad machinations of the culture that allowed such a moment to be understood aesthetically or such a work to be produced. Therefore, aesthetic inquiry must often extend beyond the field of aesthetics itself to the study of culture and history. Such an exploration must entail at the very least a consideration of several of the domains under which ugliness falls as well as an account of ugliness's status in the world today and historically[ii].

The Redheaded Stepchild of Aesthetics: Realizing the Marginalization of Ugliness

Perhaps some of the opening ideas are a bit overstated; ugliness has not been *completely* left out of the conversation concerning aesthetics[iii]. After all, Socrates rather famously debated Parmenides on the subjects of beauty and ugliness, arriving at the conclusion that ugliness is more than the mere opposite of beauty, but rather a concept in its own right (Plato, n.d.). Interestingly, Morris (2016) argues that the Platonic forms have little place in the postmodern context of a world that has seen such atrocities as the dropping of atomic bombs, the Vietnam War, and the 9/11 attacks on the World Trade Center. What we will find as we continue, though, is that where the Platonic form of Beauty may not have an arguably relevant place in certain contemporary conversations that are situated within limiting historical contexts, ugliness stems from a sort of formlessness that cannot help but pervade any conversation.

Further, we *do* each have a conception of what it means to be ugly, and phenomena like "ugly dolls," and the aforementioned television program *Ugly Betty*, which ran for a total of 85 episodes (IMDb, 2016), have done anything but blot out the idea of ugliness from modern conversations. Beyond this, one criticism that I hear quite often concerning social media is that people only tend to post "happy" pictures of themselves and their beautiful families and are much more likely to only share optimistic or "positive posts," creating online profiles that make their lives look perfect. Such a criticism indirectly posits that we should all know that there is enough dirt being swept under that digital rug to fill a desert. No one wants to show their scars; no one wants to share their own ugliness. Better to keep that in a closet somewhere, festering and rotting slowly.

Despite these intrusions of ugliness into aesthetic dialogues, however, the ugly is still a minor player, the Rosencrantz and Guildenstern (Shakespeare, *Hamlet*, 1600/1997) of Beauty's great tragedy. If you, dear reader, would indulge me and do a search for the terms "beautiful," "ugly," "beauty," and "ugliness" using Google's nGram Viewer engine— which may have its limitations and a leaning toward scientific texts, but still draws from a corpus of over five million books spanning from 1800 to 2008 (Language Log, 2010)—you will find that while "beautiful" reached its peak around 1853, making up 0.014% of all words recorded in that year and "beauty" reached its peak about the same time at 0.009% of all recorded words, the highest "ugly" ever reached was 0.001% and "ugliness," the state of being ugly (as opposed to the judgment of owning that state), never reached above 0.0002%.

So, there we have it. When we talk about aesthetics, what we tend to focus on is what is beautiful; the ugly gets pushed to the sidelines. Perhaps, then, it is a bit ironic that nearly half of the texts with which I will engage in this piece have the terms "ugly" or "ugliness" in their titles. Ultimately this is irrelevant, though, as we can clearly see that they are anomalies. With this in mind, and with the understanding that studies in curriculum often seek to find a space for the marginalized, a look into the ugly, its foundations and its implications, is more than warranted.

Ugliness as Interruption

While we all have our own ideas about what is beautiful, these ideas are often mediated through advertising, works of art, television shows, and movies. That is, there are gatekeepers who often decide beforehand what beauty is for us, keeping what they consider ugly (or at least not beautiful enough to be worthy of attention) out of our sight. Douglas (2014) argues that the openness of the Internet has created a space without these gatekeepers, one that is more democratized, where anyone with an idea and a connection can broadcast that idea to the world. Because of this, and often as a statement against normalized beauty, many creators of online content purposefully uglify their creations, not only leaving the edges rough, but roughing them up on purpose.

Often, Douglas (2014) argues, this very ugliness is created out of a sense of authenticity, something to stand against the corporation-generated images that march across our web browsers. One such iteration of ugly content is the meme series "Nailed It." These memes, which pair highly stylized photographs of crafts or "beauty poses" with failed real-world attempts at re-creating the same crafts and images "normalize imperfection, counteracting the effect of magazines, TV shows, and corporate websites that use technical tools to build an unattainable simulacrum of the world" (Douglas, 2014, p. 327). While the case for an actual normalized ugliness is a bit of a longshot, it is safe to say that these images do disrupt the constant stream of beautified images by which we are bombarded. Here, we find that the arts can "help us to learn new things about the world by interrupting us and taking us to other places so that we can 'release the imagination'" (Morris, 2016, p. 33). This "releasing the imagination" is, of course, a reference to Greene's (1995) work of the same title. Significantly, Greene writes in this piece that "[aesthetic] experiences require conscious participation in a work, a going out of energy, an ability to notice what is there to be noticed in the play, the poem, the quartet" (p. 125). That is, aesthetic experience requires *work*, it is active. In a strange way, an ugly aesthetic not only works toward challenging common notions of beauty, particularly those instances where beauty is simply manufactured, but also creates a new ground on which surprising instances of beauty may exist. This is not to say that there is any beauty in this ugliness or that beauty needs ugliness as a grounding binary, but rather that through exposure to ugliness, we have a new means by which we can judge when a thing is beautiful on its own versus when it has been manipulated to appear so. However attractive the beautiful appears, this sort of aesthetic goes, at least the ugly is authentic. Things are awful. Accept it.

There is a danger with this line of thinking, however. Internet Ugly is ultimately a statement against and an aesthetic that arose out of *manufactured* beauty. Even though I argue that this sort of aesthetic does create a new space for authentic, natural beauty, it also threatens to distract us from it, opting for the eternally ironic. When such is the case, this sort of ugliness (which is itself manufactured) runs the risk of being a hidden mundanity, a bad interruption that does not "generate anything but annoyance. So [we] mustn't romanticize the notion of interruption" (Morris, 2016, p. 36). That is, when the ugly interrupts just for the sake of interrupting, any self-reflective end that it may have achieved is lost in ambiguity, neither one thing nor another; it's nothing special, just ugly.

Eschewing the Physically Ugly

Regarding ugliness and monstrosity, Henderson (2015) tells us that the latter "could be didactic, derivative, comic or commercially valued" (p. 75). While the latter two of these could be rich digging grounds for cultural studies, it is the former that is most pertinent for this particular study. Given this, the didactic nature of ugliness comes to us strikingly in one tale surrounding the mythological Irish king Niall, as well as through tales of the legendary Dame Ragnell.

As the story goes (cf. Bard Mythologies (2018), for example), when the fifth-century Irish high king Niall of the Nine Hostages was a young boy, he and three of his companions were seeking water and came upon a well. Before they could receive the water, the ugly, decrepit, wrinkled old hag at the well challenged them to give her a kiss (in some versions of the story, the challenge is to sleep with her). Only Niall met the challenge, and upon doing so, the hag transformed into a beautiful woman. This woman revealed to Niall her metaphoric nature as Sovereignty, informing Niall that only he among his companions was truly fit to take on the sovereignty of Ireland because he was willing to accept the ugliness that such a task entailed. What is implicit in this tale is that whatever beauty there may be in the fame and wealth of sovereignty is starkly overshadowed by the harshness and ugliness wrapped up therein.

Consider this in light of Diane Lee's (1991) argument that for teachers to be "authentic professionals, they [...] have to reject notions of fixed values, fixed goals, fixed objectives, fixed truths" (p. 119). The classroom is a messy place, and while it may be easier, tidier, more pleasant, to work out of a fixed set of standards and objectives, whatever apparent beauty may come from such a set-up is ultimately a denial of the complexity of any given classroom situation, a shutting down of the imagination. Considering that Lake (2015) tells us that imagination "emerges out of union of inward personal meaning and the external world" (p. 128), this fixed-in-place aesthetic is also a shutting down of personalizing meaning within the classroom. Here's the kicker that the hag and Lee reveal, then: true sovereignty in the classroom is a matter of giving over to possibility, of embracing the ugliness of the unknown and allowing complex, monstrous situations to reveal themselves as they are and further allowing them to tear down whatever illusions of control we believe we have.

Stories that evoke the character of Dame Ragnell share some very similar themes, but complicate the notion of sovereignty even further. In the medieval text *The Wedding of Sir Gawain and Dame Ragnell* (Anonymous, 1450/2006), for example, Gawain and King Arthur must find the answer to the riddle "What is it women most desire," to avoid Arthur's beheading. Gawain and Arthur each quest for the answer, and Arthur eventually comes upon Dame Ragnell, a hag who claims she has the answer to his riddle, which she will reveal under one condition: she must be allowed to wed Gawain, and to do so publicly. While Arthur is loath to let his friend take on such a horrid burden, Gawain accepts, and Ragnell reveals that what women most desire is sovereignty. Nice answer, but this is not the end. Ragnell is not always a hag. In fact, she reveals to Gawain that she is cursed to spend half of her days as a hag and half of her days as her actual beautiful self. After this revelation, she gives Gawain a choice: should she be beautiful in the day and ugly at night, or beautiful at night and ugly during the day. The former would create a situation wherein Gawain could have a beauty on his arm at court and earn public praise, but be faced with sleeping next to and making love with her haggish form. In the latter case, Gawain could sleep next to and make love with the beautiful Ragnell in private, but be the butt of public jokes in having a hag on his arm at court. As it turns out, Gawain suggests that she make the decision herself, and doing so breaks the curse altogether. If Gawain had made the choice, he would have denied her the one thing that, according to the tale, women actually want: sovereignty. Since he gave her sovereignty in this situation that really had more to do with her life than his, she was freed.

So, there's sovereignty and there's sovereignty. The notion of sovereignty that we get from the tale of Niall is that it is ugly, but that the ugliness of being a ruler must be faced and embraced if we are to experience any beauty at all. With Ragnell, however, we must not only accept the ugliness of sovereignty, but be willing to extend sovereignty to others and allow them to make their own choices, not ruling over them but partnering with them as they make decisions for themselves.

To this point, we have dealt with characters who have either shrunk away from ugliness, like Niall's companions and King Arthur, or who have accepted the challenge that ugliness presents. These are not the only responses to ugliness, however. Often, we respond to ugliness with violence. Henderson (2015) tells us that although ugliness through deformity was a sign of divinity in many areas before the Greco-Roman era, by the classical period, ugliness of body, through notions of physiognomy, became equated to ugliness of spirit, suggesting that those who were deformed were made so as a mark of their inherent evil. Further, Eco (2011) writes that "in most cases the many victims of the stake were accused of witchcraft *because they were ugly*. And, with regard to this ugliness, some people even imagined that during their hellish Sabbats they were able to transform themselves into attractive creatures" (p. 212). Here again we have the trope of ugly creatures, through the use of spells, magically becoming beautiful, but what is important for our current discussion is the violence that ugliness begets. With this in mind, and if ugliness "has long posed a challenge to aesthetics and taste, [...] complicating questions about the human condition and the wider world in which we live and interact" (Henderson, 2015, p.9), it makes sense that those who want to live in a world devoid of spiritual filth would want to destroy the physically ugly.

This thinking, however, is fantastical, a delusion, and allows us to see the very *human* ugliness that arises from that which makes us uncomfortable. That is, an ugly response to perceived ugliness does little more than add to the pile. Further, the relation may not be so simple. Eco (2007) clarifies for us that whereas beauty is finite and limited in its scope, ugliness is infinite "like God." Not only does such an understanding of ugliness render the concept unfathomable in itself, it also makes ugliness an infinite *possibility* for *us*. If ugliness is infinite, then ugliness always risks becoming *our* possibility. Destroying the ugliness before us then, is essentially destroying the reminders of our own possible ugliness, physical *and* spiritual.

Perceived ugliness can inspire us to do more than just destroy *it*, however. There are the occasional instances where it can also drive us toward destruction in general. Consider the debut of Stravinsky's (1913/1989) ballet *The Rite of Spring*. When the Ballet Russes premiered the piece in Paris, an all-out riot ensued. While descriptions of the debacle vary, and, with descriptions of audience members drumming out rhythms on other members' bald heads and sword fighting with canes, tend toward the cartoonish, it is clear that there was an upheaval in the theatre due to either a) the consistent musical dissonance, b) the downright clunkiness of the dance, or c) a strange combination of the two. According to Hewitt (2013), who quotes one critic of the time as having written that the "music always goes to the note next to the one you expect" (para. 8), it was more than likely that the dissonance was the true key to the outrage.

One interesting thing to note here is that the performance was completed. Despite the disruptions, the ballet ran without halt from the "almost strangled bassoon melody" (Hewitt, 2013, para. 7) that begins the work to its catastrophic end that reveals a certain mechanical quality to so many human rituals. However much violence the piece may have inspired, the music itself was not stamped out. This suggests a muddier relationship between ugliness and destruction than has been discussed up to now. While physical ugliness can drive us to attack the offending person or object directly so as to be done with it, aural ugliness, which requires a different type of perception and set of associations, can inspire a whole new level of ruination. Whereas the prospect always exists for projecting the possibility of physical ugliness onto ourselves, we can never *be* an ugly sound, we can only experience them. It appears that this sort of ugly experience, removed ever so slightly from what we can point directly at (for pointing at the violinist is not pointing at the music he is making any more than pointing at the notes on the score is) can drive us toward whatever it is that we can get our hands on, just to have done with *something*.

Skeletons in the Closet: Ugly Emotions

The classroom is a strange place. Try as we might, the classroom situation is always manufactured. The students who come into our rooms and sit in the desks that we've arranged and participate in the activities and discussions that we've prepared for them do not do these things naturally. While each student may know some of their classmates, they ultimately did not group themselves. Nor did they (often, anyway) choose to be on *our* rosters. Yet there they are, with all of their intellectual and emotional strengths and baggage, trying to gain what they can from what we have to offer them. Such a situation often creates space for emotions and thoughts that we cannot quite name, or that are ambiguous in nature. These are the emotions that Ngai (2005) calls "ugly feelings." While we may commonly associate violent urges with ugliness of emotion, Ngai argues that the clarity of these feelings set them into a different category, and that it is the feelings that are less definite in their nature that are truly ugly, largely through their lack of tangible form. While there is a case to be made for both sides of this, let us begin with Ngai's thought. From there, we will move beyond feelings (which may arise arbitrarily) to thought, which is, all things considered, more purposeful.

Ugly Feelings

One of the feelings that Ngai describes as ugly is anxiety. Anxiety's ugliness stems from its lack of a concrete object and its projected nature into possible futurity. It is a weird space that consistently imagines harmful futures for particular areas that can often stop us in our tracks[iv]. Ngai writes that anxiety is characterized by less "an inner reality which can be subsequently externalized than as a structural effect of spatialization in general" (2005, p. 212). Places, and the possible futures that we project onto them, evoke anxiety, and the classroom is no different. Whitehead (1929) speaks of just this sort of curricular anxiety in stating that the England of his day was unsure whether to produce amateurs with generalized knowledge or experts with specialized knowledge. Whitehead's answer, of course, was that the issue is much muddier, and that curricula must be developed by those who are directly involved in their implementation for those who will most directly benefit; quite an anxiety-driving task of itself when one does not feel free to create. Still, perhaps it is better to be anxious about *how* to create a thing than to have anxiety over *what to create in the first place*.

While anxiety has its foundation in uncertainty and imagined possibility, the ground for anxiety in the 21st-century classroom is, ironically, beyond sturdy, for both students and for teachers. Beyond the simple idea that we're herded into rooms with people we do not (at first) know, many of whom we do not trust, the constant monitoring of students by teachers and administrators (and let's not forget the policing that students do of each other), as well as that of teachers by administrators, the state, students, and parents, create the possibility of schools being bona fide anxiety factories. Every new person thrown into the mix re-places a place, creating new possible sources of anxiety.

What's more is that while we look to technology to help us create new bonds and connect with our world in meaningful new ways, Dimitriadis (2015) informs us that reform efforts toward incorporating technology into curricula to meet the needs of a changing world economy "underscore a deeper anxiety about how the world is changing and how our educations systems fit into this evolving landscape" (p. 135). In an odd way, then, the anxiety about ensuring that American students will be ready to meet the demands of the increasingly digital world drives curriculum reforms that do little more than re-channel anxieties.

This anxiety is, of course, not only limited to the classroom. Issues of identity, particularly cultural identity, can be a major source of anxiety. When one's culture has been a grounding entity for how one defines oneself, slowly encroaching globalization and the muddying, sterilization, and nullification of cultures can be a destabilizing force. Again, Dimitriadis tells us that popular culture today "can only be understood against the backdrop of the massive social and technological shifts associated with 'globalization'" (2015, p. 136). This is problematic when we consider that, largely, individuals base their identities on those things with which they can connect and identify, and that pop culture offers a very limited, tailored set of identities from which to choose. In this way, a globalized identity threatens to flatten the categories with which an individual can identify, marginalizing those categories and, to an extent, uglifying them when they do not mix individual authenticity with a globalized identity. When the ugly becomes, as we have seen, that which we must be rid of, what we may authentically identify with often becomes the thing we must purge from our world, doubly creating plastic identities and ugly inner lifeworlds.

The question becomes, which of these uglies, if either, is acceptable, the one to be embraced? With this question in mind, it must be said that one large part of educating is building an environment of trust wherein students can explore their own ugly feelings with the instructor and with each other. The 21st-century educator must explore not only ideas and projections of students' possible beauty, but also the avenues of ugliness that they must travel. This is a narrow path, indeed. Thacker (2015) writes that the "mourning voice of Greek tragedy constantly threatens to dissolve song into wailing, music into moaning, and the voice into a primordial, disarticulate anti-music" (p. 24). Standing upon the backbone of tragedy, we must ever be alert to the dissolution of our songs. Given such a situation, it would seem that we would be better served by letting ugliness lie beneath the metaphorical rug, and yet to do so would rob any experience of its authenticity. On this note, Pop (2014) questions whether beauty and ugliness can coexist, and, utilizing an argument of degrees and comparison, concludes that the two are ultimately co-dependent. While some of Pop's methodology and reasoning is a bit dubious (his claim, for example, that "to be beautiful means 'to be lovelier than' and to be ugly 'to be less lovely than'" (p. 175), have little ground, for one can experience an instance of beauty or ugliness without necessarily having any experience with which to compare it), the notion that the two consistently intermingle within an individual's experience, informing those experiences from behind the scenes, is hardly refutable.

Finally, and briefly, I wish to discuss that emotion that makes itself so readily available in the classroom: shame. Shame, Henderson (2015) tells us, "suggests another kind of ugliness, akin to emotional 'dirt' (in the sense of 'matter out of place') that soils the soul" (p. 41). Shame arises when we feel as if we've felt or done and internalized something that "doesn't belong," a feeling that develops, ultimately, from having unrealistic ideas about what others *actually* feel and experience themselves. In the song "Delicate Cycle" (Bavitz & Dawson, 2013) by the anti-folk/hip hop duo The Uncluded, Kimya Dawson sings about growing up working in a laundromat that her father ran. She goes on to tell us that the first time she lived in a house with a washer and dryer at the age of 26 was the "year [she] bottomed out," speculating that it was the lack of "community that comes from / hauling your big old load out in public and airing your dirty laundry" that caused her life to fall apart. Her bottoming-out derived from no longer being part of a community that aired its dirty, sweat-stained undies and smelly socks. Shame, the argument goes, disappears in communities where people openly share these simple, if unpleasant, secrets.

The classroom should be no different. When we can openly share our successes (teachers especially) then we create a ground where possible failure does not have to be completely stultifying. It is on this type of ground that students actually feel free to take intellectual risks and not feel isolated from their peers through the shame they could possibly feel if they are unsuccessful. The emotional filth of shame gets a thorough wash and rinse when communal ugliness gets pulled from the bottom of the hamper.

Ugly Thoughts

Of course, no exploration of mental ugliness would be complete without consideration of that ugliest of philosophies, pessimism, with its embrace of doom and gloom. These terms deserve some discussion in their own right. Thacker (2015) explains that what comes out of an understanding that all things will end (doom) is "a sense of the unhuman as an attractor, a horizon towards which the human is fatally drawn" (p. 20). Gloom, however, doom's atmospheric counterpoint, in its "austerity of stillness," instead of facing us with our inevitable demise, rather becomes "the horror of a hovering stasis that is life" (p. 21). In other words, either way we shake it, everything runs the risk of being terrible. Of course, it's not quite so simple. Paradoxically, then, it appears that ugliness and monstrosity can become analeptics for those who would stave off the gloominess of a stagnant existence. Let us work backward here. The gloomy individual, in her melancholy stasis, sees no end, is trapped in an infinite nothingness of the now. A mild injection of doom into this sort of pessimism, however, allows for a new sort of authenticity of Being, as it provides a sort of *telos* or *towards which* for the individual (Heidegger, 1926/1962). Instead of drifting upon a stagnant sea, we instead rush toward the gaping mouth of the Kharybdis. Could it be, then, that a doom-focused pessimism is actually a sort of cloaked optimism? Is an ugliness of thought that embraces our inherent demise preferable to an ugliness of thought that sees no possibility? Perhaps my desire to answer "yes" is simply more evidence that the "notion of an American pessimism is an oxymoron" (Thacker, 2015, p. 54).

It is in light of this understanding of ugliness that Asger Jorn's (1956/2011) proposition that "an era without ugliness would be an era without progress" ("Sensational Conclusions," para. 1) is most pertinent. The dulling ugliness of gloom, that is, can still be shaken up, interrupted by the ugliness of impending doom. Whereas gloominess acts as its own analgesic, perpetuating a cycle of endless nothingness, doom promises an end, and ends require motion. With that in mind, teleological destruction still lays the pathway for progress, for motion forward, however ugly the thing toward which we are moving may be.

Toward an Ugly Curriculum

The immediately preceding discussion, is, of course, a new imagination of the absurdist existentialist dilemma. If everything is certain to crumble, does anything ever really change? The works we think we are developing today will be forgotten a thousand years from now, and that's always been the case. Does, then, the meaning we posit into our activities and experiences remain valid? Whereas gloom would issue a resounding "of course not," the idea of doom breaks this up with a less confident "maybe." If life is absurd anyway, better to let anxiety-riddled projections toward the future go. As Camus (1955/1983) has written, "Each atom of [Sisyphus's] stone, each mineral flake of that night filled mountain, in itself forms a world. The struggle itself toward the heights is enough to fill a man's heart" (p. 123) It is in the midst of this strange chasm that we may continue onward to consider what an ugly curriculum would look like. Considering all of the above, it is perhaps the idea of asymmetry through which we can most clearly accomplish this.

Ugliness as Asymmetry

In the song "Hang Ten" by the hip hop duo Hail Mary Mallon, Rob Sonic raps briefly about his outfit. "Boat shoes, gold tooth, fanny packs," he begins, closing out the rhyme with the fact that he's "in some fancy pants and a Stüssy hat/just because [he's mother****] bringin' ugly back" (Bavitz & Smith, 2014, Track 7). Such an awkward assemblage—a little of this, a little of that—hints at a collage-like aesthetic, lacking balance or completion, borrowing from a random collection of styles that has no ground beyond that of the particular individual. Consider here Rosenkranz's (1853/2015) ideas that the "abstract fundamental definition of all beauty is [...] unity," and that the "opposite of unity as abstract disunity would thus be the absence of an outward limit or interior differentiation" (pp. 63, 64). For Rosenkranz, beauty needs form, and that form should have some semblance of symmetry, wherein every part has a relation to every other part, but is distinguished from them in such a way as to not only counterbalance them, but also to be worthy of contemplation in itself. Random assemblages of objects miss the mark here.

The ugliness of asymmetry is not limited to obvious and outward physicality. There can also be asymmetries between ideologies and their realities. For example, Henderson (2015) reminds us that the "'beauty' of Chinese footbinding and Victorian corsets crippled or caused broken bones, while the art of ballet turned a woman's body into a 'deformed skeleton' according to the mother of modern dance, Isadora Duncan" (pp. 16-17). To better illustrate this point, I would like to direct my readers to Jo Farrell's (2014) "Living history project", which is a visual documentation of the practice and effects of Chinese footbinding. There are many unsettling images in this gallery, but one image that is particularly striking is a photograph of the feet of a woman Farrell identifies as Yange Jinge. Yange Jinge, now aged many years, had her feet bound as a young girl. The image that focuses directly on the bottoms of Yange Jinge's feet shows, among other things, three toes per foot (the middle to the smallest) that are nearly perfectly absorbed into the bottom of her feet, so bent and stepped-on that they appear to be little more than oddly shaped wrinkles. What we must consider is that this deformation of the feet would have occurred when Yange Jinge was still very, very young. Here, then, we can see quite plainly the barbarity that so-called beauty can mask, for surely these feet were not intended to be seen out of stockings or shoes. The ugliness here is not even so much of the physical makeup of the feet themselves, but rather in the violence that we must understand that it took to create these feet. The ugliness, that is, occurs in the theoretical asymmetry of achieving apparent beauty (as well as the loveliness that said beauty is supposed to represent) and the physical means of achieving it.

Often, I challenge my students to imagine how they would behave in situations such as whether they would go along with a discriminatory law or what choice they would make if faced with the infamous trolley problem. Regarding the former, students tend to state that they would not go along with such a law, though many admit that while they would not *want* to, they probably would if it came down to having to suffer some sort of penalty. Regarding the trolley problem, students tend to try to skirt the problem, replacing the parameters of the thought experiment with their own terms that soften the choices they are required to make. When conferencing with students about these experiments and bringing attention to the fact that they try to change the rules, students often respond with something like, "I don't want to have to make that kind of decision." It's not a bad response, really. Who would? This, however, is why imagination is important. Eisner (2002) tells us that imagination "gives us images of the possible that provide a platform for seeing the actual, and by seeing the actual freshly, we can do something about creating what lies beyond it" (p. 4). That is, while we may not want to be faced with ugly decisions, and while we may be of several minds about making them, imagination allows a glimpse into our psyches so that we can work toward mending the imbalance between the selves we desire to be in our minds and the selves that we present to the world through our words and actions.

Ugly Connections

Eisner (2002) tells us that aesthetic experience "is potential in any encounter an individual has with the world. One very important aim of arts education is to help students recognize that fact and to acquire an ability to frame virtually any aspect of the world aesthetically" (p. 232), as well as the fact that the arts "liberate us from the literal; they enable us to step into the shoes of others and to experience vicariously what we have not experienced directly" (p. 10). What arts education does for us, then, is open for us not only our own possibilities, but the possibilities of others. This may not always be a welcome experience, though.

It is important to note that, according to Simpson (2014), for psychological and philosophical theorist Theodor Lipps, an originator of theories concerning *Einfuhlung* (empathy), empathy was "not a sensation in one's [own] body, but feeling something, namely, oneself, into the [a]esthetic object" (p. 123). We write our lives onto the objects with which we share moments of empathy, but this projection is not limited to objects, as it is possible "in all intersubjective encounters" (p. 123). Every moment is a possible gateway into shared feeling, and every moment of shared feeling is a ground for aesthetic experience. This is important to our current discussion because Simpson (2014) carries the argument forward, reasoning that since positive *Einfuhlung* was a "harmonious feeling of love, freedom, and confidence in the face of a beautiful person, object, or work of art [... and in] such a context, ugliness and negative empathy threaten not only the aesthetic participant, but the optimism of *Eihfuhlung* theory itself" (p. 127). Here is the idea. When we have an aesthetic encounter, a sort of identification with the aesthetic object occurs. When that encounter causes us pain (negative feeling) we believe the object ugly and reject it. Empathy, it appears, is quite a loaded gun. On the one hand, we want to connect with others, to feel along with them, to open ourselves up to their pain. On the other hand, though, experiencing that pain can turn us off from being empathetic because...well...it hurts. Since such is the case, the educator who would invite his students toward authentic empathy must not delude himself into a sunshine and rainbows, fluffy version of the emotion, but rather see it and respect it for the bundle of ugliness that it can be.

While this section is largely predicated upon ideas that come from Eisner, we must keep in mind that Eisner's main focus is on arts education. However, there is no reason why Eisner's ideas cannot be applied to any sort of education. That is to say, it is not out of the question to wonder why a Social Studies or English or even a Mathematics curriculum could not be tailored toward realizing and embracing aesthetic experience. If we are to be transparent in our delivery of history, could we not invite our students to feel along with historical monsters? Would English teachers do their students a disservice in asking them to develop relationships with fictitious villains and to see them as real possibilities for humanity? Or how about this: H.P. Lovecraft is rather famous for creating nightmarish landscapes wherein the geometry is simply *wrong*, considering the Euclidean understanding we currently have of that branch of mathematics. Graham Harman (2012b) writes that nothing

> is more Lovecraftian than his repeated vague assaults on the assumptions of normal three-dimensional space and its interrelations, as learned by students since ancient Greece. For this reason, nothing could be more threatening than the notion that something is 'all wrong' in the presumed spatial contours on which all human thought and action is based. (p. 71)

Suppose a Geometry teacher actually incorporated Lovecraft's (1926/2014) "The call of Cthulhu" into her curriculum simply for the sake of having her students empathize with the anxiety derived from the vagueness, the wrongness, the *weirdness* the characters experience in discovering a place *in our world* where the geometry is *not of our world*. Are we treading dangerous waters by even mentioning this as a possibility?

All of this is to say that while it is "inclinations toward satisfaction and exploration that enlightened educators and parents wish to sustain rather than to have dry up under the relentless impact of 'serious' academic schooling" (Eisner, 2002, p. 5), there is no real reason why the two have to be mutually exclusive. We can have "serious" academic schooling that invites a sense of playfulness...provided we are prepared to deal with the ugly, messy thoughts and emotions that come from blending them.

Monsters

After the immediately above, some subsequent discussion of monstrosity—at least in an introductory sort of manner—is necessary. For it is a monstrous sort of ugliness with which we are dealing once we start positing notions of things being other than they are. While monsters fall under several different categories of Horror, it is the Unnatural, as I have theorized it (Grant, 2019) that is of most interest here. Unnatural creatures like werewolves, zombies, and Frankenstein's monster *become* monstrous because they defy cut-and-dry categorization through hybridity. Werewolves are a blend of the human and animal; zombies are dead flesh imbued undeniably with life (at least when we consider basic biological animation life—this is to say nothing of any *quality* of life). These monsters are what they should not be and should not be what they are, and are monsters *to us* because they do not allow us easy access to their being. While this is not the only reason such creatures are terrifying (arguably, a greater reason for their being so is that, in the stories that surround them, they are eternally devoted to wiping out whatever human life happens to be in their way), it is an undeniable one.

While Lyotard (1979/1984) warns us against the creation of grand narratives, and Pinar (2009) warns us of the concretizing and stifling dangers of identity politics, people do tend to construct entire narratives of themselves and those with whom they come most closely into contact *through* the guise of identity, and those narratives are intensely limiting. Bob is X thing. Ginger is Y thing. Collette is Z thing. This is how they function in my life, and while they may have lives outside of my own, it is really only their connections with me that matter. While we may want to argue that we keep these narratives open for future editing, be honest with yourself. When is the last time someone you considered your friend did something *out of character*? How comfortable were you with that? Did you accept it like it didn't even happen? Write them off altogether? Or did it take some getting used to? What is this *getting-used-to* other than an adjustment to something that was originally monstrous, but that we are willing to move beyond because of our connection to the would-be monstrous individual? Outside of the narratives that we construct for them, or the ways that we incorporate them into our lives, even those with whom we are intimately connected are steeped in *Otherness* and monstrosity.

What, then, of the teacher who also engages daily in the work of scholarship and theorization? Are they not similarly monstrous, bleeding across the edges of what we expect, *need*, of our teachers and theorists?

Even though one way out of the cycle of monstrosity of otherness with reference to the others with whom we involve ourselves is a taking-to-heart of Greene's (1995) notion that being a self is a process of creation, this is not so easily applicable when it comes to *roles*. *Roles* are not *selves*. A teacher is a teacher because they teach. Theorists are theorists because they theorize. Teachers can utilize the work of theorists in their teaching, and theorists can theorize about what it is to teach. These ideas keep everything neatly and tidily in their categories, actors relegated to their roles. But this is overmining (Harman, 2011, 2012a, 2013) at its finest, and is reductive of the *being* of teachers and scholars, limiting them to the systems to which our developing-and-never-finished imaginations can connect them.

The monsters of imagination live in caves and dark places for a reason. Their ugliness, and the ugliness that they reveal to us (*monstrare*) about ourselves drives us to shun them, to silence their howls and shrieks. There is no place for the category-blending in polite society. Better not to look at that. Better not to listen.

Conclusion

The Greek myth of Orchis (cf. Henderson, 2012) tells the tale of the son of a satyr and a nymph who attempts to take sexual advantage of a high priestess during a Bacchanal (which would hardly be out of the ordinary, considering the highly sexually charged nature of the festival) and ends up getting torn to pieces by wild beasts. The cause of his dismemberment is more to do with the sacrilege of attempting to take a priestess, who is to remain sexually "pure," than with the attempted rape itself (on this, we should keep in mind that for the Greeks, nymphs and satyrs were very much sexual beings, having little understanding or regard for human mores regarding sex and purity, seeking only pleasure and frivolity). Orchis's father pleads with the gods to restore him, and they do...as a flower, the orchid. Beautiful ending, right? Eh. Not so much.

The character Jonathan in the film *Decay* (Haskins, Huling, & Wartnerchaney, 2015) troubles over the gods' decision to re-incorporate Orchis in this manner. While his unnamed imaginary neighbor attempts to convince him that Orchis ends up being eternally beautiful, Jonathan, having lost his mother to her own psychosis early in his life, protests, obsessed with the idea of rot. Whatever beauty Orchis may have, he argues, comes from nothing but layers of rotting wood. Jonathan has reversed the popular notion of finding beauty in ugliness to uncovering the ugliness, the rot, the decay that fuel the beautiful. This aesthetic flip is beyond important. While it is popular and commendable to seek the beautiful in the midst of ugliness, to deny that beauty grows out of ugliness is to deny a full understanding of the experience of beauty.

Regarding curriculum, and most particularly the curricula of students who sit in desks organized by teachers who have been told what subject matter is most important to relay to their pupils and the best practices for doing so, these sorts of experiences seem almost moot. While the roots from which we derive our modern term "ugly" originally denoted what was to be feared or dreaded, newer conceptions of the term allow us to see the world from different angles, troubling ideas about what we are to fear and what we simply deem not worthy of our time (Henderson, 2015). Whether it is the case that we must do away with what we fear (ugliness and its possibility for us), or the ugly is just that which we do not want to talk about because it is not apparently worth our time, completely ignoring the ugly flattens our world, stripping the beautiful of whatever differentiating value it may have had. If we look toward what it means for an education to be standardized and anaesthetized, stripped of local flavor and the daily needs of particular students in particular classrooms, we can easily see that what was once intended to create a complex ground by which students could understand and participate in beauty becomes little more than polished linoleum. In a not-dissimilar way, curricula that tend toward so-called positive experiences and understandings of history (i.e., those that don't allow for the "ugly realities" of life) are much more in vogue than those that dig into the out-of-place dirt, the decaying historical wood, and the very ugliness of our being, making beauty an inauthentic commonplace, awaiting interruption. When such is the case, perhaps a healthy dose of ugliness is just the thing to wake us up.

References

Anonymous (2006). *The wedding of Sir Gawain and Dame Ragnell*. Retrieved from http://sites.fas.harvard.edu/~chaucer/special/litsubs/romances/wedding.html. (Original work published 1450)

Bard Mythologies (2018). *Niall of the Nine Hostages*. Retrieved from http://bardmythologies.com/niall-of-the-nine-hostages/

Bavitz, I., and Dawson, K. (2013). Delicate cycle. [Recorded by The Uncluded]. On *Hokey Fright* [LP]. Minneapolis, MN: Rhymesayers Entertainment.

Bavitz, I., and Smith, R. (2014). Hang ten. [Recorded by Hail Mary Mallon]. On *Bestiary*   [CD]. Minneapolis, MN: Rhymesayers Entertainment.

Berman, L.M., Hultgren, F.H., Lee, D., Rivkin, M.S., Roderick, J.A. & Aoki, T. (1991). *Toward curriculum for being: Voices of educators*. Albany, NY: SUNY Press.

Camus, A. (1983). *The myth of Sisyphus and other essays*. J. O'Brien (trans.). New York, NY:

Vintage International.

Dimitriadis, G. (2015). Popular culture as subject matter. In M.F. He, B.D. Schultz, & W.H. Schubert (Eds.) *The SAGE guide to curriculum in education* (134-141). Thousand Oaks, CA: SAGE.

Douglas, N. (2014). It's supposed to look like shit: The internet ugly aesthetic. *Journal of Visual Culture*, 13 (3), 314-339.

Eco, U. (2007, December 14). On the history of ugliness [video file]. Retrieved from http://videolectures.net/cd07_eco_thu/?q=umberto%20eco

Eco, U. (2011). *On ugliness*. New York, NY: Rizzoli.

Eisner, E. (2002). *The arts and the creation of mind*. New Haven, CT: Yale University Press.

Esch, M.S. (2010). Rearticulating ugliness, repurposing content: *Ugly Betty* finds the beauty in ugly. *Journal of Communication Inquiry*, 34(2), 168-183.

Farrell, J. (2014). Yange Jinge detail [digital photograph]. Retrieved from http://www.livinghistory.photography/images.html

Grant, J. (2018). Layers of rotting wood: A meditation on the curricular value of the ugly. *Cogent Education* 5(1), 1-14.

Grant, J. (2019). *The curriculum of horror: Or, the pedagogies of monsters, madmen, and the misanthropic*. New York, NY: Peter Lang Publishing, Inc.

Greene, M. (1995). *Releasing the imagination: Essays on education, the arts, and social change*. San Francisco, CA: Jossey-Bass.

Harman, G. (2011). *The quadruple object*. Alresford, Hants, UK: Zero Books.

Harman, G. (2012a). *The well wrought broken hammer*. New Literary History, 43 (2). 183-203

Harman, G. (2012b) *Weird realism: Lovecraft and philosophy*. Alresford, UK: Zero Books.

Harman, G. (2013). Undermining, overmining, and duomining: A critique. In E.J. Sutela (Ed.), *ADD metaphysics* (40-51). Greater Helsinki, Finland: Aalto University Digital Design Laboratory.

Haskins, M., Huling, C. (Producers) & Wartnerchaney, J. (Director). (2015). *Decay* [motion picture]. USA: Ghost Orchid Films.

Heidegger, M. (1962). *Being and time*. J. Macquarrie & E. Robinson (Trans.). San Francisco, CA: HarperSanFrancisco. (Original work published 1926)

Henderson, H. (2012, January 5). On nymphs and satyrs: Orchids. Retrieved from https://www.science20.com/fossil_huntress/blog/nymphs_and_satrys_orchids-85911

Henderson, G.E. (2015). *Ugliness: A cultural history*. Chicago, IL: University of Chicago Press.

Hewett, I. (2013, May 16). The rite of spring 1913: Why did it provoke a riot? *The Telegraph*. Retrieved from http://www.telegraph.co.uk/culture/music/classicalmusic/10061574/The-Rite-of-Spring-1913-Why-did-it-provoke-a-riot.html

IMDb. (2016). *Ugly Betty*. Retrieved 30 August, 2016, from http://www.imdb.com/title/tt0805669/?ref_=fn_al_tt_1

Jorn, A. (2011). Form and structure: On the cult of the "new" in our century. K. Knabb (Trans.). Retrieved from http://www.bopsecrets.org/SI/asger-jorn/form.htm. (Original work published 1956)

Lake, R. (2015). Curriculum imagination as subject matter. In M.F. He, B.D. Schultz, & W.H. Schubert (Eds.) *The SAGE guide to curriculum in education* (127-133). Thousand Oaks, CA: SAGE.

Language Log. (2010, December 16). Humanities research with the google books corpus. [Blog post]. Retrieved from http://languagelog.ldc.upenn.edu/nll/?p=2847

Lovecraft, H.P. (2014). The call of Cthulhu. In Milton Creek Editorial Services (Eds.). *The complete fiction of H.P. Lovecraft* (381-407). New York, NY: Quarto Knows. (Original work published 1926)

Lyotard, F. (1984). *The postmodern condition: A report on knowledge*. (G. Bennington & B. Massumi, trans.). Minneapolis, MN: University of Minnesota Press. (Original work published 1979)

Morris, M. (2016). *Curriculum studies guidebooks (Vol. 2)*. New York, NY: Peter Lang Publishing, Inc.

Ngai, S. (2005). *Ugly feelings*. Cambridge, MA: Harvard University Press.

Pinar, W.F. (2009). *The worldliness of a cosmopolitan education*. New York, NY: Routledge.

Plato. (n.d.). Parmenides. B. Jowett (Trans.). Retrieved from http://classics.mit.edu/Plato/parmenides.html

Pop, A. (2014). Can beauty and ugliness coexist? In A. Pop & M. Widrich (Eds.). *Ugliness: The non-beautiful in art and theory*. London, UK: I.B. Tauris & Co, Ltd. pp. 165-179

Rosenkranz, K. (2015). *Aesthetics of ugliness: A critical edition*. A. Pop & M. Widrich (Trans.). London, UK: Bloomsbury Academic. (Original work published 1853)

Schubert, W.H. (1991). Philosophical inquiry: The speculative essay. In E.C. Short (Ed.), *Forms of curriculum inquiry* (61-76). Albany, NY: State University of New York Press.

Shakespeare, W. (1997). *Hamlet, prince of Denmark*. In B. Bevington (Ed.), *The complete works of Shakespeare* (updated 4th ed.) (pp. 1060-1116). New York, NY: Longman. (Original work published 1600)

Simpson, K. (2014). I'm ugly because you hate me: Ugliness and negative empathy in Oska Kokoschka's early self-portraiture. In A. Pop & M. Widrich (Eds.). *Ugliness: The non-beautiful in art and theory*. London, UK: I.B. Tauris & Co, Ltd., pp. 122-140

Stravinsky, I. (1989). *The rite of spring*. Mineola, NY: Dover. (Original work published 1913)

Thacker, E. (2016). *Cosmic pessimism*. Minneapolis, MN: Univocal.

Vallance, E. (1991). Aesthetic inquiry: Art criticism. In E.C. Short (Ed.), *Forms of curriculum inquiry* (155-172). Albany, NY: State University of New York Press.

Whitehead, A.N. (1929). The aims of education. In *The aims of education* (Chapter One). Retrieved from http://www.anthonyflood.com/whiteheadeducation.htm

notes

[i] Before beginning, I should note that what follows is a revision of an article that I first published in *Cogent Education* (Grant, 2018). Since the publication of that article, I have taken some ideas further, and decided that some of the images that I presented weren't absolutely necessary in all of their grotesquerie, that perhaps I would do better to allow readers to imagine what I was presenting and explore the ugly monstrosities of their own psyches rather than confront them with it directly. That being said, the general premise and ultimate conclusions are the same, but the work as a whole is now better suited to this volume of works.

[ii] I should note here that readers need to be conscientious about what occurs in a meditation, as there will be some who demand an insight into my "approach" for the term. To those readers, I will give a nod to the Zen koan wherein a student trying to meditate becomes frustrated with his master, who makes incessant noise during the student's meditations. The student says to the master, "Can't you see I'm trying to meditate?" To this, the master remarks on the young student's foolishness, reprimanding him with the question, "How can you *try* to meditate?!" There is no algebra of meditation; it occurs organically, and so this exploration will be a bricolage of sorts, allowing thoughts to emerge and be explored as they arise and are relevant to the discussion.

[iii] I should also note that some readers, at this point, will begin to complain that I'm being unclear about what I mean by "ugly" and "ugliness," requesting that I provide some sort of hardline definition and framework for the terms. Too bad. Such a mindset completely misses the point here, and begs that I perpetrate a performative contradiction, in that such an undertaking would seek to tidy up something that is messy, to sanitize the ugly. Say the word to yourself. "Ugly." Allow images and feelings to come to your mind. *That* is what I'm talking about. Definitive enough? I'm sorry. Maybe that very last bit was a little ugly of me.

[iv] Readers may here wonder something to the effect of, "but are there other interpretations of 'ugly emotions'?" There probably are, just as there are multiple interpretations of just about everything. Ngai, however, presents an astute and focused study on the matter, and so holding on to her theories should be just fine for our purposes.

Chapter 4

My Story

Science, Ethics, and the Poietic

John Cato

Madame Poole loves my story. We have talked numerous times about it. I think she just likes to hear it. She even convinced her husband, "the Reverend" Jerry Poole to invite me to their church to tell my story to the young people of the church who had just graduated from high school. She thought that my story would be able to help them in their lives. And, of course, I said I would love to.

It is a nice church. The congregation was polite and inviting. The young people were attentive, but I am sure that they were thinking about what they had planned to do after the service. Heck, I was probably the fifth or sixth speaker for them in the last several weeks. As "the Reverend" spoke, I gathered my thoughts together. Where to begin my story? Where to end it? How much of the truth is necessary to get across a point? I certainly want it to be said that I gave an ethical account of myself, especially in a church! Somewhere between my nervous knees shaking and my continuously folding the program in half, as if my name would suddenly disappear on it, I heard "the Reverend" give my introduction, and began my story:

Where does one begin a story about themselves? Like Piscine, Yann Martel's character in the book *Life of Pi* (2001), I have been asked to give an ethical account of myself, so "I begin my story of myself only in the face of a 'you' who asks me to give an account" (Butler, 2005, p. 11). Therefore, I'll begin my story when I was in seventh grade. My first memories of science are in the seventh grade—rather, my first time in seventh grade. I was in Mrs. Garner's class that year, where I sat on the far-left side of the room and near the back of the room. I remember a nice girl named Yasmine sat in the front of my row. One of her

David P. Owen, Jr (ed.), Field Theory: Curriculum Studies at Work, 61–76.

responsibilities was to walk down the row each day and check to see who did their homework, and report that to the teacher. Each day, Yasmine would walk the row, and when she would get to me, I would offer up some excuse for why I didn't do it. I even remember once trying to pay her off—but she didn't take the money. I remember those kinds of things very clearly.

Another memory I have about seventh grade science that year was I did really well in class—or at least I made good grades on tests and quizzes. I even made the science bowl team. Although she never admitted it, I am sure that Mrs. Garner was shocked. I can still remember the tryout. We were sitting in Mrs. Garner's room near the windows. While I don't remember every question, I do remember the question that put me on the team. I was tied with another student, and I remember Mrs. Garner asking me, "What is the name of the water that runs along the beach and perpendicular to the ocean waves?" I don't know how I knew—I don't even like the beach, and I have never liked trivia—but I did know. I remember Mrs. Garner's face when I got the question right. I think she wanted a recount, only there were no hanging chads in this contest. I was on my way to the Science Bowl as the only member on the team who was failing science.

I also remember parts of the competition. Those memories are mostly just images of stairwells and kids eating lunches out of those white boxes. I do have a foggy memory of being upstairs and looking down into a lobby where there were many people, so it must have been a big deal. Maybe it was regional. My only other memory from that day was I remember talking with Mrs. Garner—about what I have no idea. We sat on the stairs and we talked. I wish I could remember what we talked about. I wonder if she was trying to figure me out—perhaps she already knew.

I think if I had understood the idea of failing and being held back, I am certain I would have brought that up with her on those stairs. Regrettably, I don't remember much of school after that competition, but I do remember one thing about it: I failed—or I was retained, if you prefer sugarcoating it. Yeah, good old Mrs. Garner gave me an F for the year, or that was my understanding of how that happened. Not all was lost, however, because in lieu of repeating, I could go to summer school to make up the class. I don't know how my mom found out about my failing because I wasn't in the habit of bringing home report cards. I don't think she had seen a progress report or report card since I was ten. My guess is that someone from the school called her. I do remember the day we discussed it, though. We were in our red Rabbit driving to my grandparents, and when we were almost there, I brought up the topic of going to summer school. I am sure that my reasoning went something like: this is a tough topic, there is little time left in the car, she'll want to talk to my grandmother when we arrive, so I should do it now. I can take you to the very spot on the road where we were when I brought it up. She replied, "Better luck next year." My mom had just told me—clearly—that I would be sitting in the seventh grade again next year. Looking back on it, I certainly misplayed that. I think I should have asked her earlier in the morning while she was still sleepy. Live and learn.

I forgot to mention why we were going to my grandparents' house—I was moving in with them. My mom—single with three boys—could not handle me anymore. I had become too much. I wasn't bad, though. But I clearly was in trouble. She knew it, and she knew that being with my grandparents might help me. I admire my mom in many ways. She was never afraid to do what she thought needed to be done for her children, even if it meant giving them up, because giving them up is not giving up on them.

It was a long summer. I remember switching bedrooms a couple of times. My grandparents had a big house in a gated community, and I had arrived in a Rabbit. I can still remember the big closet in my new room. Nothing was hanging up in it because everything was shoved into a pile on the floor. I even had my own bathroom. That was really nice. Not having to share a bathroom with my two brothers meant I could brush my teeth in the morning without having to move someone's cup—and I don't mean the kind you drink out of—first. Part of why the summer was so long was because I had to have my tonsils taken out. At least I would go through seventh grade again without them, because I was always getting sick. I never missed school, but I was always getting sore throats. Even though my grandfather was a physician, he attributed it to my birthday. Some planet was forever cursing me.

Though I had a mad crush on Felicia Riddlehoover, I also had to give up going to see her dance on her roller skates at the roller rink because I almost died for the second time. The first time occurred when I was the victim of an attempted kidnapping-murder-suicide, but that's another story! Returning to this story, several planets got together and really tried to get me because I had an allergic reaction to the anesthesia. So much for tons of ice cream! I was practically in a coma. I say practically because the only thing I remember from my week in the hospital was a nurse giving me a suppository. Felicia never visited me, either. Maybe she couldn't get a ride to see me. Or maybe she wasn't into the chubby kid who wore the rented skates. I don't know, but we never talked again.

The only small positive to the planets attempting to kill me was that I lost weight. I must have lost twenty pounds. I also grew some, but that had nothing to do with the attempted murder. After my recovery, it was almost time to return to school. But one problem still existed: I had failed, and I had not come up with any way to ensure I'd pass this time. Even though pulling it out at the very end had been my specialty, I was shaken and needed something more certain. If I had failed once, I surely could fail again. Felicia might be okay with being a year ahead of me now, but I was sure once she got to high school, a fourth-year seventh-grader was not going to be on her radar.

One night while I was watching TV, there was a commercial for a product called, "*Where There's a Will, There's an A.*" I convinced my grandmother to buy it for me. No reason to talk to my granddad, because he would just tell me it was up to Jupiter. That was one thing about my grandmother: If I asked her for an elephant, she would have bought one. This was in the day of "four to six weeks for delivery. Sorry, no CODs." So I waited. Finally, the program came in, and I remember sitting on my bed reading it from beginning to end. I don't remember much about it, but I do recall that one of the main things it noted was that I needed to have a *goal*, a concept that would save me several times throughout my life.

The bells rang, school started, and I was assigned my classes. Some of my teachers I had the year before, but others were new. One of them took us to the library sometime during that first week. Completely by chance—or the planets—I was sitting at a table next to a book entitled, *How to get Into a Service Academy*. I checked out the book and read it when I got home. My grandfather was always talking about West Point and the great leaders that went there. Then he would proceed to tell me their birthdays and how that is what made them great. But the *goal* of going to West Point resonated with me. I remember sitting on my bed and making a conscious decision that I was going to go to West Point. I outlined the requirements they gave and their suggestions for getting into West Point. Yikes! They look at my grades—that's not good. So I knew I had to change my grades going forward. Consequently, I decided to be the best student in school—I was always nervous saying it out loud because I didn't want the planets to get wind of my plan. It was at this point, eight years into my formal education, when I actually became a student.

My second time in seventh grade was much better. It was also then when I first remember having a teacher actually trying to engage with me about science. His name was Mr. Jones, my new science teacher, and he asked me to stay after class one day. I did, and he asked me if I wanted to "help out" by washing glassware, putting away lab materials, and setting up labs. I said I would, and I began spending many hours outside of class with Mr. Jones. He was a very kind and decent man. He also had a bookcase full with books beside his desk, and he said I could take a book home to read if I wanted. I don't know why, but one day I was looking at the bookcase and noticed a big, yellow book with red letters. It was Mr. Jones's college physics book. I asked if I could take it home to read. I am sure that he thought to himself that was a ridiculous request, but he didn't try and stop me. I remember carrying that book around with me everywhere. I found physics very interesting—at least the parts I could understand, which wasn't much. I think of Mr. Jones often, and I wish I had gone back after college and told him that I had majored in physics. I wish I had told him how much I appreciated his showing an interest in me. I had chances, because he was still teaching when I graduated. Perhaps Mr. Jones's final lesson to me would be not to take time for granted. Do what you need to do immediately because life is short, and what you think you have plenty of time for, you may not. You see, Mr. Jones and his wife were murdered—they were shot and burned by their own son.

After finishing the seventh grade for the second time, my mom transferred me to a new school district so that I would be in the zone my grandparents lived in. Changing schools allowed me to make a fresh start. Everyone knew me at my old school and knew that I was a year behind. At my new school, however, no one knew me or that I had failed. I was able to start fresh, and this time start as a good student. My new school did some things differently than my old school. For one, there was a Student of the Month at my new school. I remember at the end of August being called to the office and informed that I was named Student of the Month. Wow! That certainly had never happened. But then in September, I was named it again. And again in October. After the October award, the principal told me that they were making it so that a student couldn't win it more than once because it wasn't fair. That was my last Student of the Month in middle school. I was never tested as being "Gifted," so I was not in the gifted classes. That really set off fireworks within the school, and I think was part of the problem. I am certain other students in the past had been multiple recipients, but they were gifted students—at least that was what my new friend Robby told me. All my awards really seemed to rile them up. After all, how could I be better than them? This matter was more or less settled, interestingly enough, in science class. Somewhere near the middle of the first semester, there was a test that everyone had to take. I don't know what it was or why we had to take it. But I remember there was one perfect score on the test. Only one student knew the earth wasn't round, but shaped more like a gourd. There was a near-riot after the teacher passed back the tests, too. All those "Gifted" kids had a hard time accepting that they didn't get the right answer. Finally, the teacher revealed that I got the question right, and consequently, she would not throw out the question. She even asked me if I guessed. I said no, I just remembered hearing that somewhere. That was my first realization that I have a pretty good memory. Had the same thing happened on that science bowl question?

Good memory or not, I am uncertain about when I took the Iowa Test of Basic Skills. On it, there were different parts of the test, and I recall thinking the science section was easy. I was surprised, however, when my score report came back. I had earned a perfect score in science. Not only that, but the science section itself was subdivided into sections, like life sciences and physics. Looking back, I am surprised that a counselor did not ever call me in and say, "Hey, you might be good at science." No, I think I would be surprised if they had.

My last memory of eighth grade was that I took my first "official" step towards getting into West Point. In my borrowed book, I learned about how I must get a nomination from a Congressman or Senator. I decided to write my Congressman, Doug Barnard, and ask for a nomination. Unfortunately, what I received from his office was a form letter stating that getting into West Point is tough, that there are only a few slots, that nominations are very competitive, etc. Probably the most important part was that I was informed that I could not start the process until I was a junior in high school! I guess Saturn was not in the right place that day.

Having now finished middle school, I was off to the big high school. Things there were not much different from my last two years of middle school. I was a good student with only one goal. Everything I did was to stay on target to meet my goal. Finally, my junior year arrived, and I wrote again to Congressman Barnard. Again, I received a form letter, much like the previous one, but this one contained an additional part that had instructions regarding how to apply, and said that my file had been started.

Senior year arrived, and when it was time to do my application, I sat down and did it. It can be called arrogance or naïveté, but I only applied to one school. I didn't even put in for financial aid—just in case. There was no plan B. That seems to be one of my characteristics. Now, I just waited. Finally, sometime around March, I got a phone call from Congressman Barnard's office informing me that I received his primary nomination (read as "his top choice"). Now, I had to wait to hear from West Point to find out if I would actually be accepted. Sometime around the beginning of April, I received a package from New York. I opened it up, and inside was a leather-bound acceptance letter to the United Stated Military Academy at West Point. I don't remember much between then and 29 JUN 1992, better known as "R-Day" by me and the other incoming cadets. What I do remember was the phone calls of congratulations, and I remember running into a few teachers around town who were amazed that I even graduated high school. After all, I had failed the seventh grade.

All incoming cadets, better known as plebes, take chemistry, and my chemistry professor was CPT Buechner. CPT Buechner was famous because he had stopped a rape when he was a cadet. I was very excited— a hero was teaching my first class. One interesting thing about West Point is that students sit in order of class rank. I was in seat three, which meant that there were only two other cadets higher than me. After each test, all the classes are re-sectioned, meaning we were re-ranked and given new classes and seats. I remember sitting in my seat that first day waiting for class to begin promptly at 0700. I was almost the top student there. We were snapped to attention, and I remember distinctly CPT Buechner saying, "Welcome to chemistry. Take seats and clear your desk. You have a quiz." What? It was the first day! My understanding of school was that I went to class, learned, studied, and then took a quiz. Quizzes shouldn't occur until after learning the material—at least that was my experience. I remember wondering what planet it was now screwing me over as I cleared my desk. But that is not the Thayer method, and West Point uses the Thayer method. As I was to learn soon enough, the Thayer method is where you teach yourself, and you go to class only to clarify what you independently learned. Needless to say, I didn't do too well on the quiz. I got 2 out of 60 correct. I wish I could say that I went back to the barracks, gathered myself, and sailed through the rest of the course. But that 2 out of 60 pretty much sums up the next few weeks of class. All the tricks and strategies I had learned in middle school and high school were not helping me. I was fighting a bigger, faster, and smarter opponent. I didn't know what to do, so I decided to do the proper student thing and go see CPT Buechner.

One day I went to his office, and he sat me down. He asked me what I wanted to discuss and I replied, "I am failing. I don't understand what is going on. Help me." Or something like that. CPT Buechner leaned back in his chair, then he leaned forward towards me, and finally he replied, "Let me see your notebook. Show me where you did the problems I assigned." I responded that I didn't do them because I didn't understand how to do them. I must have looked pitiful, but I was actually irritated because I was used to high school teachers teaching me and *then* doing the problems. How am I supposed to do the problems before I am taught how? But what CPT Buechner said next changed my life. He essentially said, "Listen,

Cadet Cato, I will not help you until your do all the problems. I will not help you until you have made every effort on your own to fulfill the assignments. I am here to *push* you forward, not *pull* you forward. You have to decide if you want to be here. If you do, then I don't want to see you again until you have done all the problems, and then I will help you. Do you understand? I am not here to guarantee you succeed. I will be your biggest cheerleader, but I will not be your enabler." After what felt like years, I gathered my things, I said I appreciated his time, and I left. I began the long walk back to the barracks, but I think if I could have walked home, I would have done it.

Back in my room, I began to reflect upon my life. I don't know why. Maybe it was because I was the only one there. Maybe it was because none of my friends could relate to this. After all, my friends from high school were telling me about their college experiences, which amounted to skipping class and going to parties. Maybe it was because I couldn't do the problems. I sat on my bed hopeless, lost, and depressed. I was supposed to be good at school, but I was terrible. I had been good in school, but now I was bad. Maybe it was something deep in my brain that I had repressed, but it came out like a bolt of lightning and hit me like a ton of bricks. What I realized was that I *had* been here before. I had been exactly in this same situation before, and I knew exactly what I needed to do. If *Where There's a Will, There's an A* had taught me anything, it had taught me that my first step was to set a goal. I began to feel much better because I had not even failed yet. I had time. Unlike my seventh-grade experience, I had not waited until it was too late. I believed I could do this because I had done this before. I had learned that I could experience failure, profound failure, and emerge from it better. It was at this point that I made a decision that changed my life. I decided that my goal would be to simply do every problem that had been assigned and go back to see CPT Buechner. I could do that—I had to do that. I would not rest until I did that. I freed myself from the fear of failure. I had failed before and it didn't kill me. I was better after it. I no longer cared if I passed because that was focusing on the outcome. I simply had to meet my goal. I was just going to do those problems and go see my professor.

I spent the next three days doing chemistry problems—hours of problems. I was not concerned if they were right or wrong. Heck, I couldn't tell, anyway. I did what I thought I should do, got an answer, and then went on. I remember it was a Thursday night when I finally finished doing them all. Friday morning when I got to class, I was called up to the front desk. CPT Buechner handed me a piece of paper called something like a performance evaluation. They weren't grades, but they did go to the

Dean and to my tactical officer. I opened it up, and it stated, "You have been rated in the bottom 10% of cadets—signed CPT Buechner." I was stunned, and I looked up and said, "Sir, I have completed the problems and would like to come in now." He agreed, and I met him after class in his office. I wondered, though, if he thought I said that because of his evaluation. I was just following my plan.

In his office, he repeated his previous rocking motions as he asked for my notebook. I handed it to him. He opened it up and looked at every page—rocking away. He closed it and handed it back to me. I remember he looked at me thoughtfully and measured. I could tell he was thinking hard about what to say. I had no idea that I was about to acquire my first academic role model. He stopped rocking, and I braced myself. CPT Buechner quietly said, "It is you, Cadet, that is the problem. You are not a good student. That does not mean you are not smart. Those are different things." Long pause. "Do you want to be a good student?" Longer pause. "If so, then I will help you, and that is how you fix your chemistry. You fix you. You fix everything broken about you. You fix all of your bad habits. You change all of your beliefs about learning and school. Until you change you, you will always struggle at everything. Here is what I want you to do…." Six weeks into my plebe year, CPT Buechner became my first academic mentor, and he taught me *how* to be a good student. In my final evaluation of the year, he rated me the highest rating: top 10%.

Riding high into my Yearling year (sophomore), I was placed in CPT Creamer's physics class. Little did I know that CPT Creamer, with whom I still maintain a friendship, would change the direction of my life. It was four weeks into class and I was ranked first in the class. We had been given this new computer tool called email, and all questions to the teacher had to be sent by email. I was studying circular motion several days before the class would formally discuss it, and I was confused. So I emailed CPT Creamer, and he emailed me back with an answer that made me go wild. I was hooked! Physics was so cool, and I knew at that moment it was what I wanted to study! As I noted before, I make decisions fast, and I tend to be all or nothing. As the class unfolded over the year, I began to go regularly to CPT Creamer's office and talk to him about physics. Over time, I came to realize that if I wanted to do physics, then I would need to leave the Army. I was at a real crossroads. CPT Creamer encouraged me by telling me that I was really good at physics, and that if I really loved it, I should pursue it. He encouraged me to consider my reasons for staying at West Point versus leaving and doing what I loved. It was a very hard decision to make with serious lifetime consequences. But at the end of my Yearling year, I left the academy to pursue a career in physics. And I am proud to say that over the course of the next twenty years, now retired COL Creamer mentored me in both my physics education and in my teaching of physics. He is a large part of my success in physics and in teaching.

If I was going to leave West Point to pursue a career in physics, then I would have to go to school somewhere. Having had two years of college for free, I strongly wanted to finish as cheaply as possible so that I could go to graduate school. Consequently, I returned home and attended Augusta State University. Two short years later, I earned my BS in Physics with a minor in Mathematics. My wife and I accepted graduate assistantships, and I was off to graduate school for physics. We arrived so excited, but that excitement turned to devastation when we received a phone call from Valerie's mom saying that her dad had a brain tumor and had six months to live. We both had our assistantships deferred and came back to Augusta. I needed a job, so I found a job teaching in a private school. It was only for a year, so it didn't seem that bad. But the year ended, and Valerie's dad was still alive. We decided to stay another year. We decided to buy a house, Valerie got a job and started graduate school, and I continued teaching. We were blessed to have Jim for as long as we did. But by the time he passed away, we had planted roots. There was no turning back.

Jim's death wasn't the only death we experienced. I have to be honest: I grieved not going to grad school for physics. It really was what I wanted to do. And when that dream died, I grieved it hard. But I would not change anything because I would not be doing what I am doing today if I had gone to grad school for physics. I think what I do now is infinitely more important. I am able to be a role model to young people before they get too far into their education and really stumble as I did. I can be a positive role model. That is what I had. Mr. Jones, CPT Buechner, and CPT Creamer were all role models for me. They intercepted me when I was wandering listlessly and gave my life direction. And that is what I try to do for my students. That is what I want to be for you. I am someone who has failed, and in doing so, learned that with the right people in your life, with the right goals, you can succeed. That is my part of story. That is part of my autobiography.

I gathered my things together—my pen and the pamphlet—and left the podium. There was mild applause, like the kind when the losing team is announced before the winner is crowned. But I appreciated it. I would need a new shirt, however, because I sweated through the one I was wearing. I guess I could keep my coat on, but it was Georgia in June.

When the service ended, there was a graduate reception. I went mostly to see Madame Poole, but I knew it was the right thing to do. I walked in, got a piece of cake, and started eating. As the only white person there, I felt out of place. I am not sure why. We were all people and we were in a church, after all. I guess even God isn't enough to make me colorblind. Madame Poole was dressed in a multicolored animal print dress. It was beautiful, and she was very proud of it. She came over and we talked for a good while. "The Reverend" came back and thanked me for coming. I noticed over their shoulders the teens coming in—slowly. They had their hands in their pockets, looking down at their feet. I thought it odd. They seemed to be very nervous. Maybe they were scared of being in a room with all these adults asking them about their futures. I suddenly remembered that feeling, and it was indeed scary!

A small group of graduates and church members came over and surrounded me. They were asking me questions, mostly about how I liked my job and how I liked working with young people. It quickly turned into a surreal conversation. When I looked up, I could see I was surrounded now by the entire audience. Like the tiger in the circus ring Martel (2001) wrote about, I had nowhere to hide.

One graduating student asked me, "Why do you like science so much?" I always love these kinds of questions because I don't really know how to answer them. It is hard to say why I love science—only that I do. But I had to reply. "To me, science is art. While there is certainly a way in which science is done, as people like to call it, the 'Scientific Method,' that is not really how science is done at all. Science is not a set of rules and procedures like those described in school. In fact, that is an unethical portrayal of science! Cary Wolfe (2012) writes about the auto-poietic and the poietic. Doing science is interacting with myself and my environment, creating change. In that sense, it is auto-poietic. Doing science is creating something new. In that sense, it is also poietic. I think it is that aesthetic nature of science that I love so much. To *do* science is to *do* art."

Another person asked, "What was the most surprising thing to you about studying science?" "Good question," I replied. "I think the way in which there are different paradigms to describe things. We often describe new things in terms of the familiar ones. We use metaphors and analogies. In Nelson's *Economics for Humans*, she writes, 'Metaphors are commonly the way in which a general worldview or understanding is expressed' (2006, p. 44). And there can be times that the fundamental notion of metaphors and analogies breaks down. Sometimes, there is simply no metaphor or analog that we can use in order to better understand a new idea. For example, Bohr made the analogy that the atom was like our solar system, with the nucleus being like the sun and the electrons orbiting the nucleus like the planets orbit the sun. It's a story, if you will, of how it works that most people can understand. But our present understanding of the atom has no analog at all. Even so, we still use Bohr's analogy when explaining atoms to young students because it's a good enough analogy. But we don't even begin to try and explain our current model to them simply because we can't think of a good enough analogy for it to make any sense. And to me, it is so cool to think that there is a whole level of understanding of nature where our experience has nothing to relate the understanding to. Some might think that's strange—to not teach students our most current thinking about nature. Nelson writes, 'What kind of science is this, which holds to one metaphor unquestionably and throws out all evidence that might require its practitioners to think anew (p. 49)?' But, truthfully, we tell students whatever 'story' best makes sense to them at their present level of understanding. So the notion of metaphors and analogies in science and their inability to allow us to create a complete description of all nature in terms of known ideas that everyone can grasp is really surprising."

I went on to explain the importance of analogies in teaching. "As a teacher, I am constantly trying to get students to be able to understand something that they often have no direct reference to, so I try to come up with analogies. In fact, I spend a lot of time creating analogies for students so that they can grasp the concepts and understand them better. It's an art, if you will. Consider, for example, a writer trying to describe something to readers through a story or analogy. The writer has a point they are trying to make. There is some idea that they want readers to come away with. But sometimes it is simply not possible to directly turn a concept into an analog. For example, say the writer is trying to describe the taste of honey to someone who has never tasted it. The writer would attempt to compare honey to things with which the person has direct experience. The writer might write, 'Well, it's sweet and brown, kind of like Coke, but it's not Coke. It's thick, kind of like a syrup, but it's not syrup.' Only direct experience can give someone that understanding of honey. No analogy can do that. And once someone has had honey, they have now had a direct experience with something they cannot explain by analogy to anyone else. Like trying to describe honey, analogies only can take us so far in describing science—sometimes, in describing our world, only direct experience will do."

A few more questions came my way, but they were mostly general stuff. An older man approached me, and we started talking about research. He was telling me about some of the research at a local college. It was very interesting. Finally, he asked me if I did any kind of research like that.

I said no, and I said that I wasn't too keen on how research in medicine is done anyway, to which he asked me to elaborate.

"I have to be honest: I am not a fan of hospitals, insurance companies, and pharmaceutical companies. If you have ever read Conrad's *Heart of Darkness*, then you remember how he describes the conquerors. Like Conrad's conquerors,

> For that you only want brute force—nothing to boast of, when you have it, since your strength is just an accident arising from the weakness of others. They grabbed what they could for the sake of what was to be got. It is just robbery with violence, aggravated murder on a great scale, and men going at it blind—as is very proper for those who tackle darkness (2006, p. 7).

The conquerors take from the weak, and they do so violently. They claimed the Africans had no use for the gold, silver, and ivory. They said the Africans didn't appreciate what they had, and so they justified taking the valuables because 'they' understood the value and the African's didn't. They took because they could. I think hospitals, insurance companies, and pharmaceutical companies are like modern day conquerors. Patients are threatened that if they do not give their consent to give away their tissue, then they will not be able to receive the treatment. Valuable tissue is then taken from the patients and used to generate enormous profits, none of which is returned to the patients, just as the conquerors did in Africa. These modern-day conquerors are not operating ethically. There is no consideration of the patient, or of society. These entities willingly take tissues knowing how they were obtained. And they do so for fame and profit, just like the conquerors Conrad wrote about. They take from the sick what is precious and justify it by saying that the tissue has no use to the patient. They come in, take what they want—our tissue—and use it to make money because it does have value, none of which is returned to the patients. One only needs to look at how tissue is viewed by the medical community. According to the authors Waldby and Mitchell, 'Hospitals and clinics routinely take human tissue samples for diagnostic testing, and doctors excise pathological or excessive tissue during surgery. Historically, hospitals treat such tissue as "abandoned"' (2006, p. 85). Furthermore, they write that 'the tissue is tacitly considered to have no value or significance for the patient' (p. 85). That certainly seems to be an unethical stance by hospitals and doctors. The tissue can hardly be considered 'abandoned' because it was never returned to the patient. It was *taken* from the patient. Furthermore, the tissue is described as valueless to the patient, but not for the hospital. The hospitals are being very unethical in their approach to determining what is of value to the patient and for themselves."

"Really," he replied. "Do you have any examples?"

"Sure. Henrietta Lacks and John Moore come to mind. Their stories are very compelling. They were both human beings. They both had families who loved them. They both had friends who miss them. They both died too young after battling cancer. Ironically, in a strange way, a small part of them still is fighting cancer. Both Lacks and Moore had their cells taken from them as part of their treatment for their cancer, and they are now being used to generate billions for companies fighting cancer and other research. It is estimated that Moore's cells alone could be worth billions. Neither one, however, ever saw any compensation for those cells. While there is a narrow legal issue, which ultimately was decided by the Supreme Court, there is also an ethical issue. And what court is there to try that? The argument that Lacks's and Moore's cells were abandoned and valueless to them is simply nonsense. And what becomes of all those 'abandoned' tissues? Simple. They are sold, and the recipients use them to make money. Those tissues are very valuable to the hospitals, brokers, businesses, and researchers using them to make billions of dollars yearly. And how much is returned back to the sources of the tissue? None. All of these companies make money on the tissue, just not the person from whom the tissue was taken. That simply is not ethical. That is not moral. That is not poietic. That is not auto-poietic. While those cases certainly describe the unethical use of science in the life sciences, the life sciences hold no monopoly on the unethical use of science."

Another asked, "So, you don't think they should do research?"

"Of course we should do research. That is not what I am saying at all. What I am saying is that it needs to be done ethically. Just look at how patients are described by doctors, insurance companies, and research facilities. Look at the names for different entities in this tissue economy. Blood is like money because it is kept in blood banks. Internal organs are like crops because they are harvested. While they are just names, those names represent a perspective of how the conquerors view the tissues of the patients. Again, I am really making an analogy here to describe why I don't like how it's done."

Another older gentleman responded, "Well, I've never heard any of that. It seems fine to me. I say if they can cure it, then they should get the tissue."

"Well, all I can say to that is to quote J. Hillis Miller: 'Which of us…would or should want to take someone else's word for what is in a book (2001, p. 104)?' So, don't take my word for it. I would encourage you to read their stories, and to read about the research methods going on today. You mentioned cures. While there is a small effort to 'cure' certain diseases, for the large part, these companies are in the treatment business. It does not pay well or for very long to cure. The lines of drugs dispensed today are almost exclusively used to treat the disease indefinitely. Is that ethical? Shouldn't they also be using that valuable tissue that they took by force and earned billions of dollars of profit on and at least try to cure the disease?"

"That doesn't make them sound good," replied someone.

"I don't think they are. They are not acting ethically, in my opinion," I replied. "Toni Morrison writes in Beloved, 'Freeing yourself was one thing: claiming ownership of that freed self was another' (2004, p. 112-113). They own us. We all belong to them. When we go to get treatment at the doctor's office, we sign away ourselves because we don't have a choice. We want to get the treatment. If we refuse to, then they can refuse to operate or give treatment. The researchers decide what diseases to fight and what drug lines to pursue. In my opinion, science should be done to further our knowledge. But that is not what is happening. They are behaving very unethically. Like Conrad's conquerors, many doctors and researchers today are in search of fame and fortune; they just believe they are 'better' because they are scientists. Research today is about writing grants, bringing in huge sums of money, and pursuing research that might lead to finding something new that can be patented and sold to pharmaceutical companies. They are seeking to 'strike it rich' by doing such things as using the tissues obtained from patients who have no ability to profit in the research and then turning that into a massive profit for themselves. That is not ethically doing science, and I place blame squarely on the shoulders of the scientists who collude with the machine of medicine."

About then, "the Reverend" tried to come to my rescue. He stepped in and said, "One more question before we break for the day." Just then, an older man shouts, "I have to ask this. I have to say this. I don't believe you. Your story is too far-fetched to be real." I asked him what part he found so ridiculous. He replied, "There is no way I believe you failed the seventh grade! All of this happened because you failed." The crowd seemed to chime in with what can only be described as noise of agreement. I was beginning to wonder if I was going to get out of this church alive.

I took a deep breath, and replied, "Some of my story I told is not factually correct. When I changed schools, my best friend was a year behind me and at the new school, so I convinced my mom to hold me back a year so we could play football together. The rest is mostly true, but

I might have exaggerated a little here and there for dramatic effect. Is it wrong to vary the truth if it can tell a better story that helps other people?"

I have to tell you the truth: I think I was sweating through my suit. The old man held out his hand, and he said, "Son, now that is a good story, too. And I think that one is the one closer to the real truth. But you have told us two good stories. Which one is *the truth?*" I looked at Madame Poole. I could see the hurt in her eyes. Had she believed a lie? Was I an ethical person? I felt scared and I felt terrified that I was about to fail her. Failing someone you care about is far worse than failing yourself. But I had been here before. I had faced this situation before. I knew exactly what to say and exactly what to do. I gently put my hand on top of his hand and said, "I have told you two stories. One in which I failed, and one in which I did not. Which one do you like better?" The old man smiled and said, "I like the first one best. The one where you failed." To which I replied, "And so it goes with God" (Martel, 2001, p. 317).

References

Butler, J. (2005). *Giving an account of oneself.* New York, NY: Fordham.

Conrad, J. (2006). *Heart of darkness, authoritative text, backgrounds and contexts, criticism.* (4th ed. ed.). New York, NY: W W Norton & Co Inc.

Martel, Y. (2001). *Life of Pi.* New York, NY: Harcourt.

Miller, J. H. (2001). *Others.* Princeton, NJ: Princeton University Press.

Morrison, T. (2004). *Beloved.* New York, NY: Vintage.

Nelson, J. A. (2006). *Economics for humans.* Chicago, IL: University of Chicago Press.

Waldby, S., & Mitchell, R. (2006). *Tissue economies.* Durham, NC: Duke University Press.

Wolfe, C. (2012). *Before the law: Humans and other animals in a biopolitical frame.* Chicago

Chapter 5

Enter Henrietta Lacks

A Story for Science, Science Education, and Curriculum Studies

Dana Compton McCullough

Rebecca Skloot's book, *The Immortal Life of Henrietta Lacks* (2010), has potential to impact science, science education, and the field of curriculum studies. William Pinar (2004) lays the groundwork for curriculum to be a cross-curricular endeavor "as well as focus on interdisciplinary themes— such as gender, multiculturalism or the ecological crisis—as well as the relations among the curriculum, the individual, society, and history" (p. 21). Current practices of standardization and testing neglect these ideas. Science curriculum as well as other disciplines should be viewed as if they are "comprised of actual living people, not disembodied ideas which appear out of nowhere" (Pinar, Reynolds, Slattery, & Taubman, 2008, p. 5). Unfortunately, in the current culture of standardization, students are arriving in science classrooms "having had little or no first-hand experiences with science" (Berry, 2007, p. 5). Science students focus on memorization and becoming accomplished multiple-choice test takers. The resulting test scores become the only way these students are identified and can be deemed successful. Students' success should not require them to abandon their defining characteristics: "ethnicity, race, and sex, all of which are stripped away" (Pinar, Reynolds, Slattery, & Taubman, 2008, p. 304). In this scenario, "it is the people themselves along with their race, gender, sexual orientation, class and ethnicity, who are filed away through the lack of creativity, transformation, and knowledge in this (at best) misguided system" (Freire 1970, p. 72). Henrietta Lacks was filed away in a similar manner. Skloot's carefully penned account reveals that Henrietta's magnificent cells were only known by their code name HeLa (He for Henrietta and La for Lacks) for more than 25 years following Henrietta's death. Once these amazing cells began to grow in laboratories all over the

David P. Owen, Jr (ed.), *Field Theory: Curriculum Studies at Work*, 77–101.

world, they affected the field of biotechnology tremendously. The intersections of humans and biotechnology are worthy of examination in science education and curriculum studies as we consider "what it means to live in a posthuman world and what the implication of the biosciences...and humans" will be in this world (Weaver, 2010, p.3).

In this review, I will introduce you to author Rebecca Skloot, cell donor Henrietta Lacks, and *The Immortal Life of Henrietta Lacks*. These stories provide us with a multiperspective view into implications of actual science. Experimentation, laboratories, investigators studying exotic creatures in exotic places stereotypically characterize science. Should the story of Henrietta Lacks be part of science and science curriculum? Should storytelling be a component of science and science education? What are the implications of introducing Henrietta Lacks to science, science students, and the field of curriculum studies?

This narrative, *The Immortal Life of Henrietta Lacks*, rich in history, history of science, philosophy of science, society, and family, provides the reader with an example of an all-inclusive science intended by the founder of the field of science, William Whewell (1834), and foundational contributors to the field of science education, C. P. Snow (1959/2013) and Joseph Schwab (1978). The fields of science and science education become enhanced when integrated with ideas of posthuman thought and biotechnology offered by John Weaver (2010 and 2015) and Nathan Snaza (2015). Introducing Henrietta Lacks to science and science education creates a space for discourse. Although stories in science class must be told with care, the sharing of stories can create a space for students to become connected to the actors in the story, the science curriculum, and the "real" life science in the surrounding "real" world. Stories allow students to linger, connect, and become acquainted with the idea of actively participating in science. Discourse and lingering can lead to transformation of ideas and thinking.

When science teachers teach such an all-inclusive science, science instruction teaches not only basic concepts, but teaches students to think critically and become involved with the world around them. I propose that Skloot's carefully penned story of Henrietta Lacks can breathe life and social justice back into a standardized curriculum, tested-to-death students, and weary teachers. I explore how a marginalized, nameless, faceless, African-American woman, ravaged by science and society, can find her way into the conversations of science scholars, curriculum theorists, educators, and present-day high school students. I explore how the addition of the story of Henrietta Lacks can add life to the field of curriculum studies. Science should seep into the core, cracks, and crevices of present-day education and society through the relationships that evolve between science and all its participants, creating a science curriculum all-inclusive of humanity and social justice.

Meeting Henrietta Lacks

Skloot Meets Henrietta Lacks

Rebecca Skloot first heard the name Henrietta lacks as a sixteen-year-old struggling to earn a biology credit required for high school graduation. Her teacher was explaining mitosis and announced to the students that scientists learned about cell division by studying cells outside the body in culture. He wrote two words in enormous print: Henrietta Lacks. He erased the board. Class was over. Rebecca thought, "That's it? That's all we get? There has to be more to the story" (Skloot, 2010, p.4). Skloot followed her teacher to his office. She asked, "Where was she from? Did she know how important her cells were? Did she have any children?" (p.4). Defler responded by telling Skloot that there was no more. An exasperated Skloot left his office. She began researching—looking for anything she could find about Henrietta Lacks and her cells. Defler planted a seed in Rebecca Skloot that would germinate into a 10-year commitment to uncover the story of Henrietta Lacks and her cells. Skloot went on to major in journalism. At first, she wanted to satisfy her own curiosity and get her questions answered. Then over time her readers readily see that she became committed to uncover and share the stories of Henrietta and Henrietta's cells with Henrietta's family, who desperately wanted answers about a mother they barely knew.

World Meets Henrietta Lacks

The *Immortal Life of Henrietta Lacks* began selling in January of 2010. The novel has spent over two years on the *New York Times* Best Sellers list (Best Sellers, 2013). It quickly became required reading for college students at undergraduate and graduate levels. Middle school and high school literature and science teachers began using the book. In the beginning, only researchers who were having issues of contamination with their cell lines, needed or wanted to know Henrietta's story. Stanley Gartler announced Henrietta's identity and race at a scientific conference on "cell tissue and organ culture in 1966" (Wald, 2012, p. 247). Once Henrietta's identity was released, many became very interested in her story. Michael Rogers (1976), Michael Gold, (1985), Octavia Butler (1987), Hannah Landecker (1999, 2000, 2007), and Wald (2012), all published "public narratives about Lacks that put assumptions about race, sex, and gender conspicuously on display" (p. 247). In addition to these major publications, The British Broadcast Company (BBC) made a documentary called *The Way of All Flesh* directed by Adam Curtis (1997). It was not until Rebecca Skloot published *The Immortal Life of Henrietta Lacks* that Henrietta gained attention made possible via The *New York Times* Best Sellers list. Most recently Oprah Winfrey produced a movie with HBO called *The Immortal Life of Henrietta Lacks* (Wolfe, 2016). Now that everyone is reading and/or watching Henrietta's story, one must ask how this text, with such a history, will influence the teaching of science. Can Henrietta's voice be heard in such a conversation?

Rebecca Skloot opens her book with a quote from Elie Wiesel (1992), writer of *The Nazi Doctors and the Nuremberg Code*, who tells us that "We must not see any person as an abstraction. Instead, we must see in every person a universe with its own secrets, with its own treasures, with its own sources of anguish, and with some measure of triumph" (p. ix). This quote sets the tone for a story that will allow the readers to become connected to the story of Henrietta, her family, and the science behind the amazing cells. Skloot's teacher issued an invitation to his students to make personal connections with an otherwise very technical curriculum. At that time, there was not much of the story Defler could tell his students. Defler sets an example of how a story can be used to plant a seed. The seed he planted that day germinated into Rebecca Skloot's passion. Skloot tells Henrietta's story in a manner that is complete and accessible to the public. Her research is thorough and unyielding. Her story is personal. As she tells the story, the reader becomes connected to the people in the story. Others connect to the story because of their own experience with family, science, cancer, or racism. Connections are woven throughout, weaving the reader together with science, history, and humanity.

In the first chapter, Skloot describes how Henrietta jumped out of an old Buick, driven by her husband, with three of her kids in the back seat. She entered the lobby of Johns Hopkins Hospital and "scurried into the hospital, past the colored bathroom" (Skloot, 2010, p. 13). Henrietta entered "the land of the white coats" and the reader travels in time to the era of Jim Crow (Morris 2008, p.11). This meant "when Black people showed up at white-only hospitals, the staff was likely to send them away, even if it meant they might die in the parking lot" (Skloot, 2010, p. 15). On this day, Henrietta would be seeing Dr. Richard Wesley TeLinde, one of the top cervical cancer experts in the country. TeLinde "often used patients from the public wards for research, usually without their knowledge" (Skloot, 2010, p. 29). Many scientists at the time believed that "since their patients were treated for free in the public wards, it was fair to use them as research subjects as a form of payment" (Skloot, 2010, p. 29). Now the reader is introduced to the idea that science justified the use of the innocent for its advancement.

The year was 1951. Henrietta Lacks was one of 10,000 women to die of cervical cancer. This young mother died a very painful death from an extremely aggressive cervical cancer. The "tumor was biologically unique...a peculiar appearance and a neoplasm which was to prove quite resistant to radiation" (Jones, McKusick, Harper, & Wuu, 1971, p. 945). Henrietta's body was moved from the public ward, where she died on October 4, 1951, to a cold "stainless-steel table in the cavernous basement morgue. For research purposes, samples were cut from Henrietta's body, bladder, bowel, uterus, kidney, vagina, ovary, appendix, liver, heart, and lungs" (Skloot, 2010, p. 90). Her abdomen was black and charred from radium treatments, and "tumors the size of baseballs had nearly replaced her kidneys, bladder and uterus...her other organs were so covered in small white tumors it looked as if someone had filled her with pearls" (p. 90). While she lay on the autopsy table, "HeLa [cells] with a generation time of about 24 hours, if allowed to grow uninhibited under optimal cultural conditions" were taking over the world (Jones, et al., 1971, p. 947). These cells would go on to change science and medicine, as we know it. Henrietta died, but her amazing cells live in laboratories all over the world today, 67 years later. Henrietta's cells have been to outer space. Henrietta's cells have been used to test and develop the polio vaccine, chemotherapy, cloning, gene mapping, and in vitro fertilization. Her cells have become very important in testing drugs to treat herpes, leukemia, influenza, hemophilia, and Parkinson's disease. Henrietta Lacks was known only as HeLa, for more than 25 years following her death. No one, except the scientists who took her cells, knew the origin of the cells, her name, and her race.

Science Teacher Meets Henrietta Lacks

During my first doctoral course, John Weaver asked if I had read Rebecca Skloot's book, *The Immortal Life of Henrietta Lacks*. I had to admit that I had never heard of Henrietta Lacks. I had two degrees in biology, yet I had never heard her name. I went home and immediately ordered the book. When it came, I promptly dropped everything and began to read. I quickly came to a passage in the prologue where Skloot describes cells, using the analogy of a city street:

> Under the microscope, a cell looks a lot like a fried egg: The cytoplasm buzzes like a New York City street. It is crammed full of molecules and vessels endlessly shuttling enzymes and sugars from one part of the cell to another by pumping water, nutrients, and oxygen in and out of the cell. All the while, little cytoplasmic factories work 24/7, cranking out sugars, fats, proteins, and energy to keep the whole thing running and feed the nucleus—the brains of the operation... (Skloot, 2010, p. 3)

I loved the details of this description. I could not wait to share this with my students when we started our annual cell unit. I thought this passage would be much more interesting than the descriptions in their five-pound textbooks. There is so much memorization in my state's biology curriculum. The biggest disconnect seems to be that students have a "depersonalized image of science and scientists" (Hodson, 1998, p. 9). Science class can be extremely "off putting for large numbers of students and so discourages them from pursuing science further" (p. 9).

Shortly after I was introduced to this text, I was given an assignment to create a lesson in culturally relevant pedagogy. I decided on a writing activity that involved students looking at a science topic from multiple perspectives. Chapman, Hobbel, & Alvarado (2011) suggest that students look at a topic and examine the connections between chosen topics and three areas of focus: themselves, their community, and their world. This activity could be easily accomplished with any science topic—why not the components of the story of Henrietta Lacks? The project was simple. I introduced students to the story of Henrietta Lacks through several articles and the documentary by Adam Curtis (1997), *The Way of All Flesh*. Following this initial exposure, I showed students a list of possible topics for research and encouraged them to add to the list. The students chose a topic and spent time researching that portion of Henrietta's story. Next, students examined these connections: How did this portion of the story connect to the three perspectives: self, community, and world? Last, they shared their story with the class. Students wrote letters, storybooks, comic books, poetry, songs, raps, plays, interviews. Students told their story through art, speeches, brochures, and other combinations of the above.

While my students were working on their projects, I noticed that issues of social justice came to the forefront of class discussions. Students asked an enormous number of questions and took a stand for social justice as they discussed Henrietta's story and the story of her cells. Students made connections with Henrietta as a person, Henrietta as a Black woman living in a time of racism and segregation, and Henrietta's identity in relation to science. As a teacher, I noticed that the most important topic on the table might not have been the mandated science standards. Although these standards are an important part of science literacy, a well-rounded science curriculum should include much more. I decided to take what was happening in my classroom and share it with the whole school. The event was called Wear Red to Honor Henrietta Lacks. Why wear red? That is one of the most touching parts of the story. After a painful bout with cancer, Henrietta Lacks passed away at the Johns Hopkins Hospital for Negroes on October 4, 1951. Mary, Dr. George Gey's assistant, went to the morgue to collect her last sample from Henrietta. When Mary saw the body, her first instinct was to "run out of the morgue...instead, she stared at Henrietta's arms and legs—anything to avoid looking into her lifeless eyes. Then Mary's gaze fell on Henrietta's feet, and she gasped: Henrietta's toenails were covered in chipped bright red polish" (Skloot, 2010, p. 90). Mary reflected on those toenails in an interview with Skloot (2010):

> When I saw those toenails...I thought, oh jeeze, she's a real person. I started imagining her sitting and painting those toenails, and it hit me for the first time that those cells we'd been working with all this time and sending all over the world, they came from a live woman. I'd never thought of it that way. (pp. 90-91)

On the anniversary of Henrietta's death, October 4, students donned red t-shirts, red ribbons, and red beads to show homage to Henrietta. Each teacher devoted a short amount of time to discuss Henrietta Lacks with their first period class. The class project presentations fell on this day. As we went through the day, students discussed the importance of cells, but they saw fit to talk about the injustice done to Henrietta and her family. They often asked if the story would have been different if Henrietta had not been Black, if Henrietta had not been a woman. Students were contemplating issues of medical ethics, civil rights, and basic science principals with a multiplicity of lenses including their own race and cultural backgrounds. Ninth- and tenth-grade biology students were examining racism, sexism, and violations of basic human rights through science. The school construction teacher reported that two students had drawn diagrams of mitosis and meiosis on his marker board and were explaining how HeLa cells were different from other cells. They shared that cancer cells are going through uncontrolled mitosis.

How was this story creating so much excitement? At this point, my excitement was over the top. I wanted to share this story with everyone. Not everyone shared my enthusiasm. Someone asked me what Henrietta Lacks had to do with science. Another warned that I did not have time for all these stories—I should be more concerned with preparing my students for their end of course biology exam. Another warned that as a white woman telling the story of Henrietta Lacks, there is an issue of writing a "victory story" (Jupp, 2004, p36). Teaching in "multicultural settings, we as white educators can get hung up on our personal victory of making opportunities available to students that are of a different background" (p. 36). Another warned that science had nothing to do with democracy and social justice. Through careful self-reflection, and contemplation, I decided to proceed with each of these questions weighing heavy on my mind.

What Does Henrietta Lacks Have to do with Science?

Early Days of Science and Science Curriculum

The question concerning Henrietta and science rattled me to the core. What do you mean what does Henrietta Lacks have to do with science? The connections seemed very natural to me. Do you not know her cells were the first to grow in culture outside the human body? I began to question my own definition of science. What does the term science mean? Teachers must teach a list of standards that will eventually prepare students for a standardized test. On a more positive note, I hope science instruction and literacy will help my students become participants in issues of science. Some think of science as something that goes on in laboratories using strict methods, or something that takes place when someone dons binoculars, wide brimmed hats, and butterfly nets. Perceptions of science today by teachers and students of science may be very different from the early days of science. At this time "the 'learned' embraced in their wide grasp all the branches of knowledge; the Scligers and Vossiuses of former days were mathematicians as well as philosophers, physical as well as antiquarian speculators" (Whewell, 1834, p.59). In the early days it was acceptable for "a poet, like Goethe" to wander into the fields of experimental science (p. 59). In the early days of science most scientists of the day were "widely and classically trained, readers of Latin and Greek, French and German, whose interests ranged over all the natural and social sciences and most of the arts as well, who wrote poetry and broke codes and translated Plato and studied architecture" (Snyder, 2011, p.7). These scientists "conducted the experiments that struck their fancy, based on the chemicals and equipment they happened to have on hand" (p.7). They were scientists "who measured mountains and barometric pressure while on holiday in the Alps and observed the economic situation of the poor wherever their peripatetic wanderings took them" (p.7). Science was practiced in conjunction with other fields of study, including arts and humanities.

This norm in science was quickly fading and being replaced with "an increasing proclivity to separation and dismantlement" (Whewell, 1834, p.59). Whewell (1834) says "we adopt the maxum one science only can one genius fit" (p. 59). Whewell's term, meant to describe a multidisciplinary science incorporating aspects of humanity, unfortunately, officially separated those studying sciences from philosophers, poets, and workers in other disciplines. We must ask what the results of standardized teaching and standardized testing mean for our future.

Dangers of Binaries and Isolation

This dividing chasm continued to grow. C.P. Snow describes the art-science dichotomy in his lecture titled, "The Two Cultures" (1959/2013). Snow (1959/2013) believed that "the intellectual life of the whole of Western society is increasingly being split into two polar groups" (p. 4). He described these two groups as being composed of the "literary intellectuals at one pole—and at the other scientists, and as the most representative, the physical scientists. Between the two, a gulf of mutual incomprehension—sometimes (particularly among the young) hostility and dislike, but most of all lack of understanding" (p. 4). Snow (1959/2013) explained that "The reasons for the existence of the two cultures are many, deep, and complex, some rooted in social histories, some in personal histories and some in the inner dynamic of the different kinds of mental activity themselves" (Snow, 1959/2013, p. 23). Snow (1959/2013) goes on to tell us that "Western society is increasingly being split into two polar groups: At one pole we have the literary intellectuals, who incidentally while no one was looking took to referring to themselves as intellectuals as though there were no others" (Snow, 1959/2013, p. 4). The attitudes of both groups keep them from being able to find common ground and a common appreciation for the other.

Are the same stereotypes Snow (1959/2013) wrote about still in existence? After sharing with my department head that I wanted to use the story of Henrietta Lacks to teach my students about cells, she explained that there was no time for stories (literature) in science class.

Long ago, "nonscientists tended to think of scientists as brash and boastful...shallowly optimistic, unaware of man's condition" (p. 5). On the other hand, the scientists believe that the "literary intellectuals are totally lacking in foresight, peculiarly unconcerned with their brother men, in a deep sense anti-intellectual, anxious to restrict both art and thought to the existential moment" (p. 6). As a spectator situated between art and science, Snow declared "the number 2 is a very dangerous number: That is why the dialectic is a dangerous process. Attempts to divide anything into two ought to be regarded with much suspicion" (pp. 9-10). Snow tells us "The clashing point of two subjects, two disciplines, and two cultures—of two galaxies, so far as that goes, ought to produce creative chances. In the history of mental activity that has been where some of the breakthroughs came" (p. 17). Inviting Henrietta Lacks and history into science creates an opportunity for such a breakthrough. Students in my class were able to rectify this clash in science through music, art, poetry, and other forms of communication. This work required much more mental activity than memorizing a list of isolated facts that must be memorized for a standardized test.

Joseph Schwab (1978) warned against teaching science in isolation. An isolated view or one doctrine produces a "biased view of the nature of science" (Schwab, 1978, p. 72). Schwab (1978) insisted that "to teach a single doctrine should be to the student only misleading or confusing or both" (p. 72). He warned that "No single doctrine is more than a partial statement—partial in the sense of incomplete and partial in the sense of being based upon a given set of epistemic or metaphysical presuppositions" (Schwab, 1978, p. 72). Teachers not only have to consider science, but they must also consider theoretical views of science education, history of science, philosophy of science. Educators should know that the "Theories of curriculum and of teaching and learning cannot alone tell us what and how to teach, because questions of what and how to teach arise in concrete situations loaded with concrete particulars of time, place, person, and circumstance" (Schwab, 1978, p. 322). By oversimplifying science to a list of standards or facts and processes to simply memorize, "we block progress toward one of the most widely held, if impossible goals" of what Schwab calls "liberal science training" which is "to provide the student with an adequate picture of the world" (Schwab, 1978, p. 99). Schwab warned advocates of standardization that "To give a simple picture of a complicated world is not to give the scientist's picture of that world. By so doing we make the picture not only inadequate (which it will always be) but false" (p. 99). We have a moral obligation to students. Science should be composed of very complicated conversations, and students should realize that they are participants. As an educator, I am fearful that science curriculum is not evolving.

Schwab (1978) encourages us to use reflexive thinking in science. Reflexive thinking is simply a way to view things from more than one perspective— "deliberately...looking through a succession of lenses" (p. 325). Standardized education offers only one point of view, a one-size-fits-all education. Extending educators' possibilities to "weigh the alternative formulations of a problem thus achieved and for choosing one to follow further, generate alternative solutions" and trace each "alternative solution to its probable consequences" (Schwab, 1978, p. 325). Eclectic inquiry demonstrates the intersecting of theory and practice from multiperspectives in classrooms. To choose a single framework for this endeavor would be to adopt the theoretical framework of but one discipline or one portion of a discipline. The subject matter of science "comprises all-natural phenomena which can be made to yield general truths when subjected to the method of science" (Schwab, 1978, p. 68). Defining exactly what science is and "how to teach it are our problems" (p. 68). When it comes to understanding what science is, Schwab feels that "We all know what science is" and that "there is no difficulty in distinguishing its subject matter, as may be the case with the humanities" (p. 68). Why should one subject be exclusive of the other? Both can exist in a multidisciplinary approach.

Beyond Binaries, Single Disciplines and Isolation

Weaver (2010) describes curriculum studies as multidisciplinary: "phenomenological, hermeneutic, cognitive, racialized, gendered, and sexualized" and goes on to say that the field is "not biological" (p. 31). He insists, "The curriculum studies body lacks bios (life)...lacks a connection to technology that all bodies come face to interface with every day" (p.31). Just as adding the story of Henrietta Lacks brings bios and humanity to science classrooms, the entire field of curriculum studies needs the story of Henrietta Lacks. I propose that Henrietta Lacks and her amazing HeLa cells can fill this gap in the field of curriculum studies, provide a necessary link between the living and technology on a mass scale, and bring bios to the field.

Another challenge of the field of curriculum studies involves the posthuman condition. Weaver (2010) insists that it is "the challenge of the posthuman condition [to] rename and reclaim humanity" (p. 138). This process will involve the fields of biosciences, humanities, and curriculum theory. In present day science education, the battle of an isolated, disconnected, science continues. What if the starting point for school curriculum would be thoughts concerning "the meaning, purpose, and relationship of science, literature, language, history, and mathematics" (Snaza & Weaver, 2015, p3)? Can we imagine "what would a world be that did not insist on human superiority or dominance and that did not disavow the human's ecological entanglements" (p. 3)? A science full of connections instead of disconnections? Would this provide a pathway for science that students and teachers of science would find more appealing? More useful? Could this lead to a science where scientists, teachers, students, work together for the good of our society? Science and scientists must be removed from the isolated pedestal upon which they were placed during the Age of Enlightenment. Snaza (2015) tells us that "Enlightenment thought produced intermediate categories of humanness. Women, slaves, poor, and colonized natives we were conceptualized as potentially but not yet human" (p. 25). As were members of the public ward, in which Henrietta Lacks received treatment.

Skloot writes about Richard Wesley TeLinde, one of the top cervical cancer experts in the country; he justified the use of the innocent for the advancement of science...for the good of all humanity. Howard Jones, Henrietta's doctor, wrote, "Hopkins, with its large indigent Black population, had no dearth of clinical material" (Skloot, 2010, p. 30). At this time in history most were under the impression that human experimentation was only happening in Nazi Death camps. In 1947, "a U.S.-led tribunal in Nuremberg, Germany, had sentenced seven Nazi doctors to death by hanging" (Skloot, 2010, p. 131). These doctors were "conducting unthinkable research on Jews without consent" (p.131). Skloot supplies us with a detailed tracing of the creation of the Nuremberg Code, The Hippocratic Oath, and the addition of the term "informed consent" in legal vernacular. With knowledge of science comes a huge amount of responsibility. Scientists and participants of science need to step up to the plate and become guardians of how scientific information will be formulated and used in everyday life. Science must no longer be disconnected from the world in which it exists. Science cannot function as an isolated entity. "Science's rise to power supposes such a level of recruitment that soon, all-powerful, it creates a vacuum around itself," causing a "sudden decline of all the surrounding areas of culture—the humanities, arts, religion, and even the legal system" (Serres & Latour, 2011/1990, p. 87). Posthumanism calls for "forms of democratic education, curriculum and pedagogy that deconstruct the common sense, taken-for-granted naturalness of humanism, not from an anti-humanist perspective, but as a movement beyond the limits and contradictions of the humanist project while still maintaining the modernist and humanist projects of rights, justice, equity, and freedom" (Carlson, 2015, p. x).

One of the first advances in medicine connected to Henrietta's HeLa cells was the development of Jonas Salk's polio vaccine. It is interesting that HeLa cells can cause death and life simultaneously through the production of the polio vaccine and then the subsequent annihilation of polio. Viewing the story of Henrietta Lacks from this posthuman perspective requires several steps. Begin with HeLa cells being grown outside the human body. Next, these cells can serve as a proxy of an entire living breathing human being during testing of Jonas Salk's polio vaccine. Then the cells themselves become microscopic virus factories to produce the vaccine. The vaccine is mass-produced in these little microscopic HeLa cell factories at an all-Black research facility at Tuskegee institute. The vaccine is made available to the public. Mass vaccination of all...starting with the most privileged, of course. Would these individuals have declined the lifesaving serum had they known it came as the result of a Black woman and her cervical cancer? Once injected, the vaccine pulses through the body. Now we are eternally connected to Henrietta Lacks. We all crossed a "modernist boundary that might innocently create an artificial line between body and machine or artificial and natural worlds" (Weaver, 2010, p. 31). High school science students study the creation of Jonas Salk's vaccine, but the link to Henrietta Lacks and HeLa cells is omitted. I see similarities in the story of *Frankenstein* (Shelley, 1996/1818) and *The Immortal Life of Henrietta Lacks* (Skloot, 2010). This creature, Henrietta Lacks, the creation, HeLa cells, like *Frankenstein* "over-reached the human boundaries that separated humanity from the dangerous forces of nature" (Weaver, 2010, p. 35). Henrietta is part of a story that does at times seem like science fiction. When Henrietta was given immortal life through her HeLa cells, a boundary was crossed. Henrietta is immortal through her cells. Weaver (2010) defines posthuman as "the merging of humans and machines in order to enhance or improve human capabilities" (p. 11). Cells removed from Henrietta's body were kept alive through techniques developed to grow cells outside the body. Those techniques along with George Gey's "roller tube" technology created the possibility for Henrietta to enter the post human realm (Landecker, 2007, p. 112).

Impact of Stories Such as Henrietta's in Science Curriculum

Stories and Science

Skloot's story is told from a multiplicity of perspectives. She refuses to tell readers a "single story" that might create "incomplete stereotypes" (Adichie, 2009, p. 1). Chapters alternate beginning with the story of Henrietta and her family and then the story of HeLa cells. The book is a weaving together of science, history of science, Henrietta's story, and the collective stories of Henrietta's family. Donna Haraway (1989) tells us that "certain aspects of science itself may be considered a kind of storytelling practice" (p. 4). Do students need to know the stories behind the technologies and scientists that discovered knowledge concerning cells, starting with Hooke, Leuwenhoek, Pasteur, Watson, Crick, and Franklin? We share stories everyday through conversations. As Baszile reminds us, "Everything and everybody has a story" (2008, p. 253). Stories can be used as "a primary form of communication," to help "define problems," and to "identify relationships among problems," or they can be employed to help us "laugh at our problems and heal our hurts" and "help us to discover and understand one another" (p. 253). I think storytelling can be extended to help us to discover, understand science, and build curriculum.

For storytelling pedagogy to be successful, students and teachers must get beyond themselves. Both groups must step back and take a fresh look—to treat oneself as a stranger or an "other." By looking at ourselves as the other, we see the stranger within us. When examining the stranger, we can relate more to the other element in society. This examination "implicates the other in me," such that "my own foreignness to myself is, paradoxically, the source of my ethical connection with others" (Butler, 2005, p. 84). From a curriculum theory perspective, we apply this examination of the other to storytelling: "We bring all our sorted histories, hopes, and desires to the project of curriculum theory, hooking onto familiar stories and creating new ones" (Baszile, 2010, p. 483).

A storied or narrative inquiry explores this intertwining of relationships and allows us to examine the multiple dimensions present in lives, schools, and curriculum. This humanized approach allows us to "reprioritize and redirect our science and technology towards more socially just and environmentally sound practices" (Hodson, 1998, pp. 20-21). Before I introduce Henrietta Lacks, I ask my students if they have a special woman in their lives. Every hand in the room goes up. Then I ask if a student knows someone who is battling cancer. Again, every hand goes up. Then I tell them we will proceed with this story, because they all have something in common with the characters in *The Immortal Life of Henrietta Lacks*.

Donna Haraway (1991) tells us that "Natural scientific stories are supposed to be fruitful; they regularly lead people who practice science to see things they did not know about before, to find the unexpected" (p. 92). Students view textbooks as simple collections of known facts, and students assume these facts cannot be questioned. Listening to stories connected to that collection of facts allows students to connect to their curriculum. Not only do stories in science tell us how the science comes about, "they force an observer to see what one cannot expect and probably does not want to see...but such practice can only make visible what people can historically learn to see" (Haraway, 1991, p. 92). This opens much-needed discourse in science classrooms. Students also need to see that there are real-world applications to the information tightly packed into those textbooks and the real world.

In *(Post) Modern Science (Education)*, Weaver (2001) calls for learning and curriculum that allow for a multiplicity of possibilities and "alternative pedagogies" (p. 20). These "alternative pedagogies" will "break the grip of those stifling binaries that infest the minds of traditional enlightened science" (Weaver, 2001, p. 20). Science teachers must switch the dial from rote memorization to a "process of discovery and intellectual debate" (Weaver, 2001, p. 20). Too many times teachers are simply the givers of answers and expected results. Students are required to do little thinking in this process; they are only expected to know the outcome. Students can use stories to relate their results and a new way of thinking with familiar information and prior knowledge, essentially bridging the gap between the known and the unknown.

Care in Telling Stories

Before sharing stories with students, teachers should take a careful look at how to do so. *The Immortal Life of Henrietta Lacks* raises multiple emotionally charged issues. Henrietta's life, death, and the consequences of both are discussed in an extremely transparent manner. Patty Lather and Chris Smithies (1997) say such a book "walks a fine line between making a spectacle...of a struggle and wanting to speak quietly, with respect for all that it means to tell the stories of people willing to put their lives on public display in the hope that it will make it better for others" (p. xiii). The obvious problem with this book is that Henrietta was not present to oversee the telling of her story. Skloot worked carefully with Henrietta's daughter Deborah. Deborah gave Skloot permission to write the story. Lather and Smithies (1997) tell us that "We should be uncomfortable with these issues of telling other people's stories" (p. 9). We must get it right because they are not here to tell their version. While the *Immortal Life of Henrietta Lacks* continued to be a best seller, Rebecca Kumar wrote an open letter to all colleges and universities opposing Rebecca Skloot's portrayal of Henrietta's story. Her main objection was that Skloot says in the opening that the work is nonfiction. Skloot does this on the first page, first sentence of the book: "This is a work of nonfiction. No names have been changed, no characters invented, no events fabricated. While writing the book [she] conducted more than 1000 hours of interviews" (Skloot, 2010, p. xiii). Kumar says that it is impossible for Skloot to write truthfully about events that she herself did not witness: "the style and content of the story is ultimately the result of her choices...Skloot's descriptions are loaded with political implications and consequences...Skloot has control over the voices" (Kumar, 2012, pp. 3-4). When any of us tell a story either verbally or in writing, we are taking control of the story we are telling. The passage Kumar objects to from the book describes Henrietta finding her tumor while in the bathtub. Kumar questions the idea that Skloot wrote about something that no one witnessed. Why not just say, "It could have happened like this" (p. 4)? Kumar also feels that Skloot's nonfiction telling of the story in the voices of Henrietta's family "reads like a Looney Tunes character" (p. 4). Kumar (2012) says that Skloot goes "out of her way to make Black life seem strange, funny, and sometimes with her depictions of religion, misguided and uninformed. And this makes [Skloot] the voice of normalcy— authoritative and god-like" (p. 5).

Honestly, at first, I chose to brush over the article and ignore Kumar's concerns. The more I thought about it, the more I realized that there would be many opinions about *The Immortal Life of Henrietta Lacks*. Just because it is a bestseller, and I think it should be used to teach science and social justice, does not mean that it was written for that purpose alone. My biggest fear in embarking on this journey is that my African-American students may consider me racist. I did not want to exploit Henrietta's story for my personal gain as an educator, or compose my own victory story (Jupp, 2004, p. 36). My desire is not to "perpetuate" or "endorse" the blatant racism, "faced by [Henrietta] and a countless number of poor women whose bodies were and continue to be exploited in the pursuit of 'knowledge'" (Kumar, 2012, p. 5). As a white woman, I am aware that my life came with a multitude of prepackaged privileges. I know that crossing boundaries, pushing against pre-established borders of society, and attempting to understand a life lived outside of my race in a distant place and time is a complicated proposition. *The Immortal Life of Henrietta Lacks* provides a springboard for complicated conversations to occur in a classroom.

Robert Coles (1989) looks at storytelling in three dimensions: "stories, their story, yours, mine—it's what we all carry with us on this trip we take, and we owe it to each other to respect our stories and learn" from these stories (p. 30). He goes on to say that stories require a "teller's thoughtfulness, canniness, sensitivity and talent" (Coles, 1997, p. 93). The result of telling stories in a classroom is a product that reveals itself as "a kind of truth…An enveloping and unforgettable wisdom that strikes the reader as realer than the truth, a truth that penetrates deep within one" (Coles, 1997, p. 93). As a teacher using stories, one becomes more of a facilitator to oversee the discourse. Everyone's story becomes important.

How to Share Stories

Barone (2000) speaks of the journey of curriculum, "sans the blueprints" (p. 10) as one that focuses on the two-way interaction between the teacher and student, and their interactions with a curriculum. He says that "[this] kind of curriculum theory…will arise from the real qualities of the students' experiences of and their interaction with, the ongoing activities, and from the meanings that facets of the curriculum hold for them…curriculum from the students' perspectives" (p. 53). Standardization cannot work here because "[an] individual defines the world from his own perspective" (p. 56). In my classroom, I want to be what Paulo Freire (1970) calls a "humanist, revolutionary educator," putting forth efforts that "must coincide with those of students to engage in critical thinking and the quest for mutual humanization" (p. 75). For teachers to achieve these goals, we must work side by side and build meaningful relationships with our students. Teachers must invite students to the story.

Barone (2000) tells us that: "All great literature…lures those who experience it away from the shores of literal truth and out into uncharted waters where meaning is more ambiguous" (Barone, 2000, p. 61). The story of Henrietta Lacks can bring students into these "uncharted waters" (p. 61). Barone (2000) suggests that "the reader must imaginatively construct [their] own reality of what [they] read" (p. 61). We must have not only a method for narrative analysis, but also a method to generate information for analysis, and a process for gearing narrative analysis toward science. Barone (2000) offers some advice on how interpretation of text takes place. This advice can be converted into a "loose" method for sharing stories. This is good for teachers if they think a method is necessary. First, we teachers must "invite our students into the dangerous vessel which will float them away from the safety of literal truth and the twin seductions of ethical sloth and moral intolerance" (Barone, 2000, p. 61). This invitation will arrive in the form of a well-told story, offered by a very prepared and intriguing storyteller. For instance, the students can read an excerpt and then connect it to the standards being studied. I usually introduce the story of Henrietta Lacks by telling them how Rebecca Skloot was introduced to Henrietta in her biology class. We go on to reading the following description about cells mentioned earlier.

Next, "we must design activities that entice them into paying careful attention to the social and empirical world around them" (Barone, 2000, p. 62). Teachers must leave "gaps for students to fill in, holes which encourage them to actively intervene in the proceedings to assume responsibility" (Barone, 2000, p. 62). During our project work with *The Immortal Life of Henrietta Lacks*, students have explored multiple topics. Students have shared the parts of the story they discovered with each other. Students have read and developed research questions. By forming questions, students were able to "think critically about the significance of that which they have experienced, [and] wonder how it fits into their own maturing outlooks on the world" (p. 62). At the end of their research, students share their thoughts with teachers and each other. This discourse affords students an opportunity "to tear down and construct again any conclusions reached" (pp. 67). This level of engagement affords students an opportunity to engage in the world and be "ready to change it" (pp. 68). Janet Miller (2005) says, "The new ways of knowing can be strange, alien, and frightening" (p. 76). The process of rethinking all we have ever known may leave us feeling a little ignorant, but we continue to grow and grow—never returning to the ignorance that was present when we began the journey. This process of self-reflection cannot be taken lightly. In education, this work helps us unearth a multitude of feelings and attitudes from a unique perspective. Once we, students and teachers, are willing to explore new territory or text, or look at each other and the world with a different lens, real change may take place in all dimensions in those spaces of transformation. We must be willing to hear the story of Henrietta Lacks.

Connections and Transformations through Stories

The Immortal Life of Henrietta Lacks provides a goldmine of opportunities for students to connect with the standardized curriculum. With each story topic students pose questions. HeLa cells were used in the development of the polio vaccine. This vaccine would save millions of lives. This breakthrough came at a time when institutional racism was prevalent in society. In an interview, Skloot explained that "Black scientists at an all-Black institution [were] using a Black woman's cells to save millions of white people who wouldn't have let [Henrietta] sit next to them" (Skloot, 2010). Would we have the polio vaccine without HeLa cells? Would people have declined the vaccine if they had known Henrietta was Black? Where would science be without her cells? Would we know how cells live and grow in the body without HeLa cells? Without Henrietta?

Skloot shows us examples of science that goes beyond the walls of laboratories and into society. Science is considered an objective field, all about numbers, experiments, fieldwork, and healing. The lessons in science are important, but there were other lessons in Skloot's telling. Lessons that cause the reader to see other historical developments in science. When science is relevant, "worthwhile outcomes result" (Barton, Ermer, Burkett, & Osborne, 2003, p. 118). This group of researchers indicate the following evidence of such an outcome:

> Students of science begin to recognize and exercise their voice and autonomy; they learn to become agents of change in their own lives and within the disciplines of science, using their authority to challenge the traditional cultural practices of science and education. (Barton et al., 2003, p. 118).

When learning experiences make a connection with the student or the student culture, the information is embodied and becomes "meaningful and empowering" (p. 118). When students are "responding to their own questions and needs, science takes on a personal relevance that is not something that had to be learned for a test or project" (p. 118). Students intersect with science on multiple levels: "Power, access to knowledge, equity, social justice, and culture play a role in how youth experience science, but also to how youth respond to difficult situations in order to create a practice of science that has power and meaning in their lives" (p. 158). The intersections become part of their life, their story. Finally Barton et al. (2003) share that "Stories help us understand how science, schooling, and society might intersect in science education settings to help build a more socially just, critically informed and sustainable society" (p. 158).

DeBoer (1991) traces science education from the early eighteenth century to the late twentieth century. Over time, social relevance has gained ground over traditional rote memorization. DeBoer (1991) tells us "the true purpose of education was to prepare people to deal with...socially relevant questions—to equip them for the age in which they live" (p. 3). He tells us that if we look and "see what has been lost and gained by each major shift in the past," we can "head with greater vigor in the direction of social responsibility and socially relevant instruction in science" (DeBoer, 1991, p. xii).

Conclusions

Resurrection of a Living Curriculum

Just as Rebecca Skloot resurrected the story of Henrietta Lacks, science curriculum is in dire need of resurrection. Science curriculum should be "a coursing, as in an electric current. The work of the curriculum theorist should tap this intense current within, that which courses through the inner person, that which electrifies or gives life to a person's energy source" (Doll, 2000, p. xii). Just as we live with blood coursing through our veins, curriculum is living, breathing, constantly growing, and evolving. Curriculum should incorporate "all the contours of the *Lebenswelt*, the lived world, everyday life" (Bowers, 1995, p. 11). Aoki (2003) thinks of curriculum as being derived from two categories: "curricula-as-plan" and "curricula-as-live(d)" (p. 2). The first describes the mandatory subject and objectives usually created for teachers by state school boards. The second is created by the experiences of teachers and students—"a multiplicity of curricula, as many as there are teachers and students" (p. 2). Where does this pedagogy reside? Between the curriculum-as-planned and the lived curricula. Aoki calls these "sites of living pedagogy" (p. 2). The standards are a fixed entity in the classroom for teachers and administrators and unfortunately students. If the standards are not taught with elements of lived experience, there will be dire consequences. Morris (2001) warns that "Erasing lived experience, erasing human subjectivities in school life, endangers students and teachers alike because we will have no sense of who we are" (p. 2). The story of Henrietta Lacks and her HeLa cells can provide opportunities for lived experiences of students and teachers to become part of a living curriculum, the "bios" that curriculum theory is missing (Weaver, 2010, p. 31).

Two Cultures Multiplied through Discourse

Participation in discourse enables students and teachers to find a broader understanding of curriculum not only through discussions concerning science, but also by seeing connections to "cultural, historical, political, ecological, aesthetic, theological, and autobiographical" aspects of education (Slattery, 2013, p. 200). Teachers and students must also realize the "impact of the curriculum on the human condition, social structures, and the ecosphere rather than the planning, design, implementation, and evaluation of context-free and value-neutral schooling events and inert information" (Slattery, 2013, p. 200). Meaning will rise from discourse. Education should be a meaningful experience for participants. Students' personal stories cannot be discounted. Students must be considered valued stakeholders in the educational process. I propose that storytelling in science can serve as a springboard to create the needed discourse to make science meaningful to students.

Henrietta Lacks has created a lot of noise in my classroom. A space has evolved for a living curriculum full of discourse. It is in this place that we can understand how the history, culture, and philosophy of science and science education intersect with students. Transformation cannot take place without venturing outside boundaries and crossing predetermined borders. Teachers must venture outside these borders and provide an opportunity for students to venture outside the lines of the usual linear standardized education. The black box is sitting there, waiting. A scientific system inside the black box, left for only scientists, must be opened and made available to all participants of science. These participants can gain understanding and social justice by constructing connections in "spaces of transformation" (Serres, 1982/2007, p. 73). Participants need opportunities to linger in such spaces.

Spaces to Linger

The idea to "linger" is something that seems more rare to me than when I first read the term described by Aoki (1996, p. 75) and Coles (1997, p. 93). Lingering is a deliberate act required if one is hoping to find opportunities that lead to change or to new ideas. With curriculum maps and benchmarking deadlines, it is very difficult to create an atmosphere fit for lingering. We must stop; we must be interrupted for real lingering to occur. Noise must shatter our original thinking—our thought patterns for us to venture into a new space where we can compose new stories. Lingering allows us to "bring all our sorted histories, hopes, and desires to the project of curriculum theory, hooking onto familiar stories and creating new ones" (Baszile, 2010, p. 483). As we read, write, talk, and think, the conversation will continue to be both complicated and rewarding. Can we reach a place where we are fit to dwell in Jacob's house?

Weaver (2015) uses "Toni Morrison's imagery of Jacob's empty brick house in A Mercy to suggest we do not know who will count as posthuman" (p. 182). Morrison told the story to describe, "That no matter how different Jacob and his progeny were from the D'Ortegas of the world, humans were still unfit to dwell in the home fit for the cultured and civilized" (Weaver, 2010, p. 182). Will philosophers and curriculum theorists include Henrietta in the conversations of today? How about the rest of the world? What about humanity as a whole? Weaver (2015) tells us that humanity is "not fit to inhabit a posthuman world because we are still too barbaric toward one another selling everything for the right price" (p. 182). Bringing topics of science that deal with history, society, politics, and economics is a move in the right direction for creating a science that makes us fit to dwell in Jacob's house. Skloot's books can provide a springboard for all these complicated conversations to take place.

Rebecca Skloot provided this story in a manner for the entire world to hear. By introducing high school biology students to Henrietta Lacks, a space for creating stories is created. In this space, teachers can teach science, and the history of science, and show students the need for social justice to be a part of science. In this space, students can see the importance of their participation in science and their participation in bettering society and becoming activists for social justice. With Henrietta, teachers and students become co-conspirators to bring about change not only in classrooms and schools, but also in communities, society, and the world. I close with words from a ninth-grade biology student, Jhaymia Robinson:

> We can take her story and make it our own. We have the power to finally let her voice be heard! We shall make the ground shake with the heaviness of our hearts, and the sadness of her voice. Henrietta will not be silenced! She shall not be forgotten! No more will she be known as just another woman. She shall be known as the woman that gave life. The woman that cured diseases. The woman that saved humans from all the things that tried to destroy us. Henrietta Lacks is more than a woman. Henrietta is a hero. She is our hero. (Robinson, 2011)

Lives are touched, the living are connected to science, and the bios becomes part of curriculum and curriculum studies through meaningful stories such as *The Immortal Life of Henrietta Lacks*. May Henrietta Lacks become part of your complicated conversations?

References

Adichie, C. (2009, October). *Chimanda Adichie: The danger of a single story.* Retrieved from TED: http://www.ted.com/talks/chimamanda_adichie_the_danger_of_a_single_story/transcript?language=en

Aoki, T. (1996). Imaginaries of "East and West": Slippery curricular signifiers in education. *International Adult & Continuing Education Conference*, (pp. 2-8).

Aoki, T. (2003). Localizing living pedagogy in teacher research: Five metonymic moments. *Curriculum Intertext*, (pp. 1-10). New York, NY: Peter Lang.

Barone, T. (2000). *Aesthetics, politics, and educational inquiry.* New York, NY: Peter Lang.

Barton, A. C., Ermer, J. L., Burkett, T. A., & Osborne, M. D. (2003). *Teaching science for social justice.* New York, NY: Teachers College Press.

Baszile, D. T. (2008). Beyond all reason indeed: The pedagogical promise of critical race testimony. *Race Ethnicity and Education*, 11(3), 251-265.

Baszile, D. T. (2010). In Ellisonian eyes: What is curriculum theory? In E. Malewski (Ed.), *Curriculum studies handbook: The next moment* (pp. 483-495). New York, NY: Routledge.

Berry, B. (2007). *The reauthorization of No Child Left Behind: Views from the nations best teachers.* Retrieved from Teacher Leaders Network: http://www.teachingquality.org/sites/default/files/TLN%20on%20NCLB.pdf

Best Sellers. (2013, June 8). Retrieved from *New York Times*: http://www.nytimes.com/best-sellers-books/paperback-nonfiction/list.html

Bowers, C. A. (1995). *Educating for an ecologically sustainable culture.* New York, NY: SUNY.

Butler, J. (2005). *Giving an account of oneself.* New York, NY: Fordam University Press.

Butler, O. (1987). *Dawn: Book one of the xenogenosis series.* New York, NY: Warner.

Carlson, D. (2015). Forward. In N. Snaza, & J. A. Weaver, *Posthumanis and educational research* (pp. ix-xii). New York, NY: Routeledge.

Chapman, T. K., Hobbel, N., & Alvarado, N. V. (2011). A social justice approach as a base for teaching writing. *Journal of Adolescent & Adult Literacy*, 54(1), 539-541.

Coles, R. (1989). *The call of stories: Teaching and the moral imagination.* Boston, MA: Houghton Mifflin Company.

Coles, R. (1997). *Doing documentary work.* New York, NY: Oxford Press.

Curtis, A. (Director). (1997). *The way of all flesh* [Motion Picture].

DeBoer, G. E. (1991). *A history of the ideas in science education: Implications for practice.* New York, NY: Teachers College Press.

Doll, M. A. (2000). *Like letters in running waters.* Mahwah, NJ: Lawrence Earlbaum Associates.

Freire, P. (1970). *Pedagogy of the oppressed.* New York, NY: Continuum.

Gold, M. (1985). *A conspiracy of cells: One woman's immortal legacy and the medical scandal it caused.* New York, NY: State University of New York.

Haraway, D. (1989). *Primate visions: Gender, race, nature in the world of modern science.* New York, NY: Routledge.

Haraway, D. (1991). *Simians, cyborgs, and women: The reinvention of nature.* London, UK: Free Association Books.

Hodson, D. (1998). *Teaching and learning science: Toward a personalized approach.* Philadelphia, PA: Open University Press.

Jones, H. W., McKusick, V. A., Harper, P. S., & Wuu, K.-D. (1971). After office hours: The HeLa cell and a reprisal of its origin. *Obstetrics and gynecology, 38*(6), 945-949.

Jupp, J. C. (2004). Culturally relevant teaching: One teacher's journey through theory and practice. *Multicultural Review*, 33-40.

Kumar, R. (2012, August 28). *An open letter to those colleges and universities that have assigned Rebecca Skloot's the immortal life of Henrietta Lacks as the "common" freshmen reading for the class of 2016.* Retrieved from Brown Town Magazine: http://itsbrowntown.blogspot.com/2012/08/an-open-letter-to-those-colleges-and.html

Landecker, H. (1999). Between beneficence and chattel: The human biological in law and science. *Science in Context, 12*(1), 203-225.

Landecker, H. (2000). Immortality, invitro: A history of the HeLa cell line. *Biotechnology and culture: Bodies, anxieties, ethics*, 53-72.

Landecker, H. (2007). *Culturing life: How cells became technologies.* Cambridge, MA: First Harvard University Press.

Lather, P., & Smithies, C. (1997). *Troubling the angels.* Boulder, CO: Westview Press.

Miller, J. L. (2005). *Sounds of silence breaking.* New York, NY: Peter Lang.

Morris, M. (2001). Serres bugs the curriculum. In J. A. Weaver, M. Morris, & P. Appelbaum (Eds.), *(Post) modern science (education): propositions and alternative paths* (pp. 94-110). New York, NY: Peter Lang.

Morris, M. (2008). *Teaching through the ill body: A spirtual and aesthetic approach to pedagogy and illness.* Rotterdam, NL: Sense Publishers.

Pinar, W. F. (2004). *What is curriculum theory?* Mahwah, NJ: Lawrence Earlbaum.

Pinar, W. F., Reynolds, W. M., Slattery, P., & Taubman, P. M. (2008). *Understanding curriculum.* New York, NY: Peter Lang.

Robinson, J. (2011, October 4). *The immortal wonderland.* (J. Robinson, Performer) Evans High School, Evans, Georgia, USA.

Rogers , M. (1976, March 26). The double-edged helix. *The Rolling Stone*, pp. 48-51.

Schwab, J. J. (1978). *Science curriculum and liberal education: Selected essays.* Chicago, IL: University of Chicago Press.

Serres, M. (2007). *The parasite. (L. R. Schehr, Trans.).* Minneapolis, MN: University of Minnesota Press. (Original published in 1982)

Serres, M., & Latour, B. (2011). *Conversations on science, culture and time. (R. Lapidus, Trans.).* Ann Arbor, MI: University of Michigan Press. (Original work published 1990)

Shelley, M. (1996). *Frankenstein.* New York, NY: Norton.(original work published in 1818)

Skloot, R. (2010, December 13). 'Immortal' Cells Of Henrietta Lacks Live On In Labs. (N. Conan, Interviewer)

Skloot, R. (2010). *The immortal life of Henrietta Lacks.* New York, NY: Broadway Paperbacks.

Slattery, P. (2013). *Curriculum development in the postmodern era: Teaching and learning in an age of accountability.* New York, NY: Routledge.

Snaza, N. (2015). Toward a geneology of educational humanism. In N. Snaza, & J. A. Weaver (Eds), *Posthumanism and educational research* (pp. 16-29). New York, NY: Routeledge.

Snaza, N., & Weaver, J. A. (2015). Introduction: Education and the posthumanist turn. In N. Snaza, & J. A. Weaver (Eds), *Posthumanism and educational research* (pp. 1-14). New York, NY: Routledge.

Snow, C. P. (1959/2013). *The two cultures and the scientific revolution.* New York, NY: Cambridge University Press. (original work published in 1959).

Snyder, L. J. (2011). *The philosophical breakfast club.* New York, NY: Broadway.

Wald, P. (2012). Cells, genes, and stories: HeLa's journey from labs to literature. In K. Wailoo, A. Nelson, & C. Lee, *Genetics and the unsettled past: The collision of dna, race, and history* (pp. 247-265). New Brunswick, NJ: Rutgers University Press.

Weaver, J. A. (2001). Introductions (post)modern science (education): Propositions and alternative paths. In J. A. Weaver, M. Morris, & P. Appelbaum (Eds.), *(Post)modern science (education): Propositions and alternative paths* (pp. 1-22). New York, NY: Peter Lang.

Weaver, J. A. (2010). *Educating the posthuman: Biosciences, fiction, and curriculum studies.* Rotterdam, NL: Sense.

Weaver, J. A. (2015). To what future do the posthuman and posthumanism (re) turn us: Meanwihile how do I tame the lingering effects of humanism? In N. Snaza, & J. A. Weaver (Eds.), *Posthumanism and Educational Research* (pp. 182-194). New York, NY: Taylor and Francis.

Whewell, W. (1834). Mrs. Somerville on the connexion of science. *The quarterly review,* 58-61.

Wiesel, E. (1992). *The nazi doctors and the Nuremberg code: Human rights in human experimentation.* New York, NY: Oxford University Press.

Wolfe, G. C. (Director). (2016). *The Immortal Life of Henrietta Lacks* [Motion Picture].

Chapter 6

Solitude in Education

Changing the Monoculture of the Mind

Stacey T. Brown

The apple is iconic. It connotes nourishment, sweetness, knowledge, and what is forbidden, all of which are potential by-products of education. We think of the apple as wholesome and unadulterated, yet the apples we have access to, as consumers, are carefully grown through a process of genetic engineering. What we see in the produce section are the "gifted and talented" apples, chosen for their favorable flavor and aesthetic appearance. Consumers buy apples that are not grown and nurtured from seeds. They are reproduced from apples that are basically prototypes. Apples constitute one of the largest monocultures in the world. In order to grow apples that will appeal to consumers and prosper in the economy, they are grown in orchards that only grow one kind of isolated apple under very standardized conditions. There are different orchards that grow different apples, but "wild" apples that grow from the actual seed are largely unwanted because of their unique taste and appearance. Some are bitter. Some are asymmetrical. Some are smaller than the "standard" apple, while some are bigger. Most are undesirable to demanding consumers who require "sameness."

The apple represents knowledge in education, but it also represents the "products" of education: the students. If teachers are the farmers, students are the apples. Is it better practice to plant wild, unadulterated seeds in order to educate or is it better to graft knowledge? The teacher that chooses to let wild seeds grow takes many risks that include isolation and alienation from society and the educational community. That teacher may not be able to survive in the face of the highly promoted, highly profitable monoculture of education. The seeds, the students, are at risk as well. Teachers who choose to graft knowledge can do so carefully in an

David P. Owen, Jr (ed.), Field Theory: Curriculum Studies at Work, 103–119.

effort to promote biodiversity and to fight against monoculture. This teacher should avoid practices that mimic those of agricultural engineering that promote high yield and high profit for the benefit of the economy, a parallel to standardization in education. Pinar says, "Sustainability does not mean the unregulated reproduction of species" (2009, p. 6), which supports the importance of grafting versus the farming of wild apples. Sustainability of the individual in a pluralistic society is the ultimate goal, with curriculum that promotes a world where "understanding is both individual and social, 'local' and 'global,' historical and futural" (Pinar, 2004, p. 16).

Shiva says that, "The crucial characteristic of monocultures is that they do not merely displace alternatives, they destroy their own basis. They are neither tolerant of other systems, nor are they able to reproduce themselves sustainably" (1993, p. 50). How many program changes have we endured while under the mandates of standardization and under the guise that standardization works? And why? Because standardized practices do not work and they are not sustainable. Monoculture in education is an isolating practice that "renders the curriculum self-enclosed, abstract, split-off from those everyday lives not only students live, but also from those lived by their parents and those in their communities, their nation, on the earth" (Riley-Taylor as quoted in Pinar, 2004, p. 21). Standardization of curriculum places no importance on the individual or the "self-reflexive interdisciplinary intellectuality—the cultivation of 'original thought'—that constitutes curriculum theorists' aspiration for the process of education" (Pinar, 2004, p. 20). Without an emphasis on the self, we promote no cultivation of hybridity or individuality in "species." There are only good apples and bad apples that are easily sorted through social constructs that are not all inclusive. When curriculum promotes self-reflexivity, we prevent isolation and promote the sustainability of "private-and-public intellectuals" (p. 23) who value solitude and profound thought that can later be lived and shared publicly. Today's curriculum only promotes a tested learning of standards with no emphasis on the authoring of the self, and no celebration of solitude. In order to graft knowledge ethically, we must focus on "the cultivation of independence of mind, self-reflexivity, and interdisciplinary erudition" (p. 24).

We face a "cultural crisis in which work is split off from play, mind from body, soul from intellect" (Pinar 2004, p. 27) that parallels the ecological crisis concerning the isolation and production of apples that are chosen to maximize profits: biodiversity. Much like farmers who fall victim to the corporatization of agriculture, we see that "the factory model tends to reduce teachers to automata" where "the factory model school achieves social control at the cost of intelligence" (p. 28). Pinar says:

> for intelligence to be cultivated in fundamental ways, it must be set free of corporate goals. Such an idea hardly excludes instrumental reason, calculation, and problem solving as major modes of cognition. Intellectual freedom must allow, however, for meditative, contemplative modes of cognition and for exploring subjects—those associated, for instance, with the arts and the humanities—that may have no immediate practical pay-off and might not be evaluated by standardized examinations. (p. 29)

We must cultivate intelligence in the same way we must cultivate apples. Letting them grow wildly from seeds is not an ethically sound practice. The result is possible isolation or extinction of species. However, careful grafting of sustainable forms ensures the propagation of the species. In order for intelligence to proliferate, we must avoid standardized, isolating practices that dehumanize education. If we control the standards of learning that our students must master, are we aborting the possibility of a hybrid species of knowledge that our students can only produce in a more fertile field outside of this monoculture, in solitude?

The ethical grafting that is taking place with apples is a movement that wishes to promote diversity and save species of apples. This movement can be likened to *currere*. We tend to see ourselves in nature as the superior species, responsible for allowing nature to thrive or for deciding that it should not. In actuality, nature only manipulates us. Pollan says,

> We give ourselves altogether too much credit in our dealing with other species. Even the power over nature that domestication supposedly represents is overstated. It takes two to perform that particular dance, after all, and plenty of plants and animals have elected to sit it out. (2001, p. 5)

We cannot sustain ourselves without nature. Without humans, nature would go on. Nature without humans is self-sustaining. The reverse equation does not yield the same outcome. Humans can cooperate with nature for our benefit or manipulate it for our destruction. Analogous to education, Pinar points out,

> That is why we believe in education; we see how powerfully schooling crushes it, and yet, still, there is education, despite the schools. There is God despite the church, justice despite the government, and love despite the family. We educators must prepare for a future when the school is returned to us and we can teach, not manipulate for test scores. (2004, p. 127)

Morris allows us to draw a parallel between education and mysticism with a more postmodern lens:

> Why is the world unwilling to listen to the mystic? Because the world (of machines, nuclear weapons, empire) does not believe there is such a thing as a mystical experience and even if there were, to what use could it be put? Mystical language has always been thought to be heretical. No dogma needed. No church needed. No appeal needs to be made to authority. No permission needed. And there are no standardized tests for mystical experience. (2008, p. 85)

Here, the mystic is the teacher and the farmer, deeply rooted and well-grounded in their craft: their practice. Neither of them needs to quantify and see concrete results. They sense the fertility of the soil and the nutritive needs of their garden. If left to their mystical instincts, their gardens thrive, in solitude, unadulterated, biologically unaltered. Those who promote standardization foolishly believe they can control educational outcomes, yet education exists regardless of the monoculture that is present in our schools. Mysticism abounds in the world of education because:

> Mystical experience happens in psychological blind spots. The natural tendency is to ignore those blind spots and pretend that they are nothing. But the mystic knows better. An intellectual and emotional exploration of those mystical blind spots becomes necessary to unpack their significance and meaning. It is in those moments of existential crisis that one encounters the what-is. And even though study and intellectual work can open the doors of perception, ultimately the what-is cannot be known or understood or even described. The understanding that we do not understand takes intellectual work. (Morris, 2008, p. 111-112)

The authentic, organic farmer understands this and values the mystical experience that can only occur in solitude, where the real experience of learning and living occurs. The reconceptualized teacher lives and breathes this. If we approach education and agriculture with only a "process-product" mentality, we lose the *currere* that results from the blind spots of mystical experience. Standardization is a hindrance to mystical experience that produces the epiphanies that are a part of becoming an intellectual. These experiences also speak to the soul, creating a dialogue between body, mind, and spirit, in solitude. This happens agriculturally as well. Farmers must mystically know their orchard. The body, mind, and spirit of an orchard are the soil, the root system, and the sun, for the apple, carefully tended by the farmer. This ability to listen and respond to the rhythm of nature and life can only occur in solitude and is the only way to ensure sustainability.

If the teacher and the farmer are not able to tend to their orchards in the midst of mystical experience, they become at risk for isolation, for "alienation, social homelessness and disorientation, powerlessness and loss, emotional and sensorial destruction and death" (Wexler, 2000, p. 5). While this may sound extreme, and death might be metaphorical, rather than literal, the death of teaching as educational art and farming as agricultural art is a remote possibility, if we do not commit to an activism that stops standardization and monoculture in their tracks. Wexler says, "I see in the present historic moment a loss of this imaginative capacity, rooted in the loss and destruction of society itself" (p. 5). The societal implications on both sides are immense.

Standardization promotes isolation and alienation of knowledge and of people, both teacher and student. The "self-overcoming" that Pinar promotes (2004, p. 22) is impossible under these stale conditions. Wexler gets to the root of the problem by stating:

> Education is a key locus of transformative social interaction, or at least another name for it. Nevertheless, institutional education has become a major purveyor of feeling-denying contemporary cognitive performance obsession, yet another expression of the classical types of alienation and mechanical petrification of individual and social being. (2000, p. 14)

The private-and-public intellectual cannot become rooted in an institutionalized environment. That species will become extinct without the solitude that is needed to create, generate, and flourish.

Regardless of whether or not we standardize, there will be variety in our barrel of apples. Historically, when apples were grown from seeds, the apples that were not fit for eating were made into cider! There is no such thing as a "bad" apple, but monoculture and standardization have developed the myth that convinces us otherwise. Pinar says, "By tying the curriculum to student performance on test scores, teachers are forced to abandon the intellectual freedom to choose what they teach, how they teach, and how they assess student learning" (2004, p. 164), which makes the myth of bad apples an illusion of reality. Crocco et al. (1999) assert that:

> Acknowledging difference in ways that enhance opportunity and adequately account for past discrimination is a challenge still facing this country. Current debates over affirmative action and gender equity in education reveal the need to understand equality in terms other than simply uniformity of treatment. (p. 120)

Standardization does not allow for this understanding to take place. If anything, it pushes us back decades, erasing and eroding many of the battles that have already been fought and negating the activism that we are now tasked with reconceptualizing through curriculum theory. Activism is essential.

Teachers who do not band together against the monoculture of education are at risk of isolation and separation from their craft. At the same time, teachers must do the self-work of understanding themselves and their enemy and their own kind in response to friction that results from standardization. This can only happen in the time and space of solitude. Morris reminds us of how animals behave in nature, which allows us to see the potential of our own behavior:

> When animals get hurt, members of their pack sometimes abandon them. Fear of the Other and fear of death underlie these turnings. The problem is that people are afraid of what is Other, of what they do not understand and of what makes them afraid to face their own mortality. (2008, p. 2)

The survival and proliferation of the apple depends on the survival and proliferation of the farmer. The analogous reciprocity between teacher and student is inherent. Activism must be in place. We cannot face the standardization and cross the river to the other side unharmed if we do not explore the world and all of its imposed social constructs, the Other, and our interaction with it. Munro explains that production theorists "who stressed the power of individuals to come to a critical consciousness of their own world, stressed the dialectic between individual consciousness and structural determinants" (1998, p. 23). We must come to terms with the Other and be hospitable to it if we are going to negotiate resistance to standardization. Munro expounds by saying "Mechanisms of reproduction are never complete and always meet with opposition. This concept of resistance was central to critical theorists' understanding of the complex interaction between agency and structure" (p. 23). In order to be activists, we must be self-reflexive, private-and-public intellectuals who know how to find solitude and secure it for our own salvation.

How can one be a drifter without changing location? Farmers have their land and they cannot leave it. Farmers become drifters through crop rotation. They can rotate and revolve, like the Earth around the sun. Crop rotation allows the soil to regenerate. How can the teacher, particularly the female teacher, drift and remain in the same space? Munro offers an answer to this question by asserting the paradoxical yet poignant notion that "gender is constructed not as professional (male) or non-professional (female) but through and in a continual crossing of gender boundaries, which results in a decentering of the gender binary creating spaces from which to envisage a multiplicity of genders" (1998, p. 120). We can apply other social constructs in the place of gender, just as we can apply species of apples to this paradigm. We, like the farmer, employ rotation to enrich the soil of our curriculum and the foundation of our self-reflexivity. To further root the idea of activism as an individual and with others, Miller explains, "I hope for such doubled spaced understandings in order to work with others to forge educational communities and collaborations without consensus, without the pressure to merge into one position or one right answer or identify" (2005, p. 84). We must learn to navigate boundaries and spaces and not root ourselves, but rotate and revolve in order to survive and in order to play the role of activist. In this sense, solitude is not fixed. It is fluid. It transcends time and space. It defies duality. We should not seek agreement and unification, but collegiality and respect from varying perspectives. Some people prefer the Granny Smith apple over the Macintosh. That does not mean they do not like the Macintosh or do not like people who like the Macintosh. It is simply a preference of taste for the individual.

The monoculture of education does not apply to the species of students alone. Teachers also fall under this alienating practice. We are under the same pressures as the family farmer who personally cares for and tends to his apples, who resents agribusiness and suffers as a result of it. The anti-intellectualism of education that is promoted by the monoculture of standardization requires of curriculum theorists an activism that allows us

> to keep the bonds that bind alive, in order to be heard, in order to hear, in order to teach and learn. Our interest in our students is, of course, partly parental; we wish them well, independently of our self-interest. We want our students to succeed, even if our ideas of success differ from theirs. When we fight for cultural progress, we do not (only) seek our own narrow political gain; we fight for what we perceive to be in the public's—in the next generation's, the culture's—interest. (Pinar, 2004, p. 169)

The reciprocal relationship between farmer and apple, teacher and student, human and nature, is one to be fostered, not with isolated nutrients or fragments of knowledge, but through intrapersonal and shared experiences. We must perform "inner work" on ourselves, "not in the name of personal therapy, but in the cause of social reconstruction"

(p. 201). The teacher feels personal responsibility for students, just as the farmer feels personal responsibility for the apples in his orchard.

Farmers, in the true sense of the word, who are deeply rooted in authentic agriculture and sustainable practice, face the same isolating blame and hatred as educators. Farmers and teachers are no longer respected for their knowledge or their craft. They are put to task as technicians of process and then blamed when the product is not desirable. Activism is necessary to uphold the ethical standards of curricular theorists and educators everywhere. In order to break down the empire of monoculture, we must unite in "recognizing different, not minimizing it, (as) essential to democracy" (Crocco et al. 1999, p. 25). We cannot isolate pieces of knowledge and teach them in any way that is meaningful or useful. The knowledge is not sustainable unless it is a part of the garden of knowledge from which it came. Shiva says, "A number of artificial shifts are thus achieved through fragmenting knowledge. The sources of regeneration and renewal of life are transformed into inert and fragmented matter, mere 'raw material' to be processed into a finished product" (2014, p. 26).

Knowledge has place and history and a story to tell. It must be carefully transferred and grafted into the curriculum in order for it to be a viable part of one's own body of knowledge and this can only take place in solitude, not in isolation. Shiva continues: "The transformation of creativity into passivity relocates productivity in disruptive, coercive and exploitative acts, and defines it as a source of value; and simultaneously defines all other values as non-value" (2014, p. 26). Fragmented, isolated knowledge promotes passivity. It produces apples that all look and taste the same and excludes all other types of knowledge, even passing them off as *non*-knowledge. Shiva says, "Through this relocation of production and value, external control over sites of regeneration becomes not just desirable but necessary for human survival and well-being. The destructive, ironically, emerges as the savior" (p. 26). The wild apples, those we only deem appropriate for cider, might indeed be our saviors, whether they are teachers or students. They represent the Other that we must learn to embrace. They could create that hybrid species of knowledge that transcends standardization and embraces reconceptualization.

It has become increasingly difficult for teachers to remain autonomous as a result of mandates of standardization, which contributes to the lack of respect society shows the profession. Crocco et al. assert that, "Teachers [are] viewed as unable to carry out their duties without firm mandates from supervisors who [demand] frequent inspections of classrooms and [undermine] teacher autonomy by narrowly prescribing the pedagogical options available" (1999, p. 54). In actuality, supervisors overburden teachers with mandates that detract from the solitude they need to hone their craft and develop themselves as private-and-public intellectuals. It is the supervisors that are inept and uninformed, which is why they support and employ a monocultural approach to education. Tight restrictions and control allow them to supervise with the Foucauldian gaze of the Panopticon, functioning as a punishment of the body and soul:

> The man described to us, who we are invited to free, is already in himself the effect of a subjection much more profound than himself. A 'soul' inhabits him that brings him to existence, which is itself a factor in the mastery that power exercises over the body. The soul is the effect and instrument of a political anatomy; the soul is the prison of the body. (Foucault, 1979, p. 30)

The teacher and the farmer suffer this same fate under the political strings with which they are puppeted to produce a highly processed product at a high yield, at any cost to the puppets and their audience—their apples.

If we are in this current puppeted state of suspension, what do we do, in this illness of monoculture? Morris says, "Allow yourself to breakdown and then you might begin to put the pieces back together" (2008, p. 11). We must make meaning out of chaos and sadness and illness. We must rise from the fallow soil of the monoculture and rebuild: "Turning the illness into some sort of creative task. Turning the illness into something else that might be of some use to somebody else. It is all about the turning. Turning what is bad into something useful" (p. 11). The teacher and the farmer might need a turn in the cave. We try to leave the allegorical cave so we can come into the light, but sometimes the cave is imposed on us. Sometimes we even volunteer to go back to the cave. We isolate ourselves purposefully so that we can come back into the light, renewed and able to find solitude: the private-and-public intellectual, "freed from disciplinary shackles" (p. 13).

The isolation of monoculture and standardization is frightening. We have to be clever to stay free from the shackles. We must involve ourselves in the poaching that Appelbaum condones. Bringing the idea of monoculture to the field of curriculum studies is an example of poaching. I am "poaching concepts and metaphors from literary texts, and bringing them back home into the world of curriculum, where they become the raw compost for teaching and learning" (2008, p. 13). *Currere* is a part of poaching. It involves movement and risk. It involves agency and self-reflexivity. Appelbaum calls it "a clever sort of problem-solving raised to a high art, in which one needs to take what one is entitled to in many ways that require elaborate strategies and complex social relationships" (p. 13).

Agricultural botanists are performing their own acts of poaching in an effort to preserve species of apples and to sustain them forever. We must employ poaching to sustain education because:

> what tales of poachers reveal to readers is the spark of life that has been made possible through the complications of criminalization; the danger at once raises the stakes by introducing the threat to life itself as well as requiring the complex problem-solving strategies. I find, in the end, that poaching is the essence of a vital curriculum, and in the end, of 'becoming.' (Appelbaum, 2008, p. 13)

As Conrad wrote in *Heart of Darkness*, "And outside, the silent wilderness surrounding this cleared speck on the earth struck me as something great and invincible, like evil or truth, waiting patiently for the passing away of this fantastic invasion" (2006, p. 23). Appelbaum would enjoy a poaching expedition that produces this type of educational experience. He says, "learning, like poaching, must be dangerous, because, like poaching, an act vital to one's very survival has been twisted in recent history into a seemingly criminalized notion of stealing someone else's property" (2008, p. 13). Poaching is an organic, grassroots approach to reconceptualization that can destroy the monoculture of standardized education. Poaching and education are analogous to grafting and agriculture. Through poaching and grafting, ethics are implied and sustainability is realized.

Standardization employs science and numbers to quantify outcomes but the manipulation of data has not allowed the masses to realize that "standardized schools with standardized visions of success tend to produce standardized human beings" (Barone, 2000, p. 121). Through the grafting of the seed of the student into the branch, the giver of knowledge, of the tree, the body of knowledge, we can achieve biodiversity of knowledge and of human beings that "would support a process wherein teachers assist each student in the weaving (and reweaving) of profoundly educational, aesthetic experiences into a narrative, or story, of a unique and responsible self" (p. 121). Biodiversity in education is the answer to the epidemic of the monoculture of standardization.

A strong parallel also exists in the science behind agriculture and education. If the sites of industrialized farming and standardized education are a Panopticon, then they are also a laboratory, "used as a machine to carry out experiments, to alter behavior, to train or correct individuals" (Foucault, 1979, p. 203). It is erroneous to look at education or agriculture as "strict science" (Apple, 2000, p. 125). Certainly science and experimentation are a part of both fields, but there is also the ethical element of subjects, to which both teachers (and farmers) and students (and apples) fall prey. Munro asserts that:

> Professionalization in this context (means) transforming teaching in several ways: from an undifferentiated occupation to a stratified one; from a field based on an ambiguous body of knowledge to a science of teaching; and from a *laissez-faire* approach of teacher authority to a standardized vision of teaching practice. (1998, p. 21)

This renders a premature abortion of any fruitful bearing of knowledge or creativity that is unethical in the face of experimentation for economic profit. Teachers take risks and experiment every day, but not by methods that are deleterious to human souls and minds in the name of high yield and return. We must employ hermeneutic science, as "historical-interpretive modes of scientific activity that yield, not 'information' in the sense implied in the strict sciences, but an understanding of the 'social cultural life-world'" (Apple, 2000, p. 125-126).

Both standardization and monoculture claim to have the ability to yield results, to give the people what they want, but through industrialization of resources and cultural exploitation, they fail and blame teachers and farmers. Wexler (2000) asserts that "The critique of culture is of its effects in destroying any true individuality, any capacity of autonomous reasoned thought and mature, responsible action" (p. 69), which of course is taken from us through the refining and narrowing of practice. He goes on to say, "Whatever industrialization itself did not already destroy, culture finishes off. It tyrannizes the soul and confines the body. Intimate relations are reified, and there is simply no room for imagination, reflection, or spontaneity—for human being" (p. 69). Why does this continue to happen when so many casualties of education lie in the wake of standardization? Why do people demand genetically altered apples? Why do we reject queer apples and queered curriculum? Our current political and cultural structure allows "The social relations of high informational production (to) dematerialize the body and restructure time and space, unintentionally setting the stage for a mass resacralization of shared meanings" (p. 70). We are allowing time and space to be modified. We are allowing ourselves to become "docile bodies":

> In becoming the target for new mechanisms of power, the body is offered up to new forms of knowledge. It is the body of exercise, rather than of speculative physics; a body manipulated by authority, rather than imbued with animal spirits; a body of useful training and not of rational mechanics, but one in which, by virtue of that very fact, a number of natural

requirements and functional constraints are beginning to emerge. (Foucault, 1979, p. 155)

We are brainwashed; blindfolded. The monoculture of education only makes room for genetically modified apples, grafted with standardized practice. The new forms of knowledge take the places of the old. The old forms of knowledge end up in a graveyard, where isolated and alienated erudites dig them up and reassemble them like Victor Frankenstein and his misunderstood monster. This monster lives in the wild seedlings of the apples that standardization does not educate. While the monster educated himself through poaching, he was the Other and was not only rejected by his creator, but also by society. The monster says he is a victim of:

> a forced solitude that I abhor, and my virtues will necessarily arise when I live in communion with an equal. I shall feel the affections of a sensitive being and become linked to the chain of existence and events from which I am now excluded. (Shelley, 1998, p. 141)

Frankenstein created the monster with no thought to how he would exist, find connection, or thrive in a standardized world. Frankenstein failed to realize the rejection and isolation the monster would endure in society. Standardized education does not graft knowledge into these seedlings. We label them bad apples and destroy them through isolation.

Rather than grafting knowledge, standardization isolates knowledge. Jardine explores the monstrousness of pedagogy, asserting that it is

> due to the fact that some once-familiar feature of the world has been severed from its familiar place. These once-familiar features no longer fit where one would normally expect them to fit, nor do they arrive as normally expected. They thereby lose all sense of proportion. (1998, p. 126)

This mirrors standardized practice. It is unnatural. It has no rhythm. It is discordant and cacophonous. We are left with the same task as Victor Frankenstein, but it is not a labor of passion, as it is for him, and we must remember that Victor was essentially insane. Society cannot make cider out of his monster. The monster is a sympathetic character, but society finds no place for him. He is a wild apple who was unethically constructed into a living being, yet we take our chances every day through isolating and dehumanizing practices of standardization and monoculture.

Apples have aesthetic value. We paint pictures of them, we set them in bowls as decoration, and we buy fabrics and pillows with apples on them. We paint our walls candy apple red or sour apple green. We name apples after famous people and places. We name our children "Apple" and name corporations after them. The apple is art. However, just as the apple has become a victim of agricultural industrialization, one of the largest monocultures in the world, the arts have become a victim of educational monoculture. Beyer agrees that commodification and mass production have forced art to fall prey to the massive predator of monoculture. He says, "As a form of commodity exchange, art is isolated from important traditions, histories, and commitments, separated from those human and communal activities from which might be derived an important place for the aesthetic understanding" (2000, p. 20). Beyer astutely suggests that "schools 'process' knowledge, in addition to 'processing' people" (p. 55) and, to refute that practice, he says, "through homogenization, difference itself appears to be valorized, ironically, as a transcendent good, or at least as a fact of postmodern life" (p. 131). Kliebard reminds us that because education likens itself to industry, "educational activity which may have an organic wholeness and vital meaning takes on a significance only in terms of its contribution to the efficient production of the finished product" (2000, p. 65-66). Make lemonade out of bitter lemons. Make cider out of "different" apples. But, let us not run to the roadside stand in haste. Let us enjoy the making of the lemonade and the cider and then enjoy the fruits of our labor.

While aesthetics are important, Bowers suggests that in order for education to be sustainable, we must have balance. He says

> The modern view of creativity that leads educators to see the possibility of creativity in every aspect of students' experience will continue, as long as it is understood as individually centered, to be both experientially and symbolically limiting. Indeed, this is one of the ironies of modernity. (1995, p. 74)

This goes back to the idea of planting wild apple seeds. Each seed that an apple contains is unique. There is no way of ensuring what kind of apple any seed will produce. If grafting is not utilized, there is no balance. There is no guarantee that any apple will actually be edible. While we can make cider out of wild apples, we cannot live on cider alone, at least not soberly! Bowers suggests that an imbalanced approach to creativity "is also contributing to a form of culture that is ignoring a basic fact of existence: that our lives are connected and interdependent—both with past and future generations and with the larger biotic community" (p. 74). Grafting of knowledge allows for a curriculum that navigates between a cosmopolitan value of aesthetics and plurality within a collective consciousness of universality.

Todd grapples with this notion of wild apples as well. While she supports pluralism, she points out that:

cosmopolitanism aims to mould, encourage, or cultivate in youth a humanity that is already seen as 'shared,' it prevents us from confronting the far more difficult and much closer task at hand of facing the troublesome aspects of human interaction that emerge in specific times and places. (2009, p. 21)

Too much plurality, just like too many species of apples, is difficult for anyone to digest. We are all unique, but we innately seek the acceptance of universality. While the field of curriculum studies rejects social constructs, we value place and autobiography and history in an effort to connect with ourselves and with others. Todd values what is imperfect through an appreciation of pluralism, but says that it is:

rooted in a shift from a cosmopolitanism that, on the one hand, seeks to encapsulate pluralism within universal commitments or, on the other hand, seeks to ignore the very heart of cosmopolitanism right as a right of humanity by focusing solely on cultural diversity and hybridity. (p. 153)

This philosophy is exemplified in the practice of grafting. Grafting yields biodiversity. Biodiversity yields sustainability.

Under the influence of Sartre, Rowlands deduces that "A wolf does not have its being to be. A wolf can only be what it is...a wolf's essence precedes its existence" (2009, p. 38). Humans, on the other hand, "their existence precedes their essence" (p. 38). The apple operates like the wolf and we must use our consciousness to act on behalf of the apple and wolf. Those we educate, our apples, have a consciousness, but we must commune with their consciousness. We are still responsible for making ethical choices about which knowledge is worth grafting and how it should be grafted. The barrel is full of apples, all of which have a purpose and an existence. If our apple is like Rowlands' wolf, and it very well may be, then "It enjoys what it learns and wants to learn more. It becomes stronger and consequently happier" (p. 41). This is what we want for our apples. We want them to maintain the sweetness that makes them so desirable. The seedlings will possess knowledge as sweet and desirable as ours if they are grafted and nurtured in a way that supports pluralism and cosmopolitanism and in a manner that allows them to navigate both realms under the nurturing blanket of universality.

Cremin quotes Harris in his assertion that education is a process "by which the individual is elevated into the species" (2000, p. 20), which embodies the idea of grafting. Cremin says it is "a process by which a self-active being is enabled to become privy to the accumulated wisdom of the race" (p. 20). The isolated apple seed can survive the industrialization of monoculture, but for how long? Without pesticides, not long. Monocultures are not sustainable. The grafted seed can survive and proliferate on its own and can graft knowledge from others and can become a tree from which knowledge can be grafted for other seeds. This is sustainability.

To characterize the method of grafting, we go to Pinar: "It is regressive because it involves description and analysis of one's intellectual biography or, if you prefer, educational past" (2000, p. 424). This refers to the tree that holds the branch in which the seed will be grafted. The tree is the body of knowledge. The branch is the person or experience that extends that knowledge. The seed is the seeker of knowledge. Pinar continues: The method of grafting is "progressive, because it involves a description of one's imagined future; analytic because it calls for a psychoanalysis of one's phenomenologically described educational present, past, and future" (p. 424). This is where soul searching and self-reflexivity take root and germinate. Pinar finishes his description of method that can be applied to grafting: "synthetic because it totalizes the fragments of educational experience and places this integrated understanding of individual experience into the larger political and cultural web, explaining the dialectical relation between the two" (p. 424). Weaver reminds us, however, that grafting is posthuman: "No matter what technological device is grafted to biology the important point is to recognize biotechnology as yet another example of merging life (bio) with the non-human (technology) in order to re-create the meaning of humans" (2010, p. 18). This is the aesthetic experience that allows the seed to grow and navigate in multiple spaces between individuality and plurality in a posthuman world.

Apples represent wisdom and forbidden fruit to which we are all attracted. We seek knowledge, but not necessarily the standardized knowledge to which our students are subjected. We seek meaningful and purposeful knowledge, as well as knowledge that expands our appreciation for aesthetics. There is wisdom that can be seen and there is wisdom that is abstract, not able to be quantified or commodified. We seek to produce apples through the grafting of knowledge and experience that will allow our apples to grow from saplings to fully-grown, mature, and majestic trees. The monoculture that exists cannot be sustained without the pesticides of standardized testing. Pesticides can keep the apples alive and can keep the bugs at bay, but at what cost? How nourishing are the apples we are producing? Pollan discovered that crops that are a victim of monoculture had a "vitamin C decline by 20 percent, iron by 15 percent, riboflavin by 38 percent, calcium by 16 percent" (2008, p. 118). In addition:

> You now have to eat three apples to get the same amount of iron as you would have gotten from a single 1940 apple, and you'd have to eat several more slices of bread to get your recommended daily allowance of zinc than you would have a century ago. (p. 118)

Yet standardization and monocultures proliferate. Consumers buy the products because they are cheaper and more available than any product produced by more ethical and sustainable practice. The reconceptualization of education can put an end to the monoculture of education through a curriculum that promotes grafting of knowledge and biodiversity in realms of solitude.

References

Apple, M. W. (2000). Scientific interests and the nature of educational institutions. In W. F. Pinar, *Curriculum studies: The reconceptualization* (pp. 120-130). New York, NY: Educator's International Press.

Appelbaum, P. (2008). *Children's books for grown-up teachers.* New York, NY: Routledge.

Bowers, C. A. (1995). *Educating for an ecologically sustainable culture: Rethinking moral education, creativity, intelligence, and other modern orthodoxies.* Albany, NY: SUNY.

Barone, T. (2000). *Aesthetics, politics, and educational inquiry: Essays and examples.* New York, NY: Peter Lang.

Beyer, L. (2000). *The arts, popular culture, and social change.* New York, NY: Peter Lang.

Conrad, J. (2006). *Heart of darkness.* New York, NY: W. W. Norton & Company.

Cremin, L. A. (2000). Curriculum making in the United States. In W. F. Pinar, *Curriculum studies: The reconceptualization* (p. 17-35). New York, NY: Educator's International   Press.

Crocco, M., Munro, P. & Weiler, K. (1999). *Pedagogies of resistance: Women educator activists, 1880-1960.* New York, NY: Teachers College Press.

Foucault, M. (1979). *Discipline and punish: The birth of the prison.* New York, NY: Vintage Books.

Jardine, D. (1998). *To dwell with a boundless heart.* New York, NY: Peter Lang.

Kliebard, H. M. (2000). Bureaucracy and curriculum theory. In W. F. Pinar, *Curriculum   studies: The reconceptualization* (pp. 51-69). New York, NY: Educator's International   Press.

Mies, M., & Shiva, V. (2014). *Ecofeminism.* London, UK: Zed Books Ltd.

Miller, J. (2005). *Sounds of silence breaking: Women, autobiography, curriculum.* New York, NY: Peter Lang.

Morris, M. (2008). *Teaching through the ill body: A spiritual and aesthetic approach to pedagogy and illness.* Rotterdam, NL: Sense Publishers.

Munro, Petra. (1998). *Subject to fiction: Women teachers' life history narratives and the cultural politics of resistance.* Philadelphia, PA: Open University Press.

Pinar, W. (2000). Search for a method. In W. F. Pinar, *Curriculum studies: The reconceptualization.* (pp. 415-424). New York, NY: Educator's International Press.

Pinar, W. (2004). *What is curriculum theory?* New York, NY: Lawrence Erlbaum Associates, Inc.

Pinar, W. (2009). *The worldliness of a cosmopolitan education: Passionate lives in public service.* New York, NY: Routledge.

Pollan, M. (2001). *The botany of desire*. New York, NY: Random House.

Pollan, M. (2008). *In defense of food: An eater's manifesto*. New York, NY: The Penguin Press.

Rowlands, M. (2009). *The philosopher and the wolf: Lessons from the wild on love, death, and happiness*. New York, NY: Pegasus Books.

Shelley, M. (1998). *Frankenstein*. St. Paul, MN: EMC/Paradigm Publishing.

Shiva, V. (1993). *Monocultures of the mind*. London, UK: Zed Books Ltd.

Todd, S. (2009). *Toward an imperfect education: Facing humanity, rethinking cosmopolitanism*. Boulder, CO: Paradigm Publishers.

Weaver, J. (2010). *Educating the posthuman: Biosciences, fiction, and curriculum*. Rotterdam, NL: Sense Publishers

Wexler, P. (2000). *Mystical society: An emerging social vision*. Boulder, CO: Westview Press.

Chapter 7

Enter Henrietta Lacks Part II

A Play

Dana Compton McCullough

Introduction

In 2011, I was introduced to Henrietta Lacks and Rebecca Skloot's novel, *The Immortal Life of Henrietta Lacks* (2010). I immediately went to Amazon.com and ordered my copy. When the book was delivered to my home, I immediately began reading. To say I was excited about this text is a huge understatement. I quickly took the story back to my school and wanted to introduce the story to my students and coworkers. I went to my assistant principal's office and stuck my head in the door. I told her that I needed to speak with her about Henrietta Lacks. She responded without looking up from her computer, "That is not my section of the alphabet. She would be on Mr. Hooper's discipline list." I had to explain that Henrietta was not a student. She looked up from the computer and we began to discuss Henrietta. The first Wear Red to Honor Henrietta Lacks event was entered on the school calendar.

In order to prepare for this special day, I sent out a letter to introduce Henrietta to our faculty. The letter explained:

> Her name was Henrietta Lacks, but scientists know her as HeLa. She was a poor Southern tobacco farmer who worked the same land as her slave ancestors, yet her cells—taken without her knowledge—became one of the most important tools in medicine. The first 'immortal' human cells grown in culture, they are still alive today, though she has been dead for more than sixty years. (The Lacks family, 2010)

The letter invited students and faculty members to join the biology classes in celebrating the life of Henrietta Lacks on October 4, 2011. Henrietta Lacks may have died on this day, but her cells are still living in laboratories all over the world today. The letter detailed important discoveries involving Henrietta's cells. The polio vaccine was tested on HeLa cells. Other advances in science, including cloning, gene mapping, and in vitro fertilization, could not have happened without Henrietta's cells. The letter asked that teachers take just a few moments to share an information PowerPoint about Henrietta Lacks with their classes. Teachers and students were invited to wear red and honor Henrietta Lacks by keeping her story alive.

Henrietta had quickly become part of my teaching. I knew how to tell the story of Henrietta. I did not know how to share the story that detailed how Henrietta's story was influencing my teaching, my students, and my school. After much deliberation, I decided to conduct this research as part of my doctoral program. Tom Barone (1990) suggested "that the future truths [of educational research]" will include "accomplished pieces of literary fiction with educational themes" (p. 319). Could dissertation writing take on new meaning? Could the writer enter "a virtual world that offers a fresh perspective on the reader's own *Lebenswelt*" (p. 320)? I wanted to accomplish the writing of a useful story written phenomenologically conveying "a sense of personal authorship" (p. 319). Stories are shared in many ways. I explored many options: a novel, a poem, a painting, a photograph, a graphic presentation, a documentary, a conversation, or a play.

I first began writing simple conversations. These conversations were occurring in my head. They included teachers, students, my professors, and the authors inhabiting my bookshelf. I wondered what would happen if all these individuals, these voices, could meet in an imaginary setting and converse. After adding the setting, the work was reading like a play. Norris (2010) tells us that imagination can play "a major role in generating data" (p. 1). He goes on to explain that "imagination is part of our lived-world; to deny it is to deny our very existence, part of what it means to be human" (p. 28). Script writing affords the author opportunities to use his/her imagination in ways that the format of a simple interview or conversation may lack. By creating fictional settings, people from different time periods can meet and converse. In the case of this play, a professor, a curriculum director, two teachers, and science students discuss science education and the story of Henrietta Lacks. In any play, the audience and actors on stage are exposed to a form of research dissemination that "neither [affirms] nor [denies] their opinions" (p. 34). The discussion that follows a play "is a collective lived-experience of meaning in the making in flux" (p. 34). Norris (2010) calls playwriting an attempt "to take an organic approach to enter data generation" (p. 1). Following a reading of the play I was writing, I should be able to understand how the story of Henrietta Lacks can influence science, science education, science students, and science teachers.

The work presented in this chapter is a portion of a play written to explore the impact of including stories as part of science curriculum. Margaret Hoffen is meeting with a group to discuss her ideas about science education and science curriculum. Works by Tom Barone, Angela Calabrese Barton, Joseph Schwab, William Doll, Madeleine Grumet, and others provide the framework for this intellectual conversation. High school students provide noise, interruptions, and insight that inadvertently drive the conversation about science education, science, curriculum, and social justice.

As the following theatrical, fictional, somewhat nonfictional scenes unfold, I have created two fictional, composite characters: Margaret Hoffen and Delores Pequod. Margaret Hoffen is a teacher who has hope that by using alternative pedagogies in her classroom she can resurrect life in her classroom. I searched for a word meaning *hope* that could double as a surname. I found the German word *hoffen*. In order for change in education to occur, we must have hope. Emily Dickinson penned a poem about hope, comparing hope to a bird: "Hope is the thing with feathers that perches in the soul" (Dickenson, 1993). The hope that Mrs. Hoffen wants to bring to education is very similar to Dickinson's bird metaphor. Mrs. Hoffen has hope for education that "perches in [her] soul." She finds this hope at a time when a raging storm of controversy is present in education. One might call this the standardization storm—standardized curriculum, standardized testing, and standardized teaching. Rubin & Kazanjian (2011) tell us that

> Standardization and curriculum alignment are the dominant forces in education today. Due in part to the No Child Left Behind Act (NCLB) of 2001, education has become singularly focused on teaching towards the test in order to meet Adequate Yearly Progress (AYP), yet data has shown that using standardized testing does not result in increased student learning or development. (p. 94)

This raging storm involves the detrimental effects that standardization and strict curriculum alignment have, not only on students but on educators as well. Giroux (2009) cried out to our current administration to inform them that they must understand that "the crisis in education is not only an economic problem that requires funds to rebuild old and new schools but also a political and ethical crisis about the very nature of citizenship and democracy" (p. 262). There is "more at risk here than unhappy teachers and over-programed children. There is a battle looming on the horizon as to what type of society we want to live in and what type of citizens will comprise that society" (Rubin & Kazanjian, 2011, p. 103).

Margaret Hoffen wants her students to understand their role in a democratic society. She wants them to find meaning in the curriculum that she teaches. She wants them to understand that it is through learning that we can facilitate change in society. She has hope for students and fellow teachers that the standardized curriculum can become infiltrated with meaning that will translate into meaning relevant to life and living. Can her hope provide warmth, even in the "chilliest of lands" of standardization and controversy (Dickinson, 1993, p. 24)?

Herman Melville named the ship in *Moby Dick* the *Pequod*, a ship "named for the once-defeated Indian tribe" (Philbrick, 2011, p. 27). The story of Moby Dick "is the mythic incarnation of America: a country blessed by God and by free enterprise that nonetheless embraces the barbarity it supposedly supplanted" (p. 27). The *Pequod's* captain, Ahab, "has no qualms about exploiting the whale man under his employ" (p. 29). Mrs. Delores Pequod has similar characteristics. There is foreshadowing throughout Melville's story that warns us of the gloom and doom to come. Mrs. Delores Pequod represents the negative aspects of teaching and education. This character resists changes in education. She tries to cast a dark cloud on all who work toward change. Her first name, Delores, means sorrow. Delores Pequod speaks to support the status quo and support standardized testing.

This work is informed by the fields of philosophy of science, history of science, cultural studies of science, science education, science theater, works of playwrights, explorers, and high school students. The goal of the conversations in the fictitious settings, taking place without the boundaries of time, will seek to challenge the traditions of science and science education and answer the following question: How can the story of Henrietta Lacks bring life and hope to a curriculum of rote memorization and bulimic participants?

Enter Henrietta Lacks: A Play

Characters (in order of appearance)

Doris Bradley:	curriculum director
Krystal Sonnenshein:	school receptionist
Alexis:	high school student
Lydia:	high school student
Margaret Hoffen:	high school teacher
Katherine Driscoll:	university professor
Delores Pequod:	high school teacher
Wayne Cooper:	construction teacher
Matthew:	construction student
Anthony:	construction student
Jhaymai:	student presenter
Kyle:	student presenter
Charles:	student presenter
Mrs. Robinson:	teacher
Suzy:	science student

Setting:

This play is set in a large suburban high school in the southeastern United States. An educational researcher/curriculum director and a university professor meet with two science educators to discuss the current state of science curriculum at the school. Students provide several interruptions during the meeting. The action begins in a media center conference room, and then moves to three separate classroom settings.

Act I Scene I: A Noisy Meeting

Doris Bradley navigates her rental car through the school parking lot. She enters the double doors. Posters that say Wear Red October 4 to Honor Henrietta Lacks cover the entryway. The receptionist behind the window is wearing a bright red shirt and shiny red Mardi Gras beads. She has a sticker and red ribbon sticking to her nametag.

Bradley: Hi, is it Ms. Sonnenschein? What does your sticker say?
Sonnenschein: Yes, it is! The sticker is the book jacket for *The Immortal Life of Henrietta Lacks* (Skloot, 2010). You know, the 2010 bestseller

written by Rebecca Skloot. Our biology students read this book when they study cells. We are wearing red today to cell-e-brate the life of Henrietta Lacks. Get it, Cell-e-brate? You know like cells are the basic unit of life.

Bradley: Ah, yes. Clever play on words. How exciting!

(The receptionist smiles, hands Bradley a yellow visitor sticker, and gives her directions to the Media Center conference room. As she enters the school commons area, she hears music—a Duke Ellington tune. She sees a booth set up close to the Media Center door. Everyone in the booth is wearing red t-shirts that say—Not just HeLa—Henrietta Lacks. They are stacking up bookmarks, untangling red beads, and positioning red balloons. A young woman approaches Bradley).

Alexis: Would you like some beads? I can give you some if you are willing to tell Henrietta's story.

Bradley: Sure, I will take some beads, but who is Henrietta?

Alexis: Henrietta lived in in 1951, when women were nobody, and Black women were even less than nobody. She got sick and had to go to Johns Hopkins Hospital; any other hospital would have let her die in the parking lot because she was a Black woman. The doctors diagnosed Henrietta with cancer. Mary, a technician from George Gey's Lab, went to the operating room and took a sample of the tumor cells. It was her job to try to grow the cells outside the human body. No one had ever done this. Usually the cells would just die, but after two days, Henrietta's cells were growing like crazy! The cells were used to develop the Polio vaccine. Because we could grow these cells outside the body, we learned how cells work. Many medications and cures for diseases were discovered because of Henrietta's cells (Skloot, 2010).

Bradley: How is it that I have never heard of Henrietta?

Alexis: They kept her name a secret. The doctors did not want her name to be released. I think they were afraid the public would find out she was Black (Skloot, 2010).

Bradley: This sounds like a great story.

Lydia: Our teacher has us research the story and find a part of the story that we feel is important. Then we create a product to tell the part of Henrietta's story that we pick. We have to think about how that part of the story is important to science. Here comes our teacher now. Good morning, Mrs. Hoffen.

Hoffen: Good morning to you too, Lydia. Hi, Alexis. Welcome Dr. Bradley, it is nice to see you.

Alexis: Dr. Bradley, are you here for our Henrietta Lacks Cell-e-bration? Get it...Cell...Cell...like the cells in your body.

Brandley: I am hoping to stay, Alexis. But right now, we have a meeting.

Hoffen: Alexis, can you walk Dr. Bradley to the conference room? I will be right there.

(Alexis shows Dr. Bradley the conference room. Katharine Driscoll, a university professor and Mrs. Pequod, a teacher at the school, greet them).

Alexis: Hi Mrs. Pequod. Are you coming to the program today?

Pequod: No Alexis, I will not be at your program. You need to get to class.

Alexis: I do need to get back to the booth. I hope to see you later Dr. Bradley.

Driscoll: Hello Dr. Bradley, thank you both so much for volunteering to be part of this conversation. Your entire science department seems very enthusiastic about developing a program to bridge the gap between educational theory and teaching practice. As educational researchers, we need to see if our theoretical perspectives can be applied to actual classrooms.

Pequod: Wait a minute. You think I want to be part of this theory-meets-practice research project? *(She speaks very gruffly to the group).* I want to make sure you understand that we do not want to be part of your program. Our school is fine just like it is.

(Mrs. Hoffen rushes into the room dressed in red).

Hoffen: Hello everyone, I am sorry I am running late.

Driscoll: We are so glad you are here. We were excited to learn that our meeting is on the same day as your event. We want to see this Wear Red Day to Honor Henrietta Lacks firsthand. Our panel is hoping to see real-life examples of educational theory meeting educational practice.

Hoffen: Wonderful. Feel free to have some lunch, enjoy the music, and then attend our program in the auditorium. Mrs. Pequod, I do hope you bring your classes today.

Pequod: Are you kidding? We must finish our benchmark and review for the biology end of course test.

Driscoll: Let's start. I am Katherine Driscoll. My department at the university is interested in how theoretical information taught to teachers can be applied to actual classroom settings.

Bradley: I am Doris Bradley, a science educator and educational researcher. Currently, I am serving as this district's curriculum director. I want to see science taught in a manner that involves social justice, democracy, and human rights. When we work with students to "create relevant science, many worthwhile outcomes result" (Barton, Ermer, Burkett, & Osborne, 2003, p. 118).

Hoffen: It is so nice to meet you Dr. Driscoll. My name is Margaret Hoffen. I am a science teacher here.

Pequod: Excuse me, did I hear you right, Dr. Bradley? Science has nothing to do with justice, democracy, or human rights. Science is the pursuit of truth and understanding through a trial of experimentation and verifiable and repeatable results.

Driscoll: Mrs. Pequod, part of our work at the university involves an extended definition of science. I will explain my views of science and science education as the conversation unfolds today. First, I have a question: Why do we have jazz today?

Hoffen: Henrietta and her sisters would get together and dance to jazz music on Saturday nights. They loved the tunes of Benny Goodman, Louis Armstrong, and Billie Holiday. They would move all the furniture out of the living room and onto the lawn and dance until dawn inside the house (Skloot, 2010).

Pequod: You just go on and on don't you. I probably have 50 emails about her HeLa day on my computer right now.

Hoffen: She was not just HeLa. I prefer her to be called Henrietta Lacks.

Driscoll: Let us continue with our introductions. Mrs. Pequod, what can you tell us about yourself?

Pequod: It's Delores, Delores Pequod. I have 29 years in and I will be surprised if I make it to the 30-year mark. I teach whatever curriculum they tell me. There is no time for stories or jazz (she glares at Mrs. Hoffen). We have standards to teach, a curriculum map to follow, and end of course tests. I had a 91% pass rate last year.

Driscoll: Thank you all for being here. Mrs. Hoffen, why do you use stories in your science classroom?

Hoffen: I feel that it is a way to show real world connections. We must allow all aspects of our world "into our method" (Grumet, 1990, p. 107).

Bradley: I taught biology just like you two. However, I see a tremendous need for real world connections.

Pequod: My textbook has all the stories I need and it is aligned to our standards.

Bradley: Schwab (1978) tells us that

> To employ only one doctrine as a principle will give a biased view of the nature of science, and to teach a single doctrine should be to the student only misleading, confusing, or both, because no single doctrine is more than a partial statement. (p. 72)

Teachers not only have to consider science, they must consider theoretical views of science education. Curriculum theories and teaching and learning theories "cannot alone tell us what and how to teach, because questions of what and how to teach arise in concrete situations loaded with concrete particulars of time, place, person, and circumstance" (Schwab, 1978, p. 322).

Driscoll: Theory and practice, the two must come together. A new entity must be created between the two.

Hoffen: Science curriculum needs rethinking, revisioning, revising, or maybe reconceptualizing. Dr. Driscoll, let me give you a quick update about what is going on here, in this school district. We have Performance Standards that dictate what teachers should teach. I have provided each of you a copy. The desired learning is to result in predetermined prescribed outcomes. A strict curriculum map dictates the entire teaching schedule. This map not only tells when topics should be covered, it determines the sequence, and time allowed per unit. This map is packed full of science objectives. If students have difficulty with an objective, it is virtually impossible to find class time to address remediation. When students are not being tested, they are being drilled on how to be successful on standardized tests. Our district expends large amounts of energy on staff development to teach teachers the right formula for teaching, so the curriculum map can be efficiently followed, and students can be successful on standardized tests.

Driscoll: I feel that schoolteachers have a very difficult job. How can they work "amidst the distraction of government [intervening] in the intellectual lives of teachers and students" (Pinar, 2004, p. 208)? First, it was No Child Left Behind. Now schools must meet the guidelines sketched out in Every Student Succeeds Act (ESSA). ESSA holds states "accountable for focusing resources on low-performing schools and traditionally underserved students who consistently demonstrate low academic performance" (Alliance for excellent education, 2019). Both involve standardized testing. Unfortunately, standardized tests are just one moment in time. They are no more than a snapshot of what a child can do at one exact moment. An objective list can never be all-inclusive. I think it is correct to say, "Education, experience and life are inextricably intertwined" (Clandinin & Connelly, 2000, p. xxiii).

Hoffen: My students pay attention more when they are interested in what is going on in class. I find that allowing them to be stakeholders in the daily plans, and subjects to be discussed, makes them take better charge of their own learning. Cells, for instance, is such an abstract subject for students. I invite students to view cells using stories. We begin by studying Anton Von Leuwenhoek and his invention of the microscope. Then, we add Robert Hooke to the story of cells. Who saw cells first? This is a tough question to answer. Their textbook tells a story about Hooke being the first to see and name cells. Students are asked to begin researching this topic on their personal devices. Then the arguing ensues. Hooke was first. No Leuwenhoek was first! The stories help students make connections. These connections may deal with students' interests, or the value of the students' cultures that they bring to the classroom. There are relationships to consider. Curriculum is not exactly "neat and tidy," it is about the "interrelations between students, teachers, and texts" (Morris, 2001, p. 2011). Curriculum is a collection of noise in the classroom.

Pequod: Yep, with 32 students talking at once, and that intercom in the ceiling.

Hoffen: I agree Mrs. Pequod; it does get noisy. But, when I said noise, I was talking about the interruptions that disrupt our thinking. Think about a group having a discussion. Someone says one thing and the discussion is carried in multiple directions. Then someone else's thinking is sparked by a previous comment. A chain reaction of sorts is activated in the classroom. Before you know it, everyone is talking, discussing, and the conversation is growing. New ideas are created.

(The conversation is interrupted by a knock on the conference room door. Mrs. Hoffen walks to the door to find Alexis and Lydia, all smiles).

Alexis: Mrs. Hoffen, we had to bring this to you. *(Alexis is holding a black t-shirt covered in cotton balls and glow-in-the-dark paint. Immediately, Mrs. Hoffen knows that the shirt is covered with HeLa cells).*

Hoffen: Wow people…this is wonderful…*(She immediately pulls the shirt over her head.)*

Pequod: *(Speaking under her breath).* But isn't it Wear Red Day?

Lydia: The paint on our shirts is still drying. Mine has *(Mrs. Hoffen interrupts).*

Hoffen: Girls this is incredible…you have made my day. I am somewhat busy right now with our guests. Thank you so much.

(The girls run off. Mrs. Hoffen closes the door).

Hoffen: I am so sorry about the interruption. The girls are so excited about our day.

Pequod: Noise! Interruptions! How is anyone supposed to be able to get any work done around here? Why are those two girls allowed to run all over the school? Why are they not in class?

Bradley: That is not just a HeLa shirt. This young lady shared the story of Henrietta Lacks this morning when she gave me these red Mardi Gras beads. She is beginning to "recognize and exercise [her] voice and autonomy" through your project (Barton, Ermer, Burkett, & Osborne, 2003, p. 118). Wear Red to Honor Henrietta Lacks helps your students "learn to become agents of change in their own lives, and within the discipline of science, using their authority to challenge the traditional cultural practices of science and education" (p. 118). Both girls are proud to be learning science and teaching others about Henrietta Lacks. The girls are engaged "in relative science" (p. 119).

Driscoll: Thank you, Doris, for reminding us not to view the girls' visit as just an annoying interruption. Mrs. Hoffen, can you share with us the significance of your shirt?

Hoffen: *(All smiles, she picks up a dry erase marker and proceeds to the white board).* You see, this is a cell membrane. She draws a shape like the ones on her shirt. Most of what we can see with a basic microscope is a cell membrane and a nucleus. The cotton balls represent the nucleus.

Driscoll: Did the girls get cotton ball happy? There cannot be 2–3 nuclei in each cell.

Bradley: I can answer that one. Cancer cells have more than one nucleus in each cell.

Hoffen: Yes, very good. I am so proud of them. We read about cancer cells in *The Immortal Life of Henrietta Lacks*. Each student must create a product to tell part of the story...the girls decided to make shirts. They were drawing rough drafts of their shirts earlier in the week, but the giant HeLa cell shirt was a surprise! I am so excited!

Pequod: That is all fine and good, but can we get on with our meeting, minus the noise and the interruptions?

Driscoll: Yes Mrs. Pequod, we can continue.

Bradley: I have a quick question. Mrs. Pequod, do you feel the standards are insufficient?

Pequod: The standards are packed. Students have a lot of information to memorize. My fear is that the standards do reduce and water down science to a list of facts to be memorized by the students. And my other fear is that there is not enough time to cover all the curriculum. We must stick to the curriculum map.

Driscoll: Brian Heese (2015) reported that high stakes testing increases teacher stress and anxiety, decreases teacher morale, impacts teacher relationships with other teachers and with students, increases the amount of work required in the school day, and diverts funding away from instructional materials and to materials needed for testing and testing preparation. High stakes testing also influences the number of classroom assessments and the formats of how exams are written as well as how exams are weighted in a student's overall grade.

Bradley: All the science teachers in my district indicate that testing creates stress for all that are involved. My worry is that we are not teaching students what they need.

Pequod: That is why you must teach the standards according to the curriculum map. Otherwise, the students will not pass the test. There is not time for stories.

Bradley: By oversimplifying science to a list of standards or facts and processes to simply memorize, "we block progress toward one of the most widely held, if impossible goals" of what I call "liberal science training" which is "to provide the student with an adequate picture of the world" (Schwab, 1978, p. 99). You must understand that "to give a simple picture of a complicated world is not to give the scientist's picture of that world. By so doing we make the picture not only inadequate (which it will always be) but false" (p. 99). I have a moral obligation to my students. We must take their education seriously.

Driscoll: With all that is happening in education, it would be easy for "teachers to resign their professional authority and ethical responsibility for the curriculum they teach" (Pinar, 2004). In education, the process begins with a commitment to students and the school or university. Pinar (2004) tells us that

> Whatever our fate—given our betrayal by government and by powerful professional organizations, the future is not bright—we must carry on, our dignity intact. We must renew our commitment to the intellectual character of our labor. We can do so first by engaging in frank and sustained self-criticism. (p. 9)

No matter how difficult the journey, teachers must be willing to make the commitment to become more intellectual. If we want to model learning in our classrooms, our students must see us taking an active role to reflect on our own learning. I am sorry. I get a little carried away when I start talking about curriculum theory.

Pequod: So, you are telling me that if I analyze myself, my learning, that I can begin to cure all the ills of education?

Bradley: No, I am saying there cannot be a simple monochromatic view. We must use reflexive thinking, and view things from more than one perspective, and purposely "looking through a succession of lenses," standardized education offers only one point of view, a one-size-fits-all education (Schwab, 1978, p. 325). Current education is characterized by a "linear sequential, easily quantifiable ordering system," combined with expectations of "clear beginnings and definite endings" (Doll, 1993, p. 3). We as educators must realize the potential of finding a "complex, pluralistic, unpredictable system or network" upon which to build a foundation for educational experiences for students and teachers alike if we are willing to expand linear thinking (Doll, 1993, p. 3). I want to bring attention to all the key players in this situation: the teachers, students, and curriculum. I propose a "new concept of curriculum" emerging as "new relations between teachers and students" (p. 3). This new relationship of curriculum, students, and teachers will be quite complex…"Less ordered and more fuzzy" (p. 3). Such a relationship cannot be complete without considering the life experiences of each person involved, as well as the real-life consequences and applications of the curriculum taught. As educators, we must find our place in this highly textured, woven fabric. Just as threads intersect in a woven fabric—the weaving of a curriculum is like a….

(Hoffen finishes Dr. Bradley's sentence).

Hoffen: I know that quote, "fabric with brilliant threads throughout" (Krall, 1999, p. 5).
Bradley: Unfortunately, the beautiful threads, or "gaps, breaks, punctures are not only absent from the curriculum, they are seen only in negative terms" (Doll, 1993, p. 37).
Hoffen: I think teachers are afraid to break away from the standardized practices. All the stakeholders in education have potential to provide input into a new curriculum. Students' voices are being silenced, and learning prescribed:

> If students are not able to transform their lived experience into knowledge and to use the already acquired knowledge as a process to unveil new knowledge, they will never be able to participate rigorously in a dialogue as a process of learning and knowing. (Freire, 1970, p. 19)

Dialogue is a necessary entity when searching for what is worthwhile.

Bradley: I would add that teachers' voices are being silenced. Dialogue, discussion, and discourse are all necessary in finding meaning and personal connections in curriculum.

Driscoll: The teacher is the facilitator for what is worthwhile. The teacher ultimately must embrace intelligence, allowing students to leverage what they know they can successfully accomplish. As students develop this essential opportunity, their imagination, interest, and creativity allow them to create a love for their learning that may endure the travesties and injustices they face both in and out of the classroom.

Pequod: Excuse me. I personally see no problem with standardization. In addition, as far as the event going on in the commons today, I see no relation to science. Discussions concerning justice and democracy should be saved for social studies class. We have too many objectives to teach. Teaching is simple; we teach the standards, the students take a standardized test, we know that learning has taken place.

Bradley: I must disagree, Mrs. Pequod. We as teachers have the "potential for making science transformative in the lives of our students, thus creating opportunities for students to have resonant learning experiences that are educationally meaningful and empowering" (Barton, Ermer, Burkett, & Osborne, 2003, pp. 118-119).

(There is a knock on the door. Mrs. Pequod, closest to the door, gets out of her chair and answers. A group of students shows up at the door of the conference room dressed in red, wearing red Mardi Gras beads, and wanting to talk all at the same time).

Pequod: You kids must go to class.

(Alexis looks past Mrs. Pequod and around to Mrs. Hoffen).

Alexis: Mrs. Hoffen, which was a bigger problem in the 1950s—sexism or racism?

Hoffen: Both were problems.

Alexis: I think racism was a bigger problem because it affected men and women...

Lydia: I think sexism was a bigger problem, because women were impacted by racism and sexism.

(Both girls are sporting red shirts with the name Henrietta Lacks across the front in large puff paint letters. On the back of Alexis's shirt is a Venn diagram. The circle on the left is labeled "Whites," the circle on the left is labeled "Blacks."

Lydia's shirt is very similar, but her Venn diagram is labeled "male" and "female" with a large "1950" painted above).

Hoffen: An author named bell hooks writes about the racism and sexism she experienced while she was in college. She attended college in what she called "the wake of a powerful anti-racist civil rights struggle" (hooks, 2010, pp. 2-3). This was in the 50s around the same time Henrietta lived. hooks tells us "the outspoken sexism of [her] undergraduate male professors was even harsher than their covert racism" (hooks, 2010, p. 3). She experienced racism and sexism at the hand of her teachers "who appeared to derive their primary pleasure in the classroom by exercising their authoritarian power over [her] fellow students, crushing [their] spirits, and dehumanizing [their] minds and bodies" (p. 2). Alexis, can you "imagine being taught by a teacher who does not believe you are fully human" because you are Black (p. 2)? Ladies, this is a very complex issue. I know you two are having a disagreement over trying to decide who is right. Maybe both of you are. Unfortunately, sexism and racism still exist today. Both are major problems. bell hooks became a teacher. As a teacher, she believes that she must write about these problems from her perspective as a Black woman. There were not many Black women in her time writing about issues of civil rights. I think our focus has to be on making others aware that racism and sexism still exist today. Which is exactly what you two are doing today by sharing Henrietta's story. If people do not know, nothing can be done.

Pequod: *(Clears her throat loudly).*

Alexis: *(Whispers).* Thank you Mrs. Hoffen. We will Google her. I guess we will be on our way to class now.

Hoffen: I apologize once again for the interruption. Alexis and Lydia are proof that there is more to be considered than that student's grade on an end-of-course test. Science can be "difficult and forbidding, even intimidating and remains the province of experts. Few students ever achieve a personal understanding of science; few students ever really own the science they study in school" (Hodson, 1998, p. 6). That is unless the students find a way, a place, and a space that allows them to connect personally with the science.

Students and teachers need a space for teaching and learning. The learning that I desire to take place will not be something that can always be measured with a paper and pencil assessment. The learning will be evidenced by what my students carry with them outside of my classroom and into the world. The space we create will make time for students to develop their voice, their thinking, their relationship with the subject matter and the world in which they live.

Bradley: The girls' interruption was timed perfectly. This Wear Red Day as a part of science curriculum allows science to be "recast as something that youth create in the process of responding to their own questions and needs. It is not something that they have to learn for a test or for a project that they must complete to satisfy a teacher's requirements" (Barton, Ermer, Burkett, & Osborne, 2003, p. 118). The idea that you would allow the students to choose a portion of the story to tell, which gives them a space to ask questions of their own, is empowering to students. In this type of activity, "the process of doing science involves [students'] agency and authority in articulating their questions, and in constructing ways to respond to those questions" (p. 118). The girls both chose a question, and then chose how they would respond to that question.

Driscoll: The project creates a space for students to be more vocal. A space for teachers to be vulnerable. Every classroom could benefit from such spaces. Homi Bhabha was one of the first to write about in-between spaces. He wrote about these spaces in reference to cultural differences (Rutherford, 1990). Relationships naturally provide opportunities to create in-between spaces. As you introduce the story of Henrietta Lacks, you are opening opportunities for discussion of race. This is something that needs to be happening in the U. S. South daily. The story allows you to bring race to the forefront of the conversation. If you ignore your race, you become isolated. If you ignore the race of your students, they become isolated. In-between spaces created in the classroom, whether the space deals with cultural differences, relationships, or subject matter, will "flourish through the joined efforts of individuals who invent spaces for creating values for all so that all humans might live more robustly, develop capacities more fully, and become humane and educated in an increasingly diversified, complicated, and contested cosmos" (He, 2013, p. 63).

Hoffen: Cosmos. *(Speaking excitedly).* Have you studied Alexander Von Humboldt? Humboldt and I share similar backgrounds in science, characterized by empirical data and strict method. Humboldt "came to believe that imagination was as necessary as rational thought in order to understand the world" (Wulf, 2015, p. 36). In a letter "Goethe encouraged [Alexander] to combine nature and art, facts and imagination" (Wulf, 2015, p. 38). This new thinking allowed Alexander to think beyond science and see the connection of science to the world and the peoples of the world. Humboldt, who can be described as a scientist, an explorer, and a bridge builder, spent his life traveling, observing, collecting, measuring, and connecting. Humboldt wished to create bridges between "peoples, disciplines, places, and historical eras" (Walls, 2011, p. 10). Humboldt hoped to "create a zone of exchange rather than domination" (p. 10). I want to create this kind of "zone of exchange" in my classroom (p. 10).

Pequod: Cosmos? I am here to discuss educational theory, and she is spouting off stories about an explorer whose accomplishments were forgotten long ago. So long, I have never heard of him. We can barely get these students to memorize the parts of the cells, and you want to make a million connections.

Hoffen: Alexander von Humboldt predicted problems with "deforestation" and "climate change" years ago (Wulf, 2015, p. 58). Tell me that is not relevant to science education and society.

Driscoll: We keep dancing around the idea of in-between and so-called bridges. Let us get specific. How will you build that bridge between your students and science?

Hoffen: For the first set of bridges, we need to build will involve relationships between teachers and curriculum, teachers and students, then finally students and curriculum. To construct a bridge between the students and the curriculum I will first invite my students to the text. Simply put, I will tell them a story. Not just a story for the sake of a story—a well-told story that will grab the students' interest. The excerpts read to the students should connect to the standards. It is important not to tell the whole story at once. The excerpt or story shared should leave "gaps for students to fill in, holes which encourage them to actively intervene in the proceedings to assume responsibility" (Barone, 2000, p. 62). The gap is the third space. Here in this space, what is said, or sometimes what is not said, will create discourse between students and students, students and teachers, students and the curriculum...just to name a few opportunities. This is the transformative space where students can think about their connection to the story and to the curriculum. Last, the students will need to share their personal reflections with each other. The weaving together of their stories with the stories of others is how the new story, or the new curriculum, will be composed.

I wonder if science itself can become a bridge that can help students find education meaningful, help them become democratic citizens. Can education become like HeLa cells?

Pequod: How do you propose that education can be like HeLa cells?

Hoffen: Cells can become immortal. Scientists call it immortalization. Immortal "cells do not die out but continue to grow indefinitely if provided with adequate resources" (Van Valen, 1991, p. 71). As a teacher, if I can create a space, complete with adequate resources for students in my classroom to grow and learn continually and indefinitely, could love for learning become immortal?

Think about it. Students respected for who they are and the life experiences they bring to the classroom, building bridges with each other, their teacher, and their curriculum to create meaning...meaning custom-made to meet their needs. Discourse levels the playing field. Students that have performed poorly in school are able to participate and enter the conversation.

Bradley: In the classroom, discourse and "students' personal experiences with the subject matter were explicitly encouraged by the teacher and leveraged upon to delve deeper into the science content at hand" (Basu, Barton, & Tan, 2011, p. 58). This allows "deliberate connections [to be] made between school science and the relevant community knowledge students bring with them into the classroom" (p. 58). The story of Henrietta Lacks allows teachers to create this experience for my students. The activity brings the voices of students "into science classrooms in ways that foster critical democracy—not only in how teachers and students enact classroom life together, but also in how students and teachers are supported in leveraging their school experiences towards building a more just world" (p. 58).

Pequod: Here she goes with democracy in science again. Did you not hear my protest last time?

Bradley: Building these bridges and working to achieve a democratic classroom is rather complicated. A basic democratic classroom should include student participation in decision-making that "include curricular scope and focus, classroom participation structures, and rewards and punishments" (Basu, Barton, & Tan, 2011, p. 5). I am not talking about simply letting students weigh in on how things happen in the classroom. I am talking about the "social and cultural structures that maintain relations of power among students and teachers" (p. 5). In a democratic classroom "the responsibility for shared power and the protection of marginalized voices and perspectives is also elemental" (p. 6). By fostering what a real democracy is in the classroom...the discourse has a place to happen. Students get more involved with their learning.

Driscoll: I want to go back to Humboldt just one moment. What I take away from your story about Alexander Von Humboldt is the mention of the word discourse. Discourse related to curriculum involves "community politics, bureaucratic regulations, and publishing agendas" (Grumet M. R., 1989/1999, p. 235). Participants must "determine the rules of that conversation, undermining its promise of open inquiry and democratic participation" (p. 235). Does this sound like a description of a classroom? Or does it sound like life? Remember we discussed that we have to bring method into our work with students at any level.

Bradley: In an earlier comment, I said it is going to take a "complex, pluralistic, unpredictable system or network" upon which to build a foundation for educational experiences for students and teachers alike (Doll, 1993, p. 3). Sharing the story, then also the subsequent stories composed by your students, does indeed form many intersections. I imagine this approach would certainly get everyone in the classroom involved.

(The group hears a knock on the door. Ms. Sonnenschein, the receptionist, opens the door and addresses the group).

Sonnenschein: I hate to interrupt, but I have a tiny little message for Mrs. Hoffen.

(Hoffen walks to the door and joins Ms. Sonnenschein outside the door).

Hoffen: Please hurry Krystal…what is it?

Sonnenshein: You are needed in the construction room. Mr. Cooper said it was very important.

Hoffen: Okay Krystal, we will go in just a minute.

Bradley: I "use the ideal of democratic education in science to call attention to ways of being in the classroom that position youth as important and powerful participants in their own learning and that of their peers and teachers" (Basu, Barton, & Tan, 2011, p. 8). I really like what was said earlier—you bring the world into your method. Now the students see that they are "also members of a larger global society who can leverage their lives in schools towards making a change" (pp. 8-9). Democratic classrooms "position learning as a dialectic process where students and teachers learn to read the word and the world" (p. 7).

Hoffen: Students regardless of academic ability seem to respond well to the story of Henrietta Lacks, and the other stories I share in biology class. It is so sad that our students are assigned a personal value based on their latest benchmark, or standardized test score. Tom Barone (2000) suggests that we need strong poets—"students who continuously integrate the content of disciplines (the content of life) into a coherent and personally relevant world view" (p. 126). His directive given to teachers is simple yet eloquent—"aspire to empowering students within a democratic school setting to act with a sense of personal integrity, responsibility, and autonomy" (p. 126). I want to help all students realize there is a strong poet deep inside them. Our students are not blank slates. Our students come to us "as a slate on which much is already written and where the learner writes new words and phrases in appropriate spots and rearranges phrases to make room for new ones" (Klassen, 2006, p. 826). Standardized testing requires that students wipe off their slate and give the "information back in essentially the same form in which it was originally presented" (p. 826). Strong poets compose their learning. Standardization encourages that knowledge be returned to the teacher in the same form in which it was dispersed—rote memorization. David Blades calls it "Bulimia" (Blades, 1997, p. 72). Having to equate our students' learning with an eating disorder is a very sad state of affairs.

Pequod: *(She speaks quietly).* Sad? Those with bulimia will perform well on the test; that is not sad. If your students perform well, you might be able to keep your job.

(A voice comes over the intercom: "Mrs. Hoffen please report to the construction classroom room").

Hoffen: I was hoping we would not be interrupted again. Would you mind taking a walk with me?

(The group walks to the construction classroom).

Act I Scene II: New Teachers in Construction Class

Margaret Hoffen and her entourage walk into a surprisingly empty construction lab. Usually this area was humming with the sound of power tools. Then she turns the corner and sees the classroom area. Two of her biology students are working at the marker board. These two are talking to a whole class of boys. All the boys in the class are listening very intently to what their classmates are saying. Hoffen stands back, so she can listen without being seen.

Matthew: Her cells were different. They were cancer cells; they grew very fast. George Gey figured out how to make the cells grow outside the body—this way scientists could study them.

Anthony: Her cells looked like this. *(He drew the outline of a cell on the marker board and drew in two nuclei).* Cancer cells grow like crazy. They start going through mitosis repeatedly...you guys remember PMAT? Prophase, metaphase, anaphase, telophase, the steps of mitosis. We know about mitosis because scientists studied Henrietta's cells.

Matthew: It was sad that Henrietta was in a colored ward. They took her cells without her permission or her family's permission. Now that was just wrong. What is worse is that Hopkins was the only hospital for miles that would treat Black patients.

(The bell rings and the students discover their teacher and the others standing outside the classroom door).

Matthew: We did not know you were here, Mrs. Hoffen. We taught the whole class. Were you standing here the whole time?
Hoffen: I only caught the end of class. Wow. Great picture of mitosis, Anthony! You two are great teachers.
Matthew: Mr. Cooper showed us the PowerPoint you sent to all the teachers. Some of the guys had questions. I volunteered to answer. I like this story, Mrs. Hoffen. I feel bad for her family.
Anthony: I did not know that I really understood mitosis until I started talking in front of them. They really had a lot of questions.
(The construction teacher walks up to the group).
Cooper: I am sorry we interrupted the meeting. I thought it was amazing that these two had spent the class period teaching a class full of ninth-grade boys. I figured you would not believe me unless you saw it with your own eyes.
Hoffen: Thanks so much! You guys have made my day…But now you two better get to class. We will have time to talk later.

(The group makes their way through the crowded hallway, back to the conference room).

Driscoll: That is solid evidence that this story is affecting your students, Mrs. Hoffen.
Hoffen: I am still in shock. They were explaining mitosis and talking about issues of social justice. I need you all to understand that Matthew has a specified learning disability. He will only earn a transitional diploma because he cannot pass the math required by the state. At one time, the child was enrolled in three math classes. Anthony suffers from severe ADHD, and often has trouble completing assignments and working in the classroom environment. Both students excelled in biology. Did hearing this story allow them to have success in what otherwise might have been a very difficult class filled with rote memorization? Did mitosis gain meaning because they read Henrietta's story? Both students connected to the

story. Both were engaged in science and the story. Both are teenage boys. They just taught a group of teenage boys.

Driscoll: Students are on the very bottom of the power structure. We must remember, "Every individual brings value to society...more specifically to classrooms. The radical, committed to human liberation, does not become a prisoner" (Freire, 1970, p. 39). Becoming a prisoner means giving up. The radical or activist "enters into reality so that knowing it better he or she can better transform it" (Freire, 1970, p. 39). Our students need to know they can bring about change. Your young women running around giving out their red beads and wearing their t-shirts have hopes of creating change. The young men teaching their peers want to create change.

(Another knock is heard at the door).

Pequod: I will get that. *(She says this obviously annoyed, and terribly bored with the current conversation).*

Alexis and Lydia: Mrs. Hoffen, Mrs. Hoffen *(The girls speak together).* Mrs. Glover let us tell her class about our shirts.

Alexis: We told the class that the story was more than just HeLa cells...the people, the real people behind the science are important.

Hoffen: Ladies, that is wonderful. I think you had better get back to class.

Driscoll: Your students are obviously excited about what they are learning. William Ayers (2004) tells us that "school is a natural site of hope and struggle—hope hovering around notions of a future, struggle busting out over everything about that future: the direction it should take, the shape it could assume, the meanings it might encompass" (p. 20). Teachers and students must participate for there to be struggle. It is in the struggle that both groups of individuals can become educated.

Hoffen: Students must learn that they are stakeholders in their own learning and they need to become comfortable in the struggle. The students feel powerful when they are making choices about their learning.

Pequod: In my own classroom, I provide students with the answers they need to learn. All they must do is spit them back out to me. This prepares them for their state test. *(She pauses).* Is this why they become disengaged from their learning?

Bradley: We must look for changes that depart from the norm. Even small a small change "is revolutionary—it represents some departure from the original" (Deever, 1996, p. 188). We as educators and students cannot wait for our entire broken system to undergo a revolution before we are willing to change. Educators and students seem resistant to change, although "the potential exists. If not now, when? If not now, why?" (Deever, 1996, p. 188).

Driscoll: I like what you said about having to get away from the norm for change to occur. I think we have witnessed a change from the norm. Mrs. Hoffen, I see evidence that you are bridging gaps between yourself and the students in your classroom. I see evidence of bridges between the students and curriculum. This can potentially allow students to become motivated to direct their own learning and become activists for something they feel is a worthwhile cause for change.

Hoffen: We have had a great conversation. *(Looks at her watch).* I would really like to get back to my classroom.

Pequod: We finally agree on something. I would like to get back to my classroom.

Hoffen: Would you all like to come and hear some of the student presentations?

Bradley: Yes, that is a great idea.

(The group stands and walks towards the door).

Act I Scene III: Student Responses

The group follows Mrs. Hoffen down the hall and enters the classroom. They walk to the back of the room, taking seats in a row of empty desks. A student is holding a computer printout. His hands are visibly shaking.

Jhaymia: I will pull up your beat. *(She walks to the computer).*

(The music starts.)

Kyle: I call this HeLa. *(Speaks with a quiver in his voice).*
Old cells, still livin, I'm rappin bout science.
HeLa cells got labs and ethics and compliance
Ooo, but there is not an alliance.
John Hopkins took them cells—what an act of defiance
But it don't matter anyway
Look how it changed the game today
So many vaccines she led the way
Yea her cells never went a fray
Acting it out, but this isn't a school play
Ooo, Chick Chick Bang:

(Chorus)
You might just get hit with the HeLa
Sellin her cells away but guess what she ain't the dealer!
She been gone for a while, I really wish I could meet her.
A history in the making a true science leader.
Now let's get back to the facts.
Born in Virginia to be exact.
Her real name is Henrietta Lacks.
Her cells deserve to make stacks.
Her tumor cells so strong not even a rock can make a crack.
She is important to the world like fresh breath to a tic-tac. OOO
Shout out to her fam in Roanoke.
Shout out to Henrietta for helping cure polio
Her Helix so fire it catch you with that okie dokee.
She is such a hero the fam should never go broke.
(Chorus)
You might just get hit with the HeLa
Sellin her cells away but guess what she ain't the dealer!
She been gone for a while, I really wish I could meet her.
A history in the making a true science leader.
Switch it up
You might just get hit with the HeLa. (Wilkinson, 2015)

Robinson: Wow Kyle! Great job! I think we have time for one more presentation. Charles, it looks like your card is on the top of the deck. *(Charles shyly walks to the front of the room).*

Hoffen: Awesome Kyle! I wish I had that on video. Have you ever performed a rap before? I wish we had time for more discussion. *(She looks at Mrs. Robinson and then glances at her watch again).*

Kyle: Well, uh, no. I was kind of scared...but I really wanted to tell my story with a rap.

Charles: I will be honest, I had never written a poem before, but I liked Deborah's poem in the book. So here goes:

Henrietta Lacks

Struck with cancer you were

62 years ago, may seem like a blur

What happened has caused quite a stir

Regardless, your story will be heard

To doctors you were just another cell

They didn't care about you or hope you would get well

Your spirit is gone Earth was your shell

Now all we have left is your story to tell

In a way, I think you would be pleased

To see all the smiles from the lives that you eased

From cloning, gene mapping, and polio vaccines

You have helped the sick and diseased

You may be gone, but your cells are alive

In millions of test tubes is where you survive

On this day is when you died

Immortal forever-worldwide (Yang, 2014)

Hoffen: Charles, I really like your final line…Immortal forever worldwide. Tell me about poetry. Is this something you would expect to be doing in biology class?

Charles: Not really, I have never liked poetry in English class, but this seemed important. I thought it was a good way to tell Henrietta's Story.

Robinson: Alexis, you are next. *(Alexis springs out of her seat and runs to the front).*

Alexis: Remember, Mrs. Hoffen let us work in pairs. *(Lydia quietly joins her).*

Lydia: I want to talk about what it meant for Henrietta to be a woman in 1951.

Alexis: I am going to talk about what it meant for Henrietta to be a Black woman in 1951 in times of segregation and racism.

(The bell rings.)

Hoffen: We never have enough time. *(She sighs deeply, glancing sadly at her watch).* Alexis and Lydia, you two will be first tomorrow.

(The students pack up and leave Mrs. Hoffen and her committee to finish their discussion).

Hoffen: If a standardized curriculum is required, so be it. I may be required to teach the standards, but I have a lot of control in how I teach the curriculum, and more importantly, how I teach my students.

Driscoll: Students should be respected and be considered curriculum makers right alongside the teacher. All students should be privy to an education that requires "justice, democracy, and human rights" (Pinar, Reynolds, Slattery, & Taubman, 2008, p. 508). Teachers must teach students, not just a standardized curriculum posted on the concrete block wall of the classroom.

Bradley: Henrietta's story provides opportunities for discourse. We should allow teachers to bring difficult subjects, such as racism, to the forefront of discussion. *The Immortal Life of Henrietta Lacks* will keep Henrietta's story alive in the hearts and minds of all who hear. By keeping Henrietta's story alive, students can connect themselves to other stories, stories in which they can become participants or activists.

Act I Scene IV: Biology Class Down the Hall

(Suzy is working at her desk on a test review worksheet. She stops and looks out the window).

Pequod: Suzy, quit looking out the window. You have an assignment to do.

Suzy: But Mrs. Pequod, I have made good grades on all of your tests. I promise I will be ready for my end of course assessment. It is not until May. Why can't we go to the Wear Red program?

Pequod: Get busy Suzy! I have the next chapter review ready for you when you finish this one.

Suzy: Mrs. Pequod, I cannot answer this question. The question is bogus; it cannot be answered.

Pequod: Suzy, you must answer the question. I must verify that all students have answered all the questions. Your growth will determine if I get to keep my job or not.

Suzy: I cannot answer the question. She grabs her head with both hands. I am so confused. We are told it is important to think, and then told just to bubble a stupid answer.

(A student yells from the other side of the room, asking the teacher to come and help).

Pequod: Suzy, answer the question.
Suzy: Don't you need to go help him? *(She bubbles the answer on the worksheet).*
Pequod: Good job, that is right!

(The teacher puts the paper on her desk. Suzy reaches up and grasps the red Mardi Gras beads around her neck).

Suzy: Is anyone important anymore? Bubble this. Bubble that…Henrietta, your cells are an amazing part of science…but so are you! How can I get people to see that?

Final Thoughts

The purpose of these conversations was to discuss the elements of curriculum. I meant for the student interruptions to demonstrate how noise can interrupt curriculum and disrupt binary thinking. The dialogue created is an example of discourse, the most necessary element of a living curriculum. Using the text, *The Immortal Life of Henrietta Lacks*, lends itself to resurrecting life in science classrooms, by providing students with opportunities to connect their standardized curriculum to themselves. I begin by asking a series of questions: "How many of you have a special woman (mother, wife, grandmother, aunt, sister, cousin, or friend) in your life that you are close to? Have you ever been close to someone who experienced a horrible disease? Has your life or the life of a loved one been impacted by cancer?" By this time, everyone in the room has responded at least once…they notice that we all have a lot in common with Henrietta and her family. I think we will all connect to Henrietta in some way. Sometimes the connections are surprising.

The first year that I used *The Immortal Life of Henrietta Lacks* (Skloot, 2010) during our Cell Cycle unit, I noticed early on that students found the story very interesting. The discussion was exciting. The questions were thoughtful. The emotions ran high as my students voiced their outrage concerning Henrietta being in a public ward, her cells being taken without her permission, and her family having no idea her cells were still alive. Henrietta and her family seemed invisible to science. A young man in my class, Matthew—you may remember him as the construction class teacher—told me that reading about the Black scientists working in the "HeLa factory" was the first time he had ever read about African-Americans doing science (Skloot, 2010, p. 93). He said it made him feel good to know that his people helped to make a difference. I was saddened that this was the first example he had seen that he himself could become a scientist. So many students think science is something that is far beyond their reach. It seems that science is on an isolated pedestal of sorts and it "creates a vacuum around itself. Which is the reason for the sudden decline of all the surrounding areas of culture—the humanities, arts, religion, and even the legal system" (Serres & Latour, 2011, p. 87). Science will not be developed fully if the "unusual gifts of race have not thereby been developed" (Woodson, 2005, p. 5). Race being ignored in science adds to making some individuals feel invisible or unimportant in the field of science. The narrator in The Invisible Man begins by telling us that "I am invisible; understand, simply because people refuse to see me" (Ellison, 1995, p. 3). All our students in science should see themselves and others like themselves as participants in science. Without conversations concerning equity in science education, science education cannot move forward. What I propose may seem too simple: teachers must build relationships with their students and create a space where the students can connect themselves to the science curriculum. These connections spark life into an otherwise lifeless curriculum. Once the connections are made, students have an opportunity to see themselves in the center of the curriculum as active participants. Active participants who can become activists and instigate change in our world.

Time in science class should not focus on testing alone. Science curriculum should be rich with philosophy of science, history of science, activities that involve inquiry, and stories. Students can use stories to relate their results and a new way of thinking with familiar information and prior knowledge, essentially bridging the gap between the known and the unknown. Boundaries of science should be expanded to include all participants—those researching and creating new knowledge in science and those affected by this new knowledge. It is also important to tell the whole story. Students need to hear the story of Henrietta Lacks, the woman and her amazing HeLa cells. May her story complicate your conversations.

References

Alliance for excellent education. (2019). Retrieved from The every student succeeds act: Replacing no child left behind: https://all4ed.org/ESEA/

Ayers, W. (2004). Teaching toward freedom. Boston, MA: Beacon.

Barone, T. (1990). Using the narrative text as an occasion for conspiracy. In E. W. Eisner, & A. Peshkin (Eds.), Qualitative inquiry in education: The continuing debate (pp. 305-326). New York, NY: Teachers College Press.

Barone, T. (2000). *Aesthetics, politics, and educational inquiry.* New York, NY: Peter Lang.

Barton, A. C., Ermer, J. L., Burkett, T. A., & Osborne, M. D. (2003). *Teaching science for social justice.* New York, NY: Teachers College Press.

Basu, S. J., Barton, A. C., & Tan, E. (2011). *Democratic science teaching: Building the expertise to empower low-income minority youth in science.* Rotterdam, NL: Sense Publishers.

Blades, D. W. (1997). *Procedures of power & curriculum change: Foucault and the quest for possibilities in science education.* New York, NY: Peter Lang.

Clandinin, D. J., & Connelly, M. F. (2000). *Narrative inquiry: Experience and story in qualitative research.* San Francisco, CA: Jossey-Bass.

Deever, B. (1996). If not now, when? Radical theory and systemic curriculum reform. *The Journal of Curriculum Studies, 28*(2), 171-191.

Dickenson, E. (1993). *Emily Dickenson.* New York: Everyman's Library; Reprint edition (November 2, 1993).

Doll, W. F. (1993). *A post-modern perspective on curriculum.* New York, NY: Columbia University.

Ellison, R. (1995). *The invisible man.* New York, NY: Vintage International.

Freire, P. (1970). *Pedagogy of the oppressed.* New York, NY: Continuum.

Giroux, H. A. (2009). Obama's dilemma: Postpartisan politics and the crisis of American education. *Harvard Educational Review, 79*(2),250-266.

Grumet, M. R. (1989/1999). Word worlds: The literary reference for curriculum criticism. In W. F. Pinar (Ed.), *In contemporary curriculum discourses: Twenty years of JCT* (pp. 233-245). New York, NY: Peter Lang.

Grumet, M. R. (1990). On the daffodils that come before the swallow dares. In E. Eisner, & A. Peshkin, *Qualitative inquiry in education: The continuing debate* (pp. 101-120). New York, NY: Teachers College Press.

He, M. F. (2013). East~West epistemological convergence of humanism in language, identity, and education: Confucious~Makiguchi~Dewey. *Journal of language, identity and education, 12*(1), 61-70.

Heese, B. (2015). *Effects of the elimination of grade 12 provincial exams in chemistry, biology, and physics on teachers in a British Columbia school district. (Unpublished doctoral dissertation).* British Columbia, CA: University of Victoria.

Hodson, D. (1998). *Teaching and learning science: Toward a personalized approach.* Philadelphia, PA: Open University Press.

hooks, b. (2010). *Teaching critical thinking: Practical wisdom.* New York, NY: Routlage.

Klassen, S. (2006). A theoretical framework for contextual science e teaching. *Interchange, 37*(1-2), 31-62.

Krall, F. R. (1999). Living metaphors: The real curriculum in environmental education. In W. F. Pinar (Ed.), *Contemporary curriculum discourses: Twenty years of JCT* (pp. 1-5). New York, NY: Peter Lang.

Morris, M. (2001). Serres bugs the curriculum. In J. A. Weaver, M. Morris, & P. Applebaum, *(Post) modern science (education): propositions and alternative paths* (pp. 94-110). New York, NY: Peter Lang.

Norris, J. (2010). *Playbuilding as qualitative research: A participatory arts-based approach developing qualatative inquiry.* New York, NY: Routledge.

Philbrick, N. (2011). *Why read Moby-Dick?* New York, NY: Viking Penguin Group.

Pinar, W. F. (2004). *What is curriculum theory?* Mahwah, NJ: Erlbaum.

Pinar, W. F., Reynolds, W. M., Slattery, P., & Taubman, P. M. (2008). *Understanding curriculum.* New York, NY: Peter Lang.

Rubin, D. I., & Kazanjian, C. J. (2011). "Just another brick in the wall": Standardization and the devaluing of education. *Journal of Curriculum and Instruction, 5*(2), 94-108.

Rutherford, J. (1990). The third space. Interview with Homi Bhabha.

Schwab, J. J. (1978). *Science curriculum and liberal education: Selected essays.* Chicago, IL: University of Chicago Press.

Serres, M., & Latour, B. (2011). *Conversations on science, culture and time. (R. Lapidus, Trans.).* Ann Arbor, MI: University of Michigan Press. (Original work published in 1990).

Skloot, R. (2010). *The immortal life of Henrietta Lacks.* New York, NY: Broadway Paperbacks.

The Lacks family. (2010). Retrieved from http://www.lacksfamily.com/

Van Valen, L. (1991). HeLa a new microbial species. *Evolutionary Theory*, 10(2), 71-74.

Walls, L. D. (2011). *The passage to the cosmos: Alexander Von Humbolt and the shaping of America.* Chicago, IL: University of Chicago Press.

Wilkinson, K. (2015, October 4). *HeLa.* (K. Wilkinson, Performer) Evans High School, Evans, Georgia, USA.

Woodson, C. G. (2005). *Mis-education of the negro.* Mineola, New York: Dover Publications (Original work published in 1933)

Wulf, A. (2015). *The invention of nature.* New York, NY: Alfred A. Knopf.

Yang, M. (2014, October 4). *The tale of Henrietta Lacks.* (M. Yang, Performer) Evans High School, Evans, Georgia, USA.

Chapter 8

Patriot Acts

John Cato

With Archie's arrival, Britain's Prince Harry and wife Meghan's son, news outlets from around the world poured into England seeking to interview an expert on the British royal family. If there exists such an authority outside the castle, then it must be the chairman of the British Monarchist Society and the president of the Centre for British Royal Studies, Thomas J. Mace-Archer Mills, Esq. He has given numerous interviews for international media outlets, such as BBC Radio and *The Economist*, on the royal family and the monarchy (Bryant, 2018). Certainly, landing an interview with Mace-Archer Mills would be a coup for any journalist. Except Britain's Thomas J. Mace-Archer Mills, Esq. is really American Tommy Muscatellow, Jr. (Bryant, 2018). His accent? He picked that up while in high school doing the play, *Oliver!* (Bryant, 2018). And the British Monarchist Society and Centre for British Royal Studies? He made those up, too (Bryant, 2018). It was all a con.

A con is "a perfectly constructed piece of theatre" (Reading, 2012, p. 8) designed by the confidence man, or grifter, to get an unsuspecting person, known as the mark, to give over something, not by using force, but instead by using persuasion. Good cons are highly polished, with conmen repeatedly pulling cons on new marks. Cons are highly sophisticated and designed to persuade even the most cautious among us. They resemble a "tightly scripted drama with nine acts, each with its own distinct function in conveying the mark towards the climax" (Reading, 2012, p. 7). When we examine the language and structure used in cons, it becomes evident many people use similar language, structure, and techniques in order to persuade people. Even the manner in which presidents pitch their educational reform resemble the characteristics associated with a con's tightly scripted play.

Although cons have nine acts, they occur within three stages. According to Maria Konnikova's (2016) *New York Times* bestseller, *The Confidence Game*, the first stage consists of *the put-up, the play, the rope,* and *the tale.*

David P. Owen, Jr (ed.), *Field Theory: Curriculum Studies at Work*, 151–167.

During the put-up, the grifter picks a mark by sizing him or her up, an important step because, as Konnikova writes, "Size someone up well, and you can sell them anything" (pg. 56-57). To do so, the con artist carefully chooses everything down to the setting in order to ensure that he will select the right mark for his con (Konnikova, 2016). Likewise, when presidents promote their educational reforms, they choose the best setting or occasion to do so in order to ensure they will succeed. For example, when Obama wanted to make a speech to generate support for his educational reform, he chose to make his speech at the Mapleton Expeditionary School of the Arts in Colorado. According to Obama (as cited in Crummy, 2008), he chose to give his speech at Mapleton because he wanted to:

> hold up this school and these students as examples of what's possible in education if we're willing to try new ideas and new reforms not based on ideology, but on what works to give our children the best possible chance in life. (para. 4)

Although he could have spoken anywhere, selecting Mapleton, a school whose "school enrollment is 77% minority, and 63%...economically disadvantaged" (U.S. News, 2019), makes good sense because its community would be receptive to change—a desirable trait for the ideal mark. In fact, during the put-up, the grifter ultimately tries to size up a mark by determining what the mark most deeply wants. A con artist's "genius lies in figuring out what, precisely, it is we want, and how they can present themselves as the perfect vehicle for delivering on that desire" (Konnikova, 2016, p. 5). As Konnikova argues, great grifters give the mark what they most want. Similarly, presidents seek to do the same when they pitch their educational reform policies. They capitalize on the two desires that the public wants most from educational reform: 1) the desire for educational reform that will close the achievement gap (Ansell, 2011), and 2) the desire for educational reform that will lead to jobs (Manyika et al., 2017). One can see how presidents increasingly appeal to these desires by carefully selecting everything from the names they give their reforms to the language they use to tout them. For example, Obama's aptly named reform, Race to the Top, appeals to the American public's desire to close the achievement gap. Even the language used to describe it iterates that message, promising "to help *every* student learn and succeed" ("Race to the Top," n.d.). President Bush, too, appealed to this same desire. His signature education law, the No Child Left Behind Act of 2001 (2002), mandated that by 2014 *all* children would be proficient in both math and reading as well as achieve a 100% high school graduation rate.

Presidents also appeal to the public's desire for education leading to jobs. President Obama oversaw two major education reforms tied to jobs: The Race to the Top (R3T), a grant written into the American Recovery and Reinvestment Act of 2009 (ARRA) (2009), and the Every Student Succeeds Act (ESSA) (2015). A core feature present in both initiatives was his desire to advance STEM education and promote STEM careers (Handelson & Smith, 2016). Obama pushed STEM because a major shortage existed in qualified STEM workers. In an interview on NPR's *Tell Me More*, Anthony Carnevale, director of the Georgetown University Center on Education and the Workforce, said so many STEM workers are needed "because we lose so many of them along the way" (as cited in Martin, 2013, para. 5). According to John Holdren (2013), Assistant to the President for Science & Technology Director, as part of Obama's original Race to the Top grant, the grant went first to states who would:

> [put] a competitive preference priority on developing comprehensive strategies to improve achievement and provide rigorous curricula in STEM subjects; partner with local STEM institutions, businesses, and museums; and broaden participation of women and girls and other groups underrepresented in STEM fields. (p. i)

States trying to be first-round grant winners quickly altered their curriculums, making them heavily weighted in STEM courses, as well as preparing students for STEM careers. Thus, by providing grant money to states who focus on STEM education and on getting students to pursue STEM careers, more states would likely adopt those as goals. The assumption was, by having more states focus on those goals, more students would go into STEM careers. While all of that sounds promising as a means of achieving the public's desire for students having jobs post-graduation, the reform's success would require all public schools to have the necessary resources already in place to run with these changes, but sadly, that was not and still is not the case. In order to teach all the new STEM students, for example, we would need a great many more STEM teachers. That would prove to be particularly problematic because STEM careers pay much better than teaching, leading many would-be-qualified candidates to choose instead to work in STEM careers and not work in the classroom. In order to address this deficiency, President Obama (State of the Union, 2011) called on corporations to find a way to meet his goal of adding 100,000 STEM teachers over the next 10 years. But as of 2017, only 40% have been trained (Satell, 2017).

Once a con artist has identified a mark's desires, then comes the play. During the play, the con artist sets the hook in the mark by appealing to the mark's emotions, which essentially is "an attempt to lower his defenses through a bit of fancy emotional footwork" (Konnikova, 2016, p. 132). The con artist does this by gaining the mark's trust, usually by telling an emotional story. Indeed, according to Konnikova (2016), "The best way to activate strong feeling is simple: you tell a compelling story" (p. 101). This is also similar to how presidents push their reforms on the American public. For example, during President Bush's (2002) NCLB signing speech, he said:

> I read a quote one time from a young lady in New York. She said, "I don't ever remember taking an exam. They just kept passing me along. I ended up dropping out in the seventh grade. I basically felt nobody cared." The story of children being just shuffled through the system is one of the saddest stories of America. "Let's just move them through."' It's so much easier to move a child through than trying to figure out how to solve a child's problems.

Bush's story appeals to pathos by tapping into feelings that already exist in the audience: their desire to close the achievement gap. Moreover, his decision to use someone who has literally been "left behind" symbolizes the aims of his No Child Left Behind reform and has all the hallmarks of great theater.

After the play comes the rope. The rope is "the alpha and omega of the confidence game" (Konnikova, 2016, p. 132). More than just a strategy, the rope also includes how the con constructs the proposition. As Konnikova (2016) writes, if someone "is a good roper, you will soon be seeing the world as he sees it" (p. 159). Pulling off the rope requires two parts. The first part, the alpha, entails a persuasive appeal that works "by promising more" (Konnikova, 2016, p. 145). Here the con sells the mark by promising something that seems almost unbelievable (Konnikova, 2016). That occurred during Bush's signing speech for NCLB. Soon after his story about the little girl left behind, he stated, "What this bill says, it says *every child can learn*" (Bush, 2002). With the alpha stage concluded, the con delivers the omega. It involves the con artist reducing the mark's resistance to the con. This also parallels how presidents pitch their reforms. For example, Bush (2002) concluded his speech with, "We want to make sure no child is left behind." That slight change in phrasing moves the audience away from the unbelievable notion (the alpha), *no child will be left behind,* to a more acceptable one (the omega), *we don't want to leave any child behind.* And, after claiming his reforms would result *in leaving no child behind*, a statement likely to invoke skepticism, Bush dampens it by saying:

> We're going to spend more money, more resources, but they'll be directed at methods that work, not feel-good methods, not sound-good methods, but methods that actually work, particularly when it comes to reading. We're going to spend more on our schools, and we're going to spend it more wisely.

In this way, Bush's language parallels that of the rope. He increases the appeal of his reform policies and decreases the public's resistance to them through an allusion: by alluding to previous presidents' reform policies that he claims were not substantive, he successfully appeals to ethos promising to spend the tax payer's money wisely.

Likewise, Obama used similar techniques in his efforts to gain public support for his reforms. Take, for example, Obama's 2012 State of the Union Address. First, he does the play by giving an emotional story: "Jackie Bray is a single mom from North Carolina who was laid off from her job as a mechanic" (State of the Union, 2012, para. 30). Then, he follows this up with statements paralleling the rope (i.e. promises more and diminishes resistance):

> Then Siemens opened a gas turbine factory in Charlotte, and formed a partnership with Central Piedmont Community College. The company helped the college design courses in laser and robotics training. It paid Jackie's tuition, then hired her to help operate their plant. (State of the Union, 2012, para. 30)

His story about how educational reform can close the achievement gap *and* lead to a job delivers a one-two punch.

After the rope comes the tale. During the tale, the grifter explains to the mark how the mark will personally benefit (Konnikova, 2016). It's "the moment when 'Too good to be true' turns into 'Actually this makes perfect sense'" (Konnikova, 2016, p. 172). In his 2012 State of the Union Address, President Obama cinches the rope with a tale that promises the unbelievable:

> We also know that when students don't walk away from their education, more of them walk the stage to get their diploma. When students are not allowed to drop out, they do better. So tonight, *I am proposing that every state—every state—requires that all students stay in high school until they graduate or turn 18.* (State of the Union, 2012, para. 36)

We also find this in his 2011 State of the Union Address:

Take a school like Bruce Randolph in Denver. Three years ago, it was rated one of the worst schools in Colorado—located on turf between two rival gangs. But last May, 97 percent of the seniors received their diploma. Most will be the first in their families to go to college. And after the first year of the school's transformation, the principal who made it possible wiped away tears when a student said, "Thank you, Ms. Waters, for showing that we are smart and we can make it." That's what good schools can do, and we want good schools all across the country. (State of the Union, 2011, para. 38)

Again, he begins with a compelling story to prime the audience. Then, he relies on the rope to figuratively rope them into believing his reforms are highly desirable. Finally, he has them believing that they, too, can have success like that if they adopt his reforms. After all, if it can happen at *that* school, then why can't it happen at *my* school?

Not only does presidential language often parallel the con, but so does the specific reform's language. For example, NCLB's language has goals such as to eliminate the achievement gap by requiring 100% of high school students be proficient in reading and mathematics, as well as to have 100% graduation rates. Those goals appeal to the public's desire to eliminate the achievement gap (the put-up) as well as make seemingly unbelievable claims (the alpha part of the rope). And, like the omega part of the rope, NCLB also includes provisions that suggest achieving those goals might not be entirely possible without additional components coming into play, components that would likely cause the public to think, "Now that sounds more reasonable." For example, NCLB states that some students may need help reaching the proficiency goals, so it provides for free tutoring to students who meet certain criteria in order to help all students achieve the goals. Furthermore, NCLB allows for parents, under certain conditions, the ability to change their children's school. Hence, although NCLB doesn't preclude students from receiving help, it does imply that with the right system and with enough support, all students will achieve those goals, a reform which the public can get behind. By now, the tale is on and the public begins to think, "I support this reform."

But what leads the public to believe that the exaggerated promises outlined in these reforms could come true? According to Konnikova (2016), "Part of what makes it possible for people to fall for cons is most people naturally want to believe in others." As Konnikova puts it, "We want to believe in what they're telling us" (p. 5). Consequently, our desire to believe what others are telling us means "we've done most of the work for them" (Konnikova, 2016, p. 5). Likewise, when presidents tell us that they can fix the education system with their reforms, we naturally want to believe them. After all, people "need to believe in something that gives life meaning" (Konnikova, 2016, p. 4). For most parents, their children's education would certainly qualify, and who wouldn't want the best education for their children? People also want to believe because they have "a need to see some sort of justness and fairness in the surrounding world" (Konnikova, 2016, p. 5) and claims that promise to close the achievement gap speak to that. The widely held belief that schools offer us the opportunity to have a meritocracy also makes the public open to seeing them as sites that can overcome societal ills. Who wouldn't want to support reforms that would make schools, and possibly the world, better?

The belief that educational reform can deliver that is also understandable when one considers that each president presents public schools as institutions that operate in a manner consistent with a treatment effect. Malcolm Gladwell (2005) explains the difference between a treatment effect and a selection effect in his *New Yorker* article, "Getting In." In it, he writes about the "social logic of Ivy League admissions" (Gladwell, 2005, subtitle). According to Gladwell, there are two effects in play: the selection effect and the treatment effect. In the selection effect, traits are preselected and used to screen applicants. In order to demonstrate the selection effect, Gladwell uses the idea of a modeling agency. Modeling agencies look for people who already have certain desirable physical features that will meet the needs of the agencies' clients. For example, a client advertising sports gear might want to have models who look young and athletic, but a client who sells expensive clothing may want tall, slender, and young models. Models hoping to be hired must already meet the agencies' requirements because these businesses will not wait until they do. However, places that operate on a treatment effect work differently. Gladwell uses the Marine Corps as an example to explain how. Anyone who meets their minimum entrance requirements will be allowed to go to Basic Training, where the new recruits will undergo intensive training designed to turn all of them into Marines. Unlike the selection effect, the recruits enter Basic Training without already having met the Marine Corps' standards for graduation, but by the end of Basic Training, all who finish will graduate as Marines, having met or exceeded the necessary performance standards. The training that recruits receive turns them into Marines. The process they endure produces the same product regardless of who experiences it.

Although on the surface, public schools may have the semblance of operating like the Marine Corps (i.e. a treatment effect), they do not. After all, their recruits have volunteered to enlist, but public school students have not volunteered to be in school due to being required by law to attend. In addition, the Marine Corps utilizes some form of preselection through their minimum entrance requirements. But the same cannot be said for public school students. Instead, they must take every child zoned for a particular school regardless of that child's ability or motivation. In spite of that, every presidents' educational reform policies capitalize on the public's desire to eliminate the achievement gap and to guarantee employment by presenting public schools as operating on a treatment effect. They know that the public needs to conceive of their child's school in this way. They need to believe that their child's school will provide a quality education that will allow their child to be gainfully employed. They also need to believe that their child will leave school with the same education and skills as every other child in the nation. They also need to believe that the public school their child attends is just as capable of providing those opportunities as any other school.

Because the public needs to believe that, educational reform must promise that. For example, consider the two goals of NCLB: *100% of all students can read and do math proficiently*, and *100% of all high school students can graduate*. Consider also Bush's remarks during his signing speech: "Every single child, regardless of where they live, how they're raised, the income level of their family, *every child will receive a first-class education in America*" (Strauss, 2015). Such outlandish results could only happen through a treatment effect, which is what the presidents' reform policies symbolize. The idea that *any* student can learn to read at a high comprehension level and do mathematics at an advanced level disregards any cognitive limitations a child may have. But the public has to believe that the impossible is possible. They must believe that by having their children participate in certain reading or math programs, success can be attained, a clear indication of a treatment effect, and a belief integral for politicians to tap into when selling the public on educational reform. Such statements dismiss the realities of what "public" really means in the term "public school" by discounting the fact that students not only arrive at school with differing cognitive abilities, but also with other differences that continue to thwart our abilities to close the achievement gap, such as class. But through their reform policies, presidents continue to promote schools as places that operate on a treatment effect, making believers out of an American public that desires change.

Once the mark believes, the next act requires the mark to remain a believer. This stage begins by using "evidence" to convince the mark that he or she was justified in believing the con. Doing so requires the con artist to act as *the convincer*. The convincer's purpose is to make the mark believe that everything is on the up and up. According to Konnikova (2016), "The convincer makes it seem like you're winning and everything is going according to plan" (p. 201) in order to get "the mark to dedicate himself to his commitment for the long haul" (Konnikova, 2016, p. 209). A similar process occurs with educational reform. With the public having now bought into the promises outlined in a president's educational reform policies, the convincer now comes in and keeps the public believing the reforms are working by striving to provide evidence of their success. NCLB's convincer came in the form of accountability measures. NCLB measured and scored every public school and every school district in order to determine if they were meeting the goals of the reforms. Essentially, that meant NCLB required a battery of standardized tests and secondary measures, such as attendance rates and graduation rates, in order to measure student and school achievement (Klein, 2015). Schools on target for meeting the required NCLB goals were said to have "passed" Adequate Yearly Progress (AYP), while schools that did not were said to have "failed" AYP. The states released the report cards to the public in an effort to convince the public that the reforms were working, and therefore, to encourage the public to continue to support the NCLB.

President Obama's reforms also made use of a convincer. For example, in 2010, President Obama and the U.S. Department of Education released a policy pushing the connection of accountability to college and career readiness. In it, one reform called for "developing better assessments aligned with college-and career-ready standards" (U.S. Department of Education, 2010, p. 1). Those reforms led to Georgia's College and Career Readiness Index (CCRPI), which is "the new accountability system that replaces the No Child Left Behind (NCLB) Adequate Yearly Progress (AYP)" (Georgia Department of Education, 2014). Much like NCLB's report card, the CCRPI is a number generated to show how "ready" students from particular schools and school districts are for college and careers after leaving high school. States then release the CCRPI scores to the public in an effort to show that the reforms are preparing students for careers, which capitalizes on what the public desires and ensures they continue to support the reforms.

Some may ask, "what's the harm in presidents presenting us with reforms that make such outlandish promises?" After all, they appear to be well-intentioned and to have children's best interest at heart. But whose best interest does a president's educational reform policy really have at heart? Because of the election laws and how presidential campaign funding works, presidential candidates typically need to raise large sums of money in order to seek office. Therefore, it is not uncommon for a candidate to reach out to corporate leaders in order to gain their support and financial backing. Although people certainly give to candidates for all kinds of reasons, one reason could be the belief that the donor might get the ability to influence the candidate on policy. In fact, according to Spencer (2017), since "the rich are interested in advancing their agendas, they generally only donate to prospects that fund those agendas" (para. 3). One item typically found on Corporate America's agenda is jobs. Take, for example, when President Obama campaigned for reelection. He held meetings with corporate leaders such as Facebook's Mark Zuckerberg, a contributor to Obama's campaign, that were closed to the media, in order "to explore ways they [could] collaborate to expand the economy and create jobs" (*The Associated Press*, 2011, para. 5). Another example is when President Obama toured Intel Corporation with Intel CEO Paul Otellini (*The Associated Press*, 2011). While at Intel, Obama "hear[d] about the chip-maker's efforts to spur innovation and prepare workers for jobs in high-tech industries. [He] also [spoke] about the role of education in preparing workers for those jobs" (*The Associated Press*, 2011, para. 11). Furthermore, Otellini outlined for Obama Intel's own education program, one "that includes a curriculum, a competition and online resources to encourage studies in science, technology, engineering and math" (*The Associated Press*, 2011, para. 9). In addition to that meeting, "Otellini was among 20 corporate CEOs who met privately with Obama" that December (*The Associated Press*, 2011, para. 12). Furthermore, in 2017 under President Trump, a large group of tech companies, including Amazon, Facebook, Microsoft, and Google, pledged $300 million dollars to STEM education in order to increase the number of STEM workers (Spencer, 2017).

Why does any of this matter? Because the concerns that corporate leaders raise about the economy drive curriculum decisions taking place in our public schools. As Pinar (2012) argues, "while the point of the American public schools has not changed much in over the past one hundred years, the economy schools were designed to support has" (p. 36). When corporate leaders expressed a need for more STEM workers, Presidents Obama and Trump listened and responded by making STEM education and STEM career pathways integral to their reforms. While they pitch these reforms as ways to overcome the achievement gap and to guarantee future employment, they serve the president's need for campaign funding by serving the agenda of corporate leaders.

The extent to which the nation's schools have embraced educational reforms related to the STEM agenda is extensive. For example, many nonprofits emerged in order to help achieve its goals. The National Mathematics and Science Initiative (NMSI) was created and funded largely by donations from ExxonMobil, the O'Donnell Foundation, the Bill and Melinda Gates Foundation, and the Michael and Susan Dell Foundation. Its purpose is to offer grants to schools in order to increase their student participation in AP STEM courses, such as AP Calculus, AP Physics, and AP Computer Science. They achieve their goal by giving schools and school systems a grant that requires the recipients to add AP courses, encourages them to remove prerequisite requirements to AP courses, pays for students' AP exams, and pays students for passing AP exams. Since the grant emphasizes getting as many students into AP math, science, and English courses as possible, often resulting in students being in courses that are simply too demanding for them, NMSI pays to have consultants go to the schools three Saturdays a year in order to work with students on additional coursework. The grant also provides for teacher training, which amounts to learning how to get more students to pass their respective AP exam. According to NMSI's website, NMSI's presence in a school results in "a stronger corps of math and science teachers, increased student access to and achievement in rigorous STEM courses, particularly among students traditionally underrepresented in STEM fields, and greater workforce preparedness" (NMS, 2019).

Like the language used in each president's educational reform policies, the mission statement for NMSI strongly suggests the belief that public schools operate on the treatment effect. For one, it assumes that all students possess the ability to take AP STEM courses, and that struggling students can overcome their difficulties with the right help, such as the three Saturday sessions of extra tutoring. It also structures its teacher training around helping students learn to pass the exam rather than on specific teaching skills. It assumes students can be motivated by offering them financial incentives. Furthermore, by only offering those rewards for students who take math, science, and English classes, NMSI effectively discourages students from taking more arts, humanities, and languages, areas they don't want students to consider because they would be counterproductive to NMSI's goals.

Another STEM initiative promoted by the White House is CSforALL, a program designed to make computer programming an integral part of the educational experience of all students. The program is partially funded and run by the powerful National Science Foundation, and has the Department of Education serving as a main administrative agency. While this program mainly serves the function of CS advocacy through promotion and incentives, there are other programs that specifically promote CS to students and serve as a vehicle for training students for careers in STEM fields (Llovio, 2015). For example, the program Hour of Code is a global initiative in over 180 countries so far. Teachers sign their students up, and then have students complete self-guided modules to learn to code. The teachers devote one hour of teaching time weekly for students to complete the activities. In addition, summer "bootcamps" exist for students to go and learn to write code. The businesses and universities offer those bootcamps so students leave 21st-century-ready to enter STEM careers. These two examples illustrate how quickly the STEM curriculum has extended its influence beyond the boundaries of the typical school day.

In fact, entire schools now exist solely focused on teaching students to program in order to prepare them for STEM jobs. For example, according to Llovio (2015), in Virginia, a group of schools joined together to make a "new regional high school that will allow students to meet their core requirements while getting an education focused on computer science" (para. 2). This initiative, according to Lane, "create[s] a high school environment that's more reflective of modern education and preparation for the modern workforce" (as cited in Llovio, 2015, para. 8). In this new school model, students take core classes and computer science classes during their freshman and sophomore years, and their junior and senior years are spent "learning real-world job skills through internships while working toward earning a two-year degree from local community colleges" (Llovio, 2015). That is done because "research show[s] a high demand for software developers and system engineers" (Llovio, 2015). Again, a rhetoric consistent with educational reform underscores all of those notions: the belief that schools operate on the treatment effect. First, it assumes requiring students to learn coding and be proficient in CS skills is sufficient training to prepare students for STEM careers. Second, it assumes that by emphasizing those skills in high school, it will motivate students to pursue STEM careers. Third, it assumes all students who take part in those programs will grasp the skills equally and be equally prepared to enter STEM careers. Finally, it suggests to parents that schools are capable of fully preparing their children to enter STEM careers. Although not true, the "evidence" indicates the reforms are working, so the public continues to believe in them.

Even digital education initiatives steer students towards STEM education and into STEM careers. Virtual classes offer students the opportunity to free themselves from any traditional education limitations, such as the lack of a highly qualified teacher in the building. Doing so frees up scheduling so students can take whatever courses they want, whenever they want, and how they want. Additionally, this type of education has the added benefit of getting students out of high school and into college or the job market faster, thus saving money on their educations by needing fewer traditional classroom teachers. But as Dynarski (2018) points out, "Online courses are particularly attractive to school and district leaders looking for ways to trim costs [because]…teacher salaries are the key driver of instructional costs at every level of education." But proponents of these types of educational experiences operate from the assumption that all students can equally handle taking the courses within a digital environment because the digital setting provides an environment similar to a meritocracy, treating all students equally. But research done by the Brookings Institution clearly shows that online education is a "poor option for the least prepared students" (Dynarski, 2018). Furthermore, research by Bettinger, Fox, Loeb, and Taylor (2017) showed students who take online classes tend to not fair nearly as well as students who take traditional classes. In fact, they found online students are more likely to drop out of college altogether and do poorly in future courses that depend on the online course material, all of which works against the aims of educational reform. As Theberge (1981) argues, "The interests of business are unalterably opposed to those of working people and consumers. What is good for business is not likely to be in the interest of American society" (p. 32). Still, by advocating for educational reforms designed around STEM education and promising STEM careers for students, presidents can claim that they brought about the type of reform that the public desired and simultaneously benefit those companies that bankrolled their campaigns and benefit from having STEM workers.

As Spencer (2017) points out, by allowing donors to influence policy, "we cede control of our values and our minds to the whims of the wealthy." Furthermore, he goes on to say that the effect is we become subservient to the donors, which means we no longer "have a say as to how education function[s] and how society operates." But opposing a president's educational reform policies can be difficult due to the fact that presidents often persuade the American public to equate supporting their educational reform with supporting the nation. They do so through a rhetoric of nationalism. According to Ashcroft, Griffiths, and Tiffin (2007), nationalism is very much an ideology "in which specific identifiers are employed to create exclusive and homogeneous conceptions of national traditions" (p. 135). It perpetuates "the idea of nations as natural and immutable formations based on shared collective values" (Ashcroft, Griffiths, & Tiffin, 2007, p. 136). Consequently, "Nationalism [is] one of the most powerful forces in contemporary society," and "Modern nations such as the United States, with their multi-ethnic composition, require the acceptance of an overarching national ideology" (Ashcroft, Griffiths, & Tiffin, 2007, p. 136). Since nationalism is the ideology that forms a nation, whoever holds national power determines national ideology, making that difficult to overcome.

Evidence of how presidents have used the rhetoric of nationalism to garner support for their reform policies can be found in Bush's speech at the signing of the NCLB act. In his opening, Bush (2002) said, "We've got a lot of challenges here in America. There's no greater challenge than to make sure that every child...receives a first-class education." Bush immediately followed that with:

> And as you know, we've got another challenge, and that's to protect America from evil ones. And I want to assure the seniors and juniors and sophomores here at Hamilton High School that the effort that this great country is engaged in, the effort to defend freedom and to defend our people, the effort to rout out terror wherever it exists, is noble and just and right, and your great country will prevail in this effort.

By juxtaposing those two ideas in his speech, Bush equates supporting his education reform with patriotism, thereby making it unpatriotic not to support his reform.

President Obama (2008) also relied on the rhetoric of nationalism to gain the public's support for his reform. He did so through an American nationalistic ideology—the American Dream. In America, we believe that everyone has the ability to pull themselves up by their bootstraps and make it. Obama (2008) tapped into that ideology when he stated:

> That is the promise of education in America, that no matter what we look like or where we come from or who our parents are, each of us should have the opportunity to fulfill our God-given potential. Each of us should have the chance to achieve the American dream. (para. 34)

By making those statements in his education reform speech, Obama links his reforms to giving everyone the opportunity to achieve the American Dream, a notion fundamentally American. Hence, by implication, to not support his reforms would be fundamentally un-American.

Ideally, education reforms should be based on what is in students' best interests. Reforms that originate from that motivation can be deemed worthy of debate and possible implementation. But when presidential reforms serve the best interests of corporations instead of students, then these reforms are really just cons. How do we know if we're being conned? According to Konnikova (2016), if it is a good con, then you don't. In fact, "Marks insist they haven't been conned at all" (pg. 189). In fact, "When we feel that something was a personal failure, we dismiss it rather than learn from it" (Konnikova, 2016, p. 189). That makes it so much easier for con artists to continue preying on their marks. Likewise, the American public may not want to conceive of educational reforms as cons. Yet, an election system that operates as ours does leaves the public vulnerable to presidents offering reforms at the behest of corporations in exchange for donations. And as long as presidential campaigns are largely funded by corporate donations, then those donors will always be able to bend the president's ear and exert influence on educational reforms, thus taking the reforms further from what is in the best interests of students and closer to what is in the best interests of corporations. Consequently, corporations will continue to drive curriculum, and hence reform efforts, to be designed around job training and career readiness. Lost is the important curriculum question, perhaps the *most* important curriculum question, asked by Schubert (2010): "What is worth knowing, needing, experiencing, doing, helping, becoming, overcoming, sharing, and contributing?" (p. 15). When Corporate America decides the answer to that and influences educational reform, we've all been conned. And if no one seems to be the wiser, that's a pretty good con.

References

Ansell, S. (2011, July 7). Achievement gap. *Education Week*. Retrieved from https://www.edweek.org/ew/issues/achievement-gap/index.html

Ashcroft, B., Griffiths, G., & Tiffin, H. (2007). *Post-Colonial studies: The key concepts.* (2ed) New York, NY: Routledge.

Bettinger, E., Fox, L., Loeb, S., & Taylor, E. (2017). Virtual classrooms: How online college courses affect student success. *American Economic Review, 107(9)*. Retrieved https://www.aeaweb.org/articles?id=10.1257/aer.20151193

Bryant, K. (2018, June 1). The greatest royal wedding scammer has come clean. *Vanity Fair*. Retrieved from https://www.vanityfair.com/style/2018/06/british-royal-wedding-expert-imposter-thomas-j-mace-archer-mills

Bush, G. (2002, January 8). Remarks on signing the No Child Left Behind Act of 2001 in Hamilton, Ohio. *Government Publishing Office*. Retrieved from https://www.govinfo.gov/content/pkg/WCPD-2002-01-14/html/WCPD-2002-01-14-Pg26-2.htm

Crummy, K. (2008, May 28). Obama praises successful Thornton school. *The Denver Post*. Retrieved from https://www.denverpost.com/2008/05/28/obama-praises-successful-thornton-school/

Dynarski, S. (2018, January 19). Online courses are harming the students who need the most help. *The New York Times*. Retrieved from https://www.nytimes.com/2018/01/19/business/online-courses-are-harming-the-students-who-need-the-most-help.html

Georgia Department of Education. (2014). College and career ready performance index. Retrieved February 5, 2015, from http://www.gadoe.org/CCRPI/Pages/default.aspx

Gladwell, M. (2005). Getting in: The social logic of Ivy League admissions. *New Yorker, October 10, 2005*. Retrieved from https://www.newyorker.com/magazine/2005/10/10/getting-in

Holdren, J. (2013). Federal science, technology, engineering, and mathematics (STEM) Education 5-year strategic plan. Retrieved from https://obamawhitehouse.archives.gov/sites/default/files/microsites/ostp/stem_stratplan_2 013.pdf

Handelson, J., & Smith, M. (2016). STEM for all. Retrieved from https://obamawhitehouse.archives.gov/blog/2016/02/11/stem-all

Klein, A. (2015). No Child Left Behind: An overview. *Education Week.* Retrieved from https://www.edweek.org/ew/section/multimedia/no-child-left-behind-overview-definition-summary.html

Konnikova, M. (2016). *The confidence game: Why we fall for it... every time.* New York, NY: Viking.

Llovio, L. (2015, December 16). New Va. high school to focus big on coding. *eSchoolnews.* Retrieved from https://www.eschoolnews.com/2015/12/16/new-va-high-school-to-teach-coding/

Manyika, J., Lund, S., Chui, M., Bughin, J., Woetzel, P., ...Sanghvi, S. (2017). Jobs lost, jobs gained: What the future of work will mean for jobs, skills, and wages. Retrieved from https://www.mckinsey.com/featured-insights/future-of-work/jobs-lost-jobs-gained-what-the-future-of-work-will-mean-for-jobs-skills-and-wages

Martin, M. (Host). (2013, November 25). Is the STEM education crisis a myth? [Radioprogram]. *Tell me more.* Retrieved from https://www.npr.org/templates/story/story.php?storyId=247166532

No Child Left Behind Act of 2001, 20 U.S.C. § 1111 (2008)NMS (2019). Retrieved from https://www.nms.org/

Obama, B. (2008, May 28). Full text of Obama's education speech. *The Denver Post.* Retrieved from https://www.denverpost.com/

Pinar, W. F. (2012). *What is curriculum theory?* (2nd ed.). New York, NY: Routledge.

Race to the Top (n.d.). Retrieved from https://obamawhitehouse.archives.gov/issues/education/k-12/race-to-the-top

Reading, A. (2012). *The mark inside: A perfect swindle, a cunning revenge, and a small history of the big con.* New York, NY: Alford A. Knopf

Satell, G. (2017, August 26). The untold story behind the quest to train 100,000 STEM teachers. Retrieved from https://www.inc.com/greg-satell/the-untold-story-behind-the-quest-to-train-100000-.html

Schubert, W. (2010). *Handbook of public pedagogy.* J. Sandlin, B. Schultz, & J. Burdick (Eds.). New York, NY: Routledge

Spencer, K. (2017, September 30). Silicon Valley's $300M donation to STEM education is not what it seems. *Salon.* Retrieved from https://www.salon.com/2017/09/30/silicon-valleys-300m-donation-to-stem-education-is-not-what-it-seems/

State of the Union (2011). Retrieved April 26, 2019, from https://obamawhitehouse.archives.gov/the-press-office/2011/01/25/remarks-president-state-union-address

State of the Union (2012). Retrieved May 15, 2019, from https://obamawhitehouse.archives.gov/the-press-office/2012/01/24/remarks-president-state-union-address

Strauss, V. (2015, December 9). Why it's worth re-reading George W. Bush's 2002 No Child Left Behind speech. *The Washington Post.* Retrieved from https://www.washingtonpost.com/news/answer-sheet/wp/2015/12/09/why-its-worth-re-reading-george-w-bushs-2002-no-child-left-behind-speech/?utm_term=.171febeb1d52

Theberge, L., & Media Institute. (1981). Crooks, conmen, and clowns: Businessmen in TV entertainment: A study. Washington, D.C.: The Institute.

The Associated Press. (2011, February 17). Obama meets with Facebook founder Mark Zuckerberg, headed to Oregon next. https://www.oregonlive.com. Retrieved from https://www.oregonlivcom/pacificnorthwestews/2011/02/obama_meets_with_facebook_founder_mark_zuckerberg_headed_to_oregon_next.html

United States Department of Education. (2010). College and career ready standards and assessments (pp. 11). Washington, D.C.: U.S. Department of Education.

U.S. News. (2019). Mapleton Expeditionary School of the Arts. Retrieved from
    https://www.usnews.com/education/best-high-schools/colorado/districts/mapleton-school-district-
    no-1-in-the-county-of-adams--st/mapleton-expeditionary-school-of-the-arts-4274

Chapter 9

Partnership for a Drug-Fiend America

David P. Owen, Jr.

> Cocaine cannot kill my pain
> Like a freight train through my vein
> Cocaine cannot kill my pain
> * * *
> Heroin is the only thing
> The only gift the darkness brings
> Heroin is the only thing
>
> —Steve Earle, "CCKMP," 1996

These words are lyrics from "CCKMP," or "Cocaine Cannot Kill My Pain," a song from Steve Earle's 1996 album *I Feel Alright*. Earle is hard to pin down as a musician for many people; he is too country for rock and too rock for country. That alone makes him difficult enough to market easily to the music loving public, but Earle is also a recovering illegal drug addict who has never really shied away from discussing his struggles with drugs in his music. He has even spent some time in prison for drug-related crimes. However, while Earle's personal life and physical health have certainly been affected by his drug use, his music career is still thriving. He puts out critically acclaimed albums every few years, and is widely cited as an influence by a variety of songwriters—me included. He has even been able to draw on his experiences with music and drugs in a sideline acting career, in the role of an addictions counselor on *The Wire* and a street musician on *Treme* (IMDb, 2019). To my knowledge, no concerned parents' groups or politicians are currently protesting the sales of his music in stores everywhere, or speaking out against his negative influence on America's youth, even though such groups can commonly be found in the news going after musical artists for discussing exactly the kinds of things Steve Earle does. In fact, one such speaker came to my school one

David P. Owen, Jr (ed.), *Field Theory: Curriculum Studies at Work*, 169–187.

spring for an attendance-mandatory lecture to teachers on the evil influences of hip hop and its pervasive drug references.

The case of Steve Earle is certainly only one example among many of our country's complicated relationship with drugs; in countless ways every day we passionately embrace, vehemently reject, or simply ignore drugs. Perhaps this inconsistency, this picking-and-choosing approach to fighting the drug culture can be explained by the fact that the United States is a country that has always been on drugs—literally and figuratively, legally and illegally—but has never really known what to do about it, if anything at all. One of our recent presidents, Barack Obama, has spoken openly about his drug use when he was younger, a fact that has endeared him to some (for honesty?) and ruined him for others (for honesty?). The president before Obama, George W. Bush, if the news reports are to be believed, is a recovering illegal drug user, a blemish on his record that has caused him almost no trouble politically. And the president before him, Bill Clinton, openly claimed that he tried to smoke marijuana in college, but could not manage to inhale—which promptly made him the laughingstock of teetotallers and stoners alike. Can a president who used to experiment with illegal drugs fight them? Should he or she? Should any of us? And if so, which drugs should we fight? We find ourselves as a country in an unusual, difficult position today when it comes to drugs, and that position is made even more complicated when we realize that many of the major forces that have contributed to the proliferation, sale, and use of drugs in America—Romanticism, the cult of the maverick, modernism, and capitalism—are forces that also give America its identity. Could it be that a drug-free America is no America at all?

If I told people that drugs were available on almost every corner in my town, and that a significant number of our businesses had at least some connection to drug sales, and that my school was full of drugs—those people would feel sorry for me, and ask me why I have not moved. That is, until I clarified that I was talking about the weed-like spread of CVS and Walgreens, our city's reliance on and support for at least five hospitals and a medical college, and the *prescription* drugs my students use. The point here is that we have *legal* drugs and *illegal* drugs in the United States, the first of which we hold as a point of pride and the second of which we treat as a disease to be eradicated—often by the first kind of drugs.

On top of that enigma, it is not even clear what we mean by "drugs." We often call the legal kind "medicine" and the illegal kind "drugs," but we still refer to "drugstores" and "druggists" and the legal and powerful "drug industry," so that distinction is not particularly useful. We sometimes say illegal drugs are something like "artificial stimulants," or "synthetic" or "controlled" substances, but that is obviously problematic too. First of all, many "medicines" are synthetic substances, and many illicit drugs are made from plants that grow naturally. And anyway, as Sadie Plant (1999) points out in Writing on Drugs, "a vast range of neurotransmitting chemicals are already present in a nervous system that does, in fact, have its own opiates, its own cocaine, its own version of every psychoactive compound that can affect the brain" (p. 195). In short, even though many illegal drugs are made in labs, they replicate chemicals we already have in our brains normally, albeit in smaller doses. Besides, air condition and clothing are "unnatural," and no one is trying to eradicate those (thank goodness). We also talk often about the "harmful" effects of illegal drugs, even though we know that legal drugs can be just as harmful if abused; we also do not outlaw other "dangerous" things like overeating, automobiles, tanning beds, or MMA—not to mention war.

If we ignore the anti-drug commercials that claim that marijuana will make a teenager shoot his friend or run over a little girl on a bicycle and that buying drugs illegally supports terrorism, the difference between legal drugs and illegal drugs is largely the law, and a law which we have not always had. According to Marcus Boon (2002), the distinction between illegal and legal drugs "involves a dialectic of law and transgression that did not exist before World War I" (p. 7). The law he mentions is the Harrison Narcotics Act of 1914, which required the manufacture, sale, and distribution of "opium or coca leaves, their salts, derivatives, or preparations" (Chapter 1) to be taxed and regulated. This law was expanded over the years to include a variety of substances and is the basis for the War on Drugs legislation today. And while some of these substances are certainly dangerous, and I am certainly not arguing for their legalization, I think we must admit that it would be difficult to satisfactorily explain, for example, why alcohol and cigarettes are permitted and marijuana is not. We cannot forget, either, that some of our most demonized drugs were given to us in America by some of our most revered, successful companies and institutions: Bayer gave us heroin (Plant, 1999, p. 6), Merck gave us cocaine (p. 65) with help from Coca-Cola (p. 71), and morphine is still used in hospitals around the country every day. Today, though we may not know exactly why, we do know that when it comes to drugs, some things are legal, and some are illegal, and some (as in the case of our current opioid crisis) begin legal and then become illegal—the legislative equivalent of a parent who ends discussions with "because I said so."

But what is our fascination with drugs in America, anyway? Especially when it comes to illegal drugs, and the sometimes very stiff punishments for their possession or distribution and clear physical toll, why do we bother? These questions are not easy to answer, either. It seems that "different drugs have different effects" (Boon, 2002, p. 9), drugs affect people differently (see Baudelaire and De Quincey's disagreement on wine), and people use drugs for a variety of reasons. Freud took cocaine to understand his subconscious (p. 183), Balzac (p. 175) and Kerouac (p. 215) took speed to fuel writing binges, and the CIA experimented in hopes of finding a truth serum (Plant, 1999, p. 125). James Salant, writer of the drug memoir *Leaving Dirty Jersey* (2007) is not sure why he started crystal meth, listing "pent-up teenage rebellion," lack of parental attention, and the example of his older brother as possible causes (p. 19), and he writes later about a vague "pain," and "shooting drugs to swallow it up" (p. 229). Another writer who recounts her addictions, Elizabeth Wurtzel, says in *More, Now, Again: A Memoir of Addiction* (2002) that her drug use seems to stem from a wish to escape her own self-loathing: "Quite simply, it makes me feel okay to be me. Here is how I feel not on drugs: I hate me" (p. 25). Some people also try to escape physical pain; for example, Thomas De Quincey writes in what became the western world's first drug memoir, *Confessions of an English Opium-Eater* (1821/2003), that he first resorted to opium to help with his stomach pains and sleeplessness (p. 21). William S. Burroughs claims in *Junky* (1953/2003) that he ended up a drug addict simply because he did not have "strong motivations in any other direction"; he says he "tried it [junk] as a matter of curiosity" and "ended up hooked" (p. xxxviii). Still others seem to turn to drugs to escape some of life's harsh realities. As Langston Hughes recounts in "Junior Addict" (1967), "It's easier to get dope / than it is to get a job" (p. 13).

One writer, though, seems to find something particularly American about drug use. Though many dismiss Hunter S. Thompson's *Fear and Loathing in Las Vegas* (1971) as the ravings of a drug-addled madman, showboating his irresponsible, often reprehensible behavior for an American public always eager for vicarious thrills, this summation of the work is far too simple. Thompson even admits in the jacket copy that only a "lunatic would write a thing like this and then claim it was true" (p. 210). And while many will no doubt be tempted to write this statement off as a liability-shirking excuse, an observant reader will notice that there is something decidedly literary about Thompson's wild tale; indeed, there are places where the narrator is suddenly far too lucid in his ranting about our culture, and speaks with far too much force and clarity for his supposed condition. Probably people of all nations in all of history have used drugs in some way; however, what Thompson may be causing us to consider is whether or not America's habit is one that it can kick. There is a reason, maybe, that Thompson sums up his "assignment" in Las Vegas thusly: "The American Dream. Horatio Alger gone mad on drugs in Las Vegas. Do it *now*: pure Gonzo journalism" (p. 12).

Once this statement by Thompson registers, other comments on America seem to rise up out of the illicit fog. Perhaps most tellingly, there is the mission statement agreed upon by the author and his accompanying attorney:

> But our trip was different. It was a classic affirmation of everything right and true and decent in the national character. It was a gross, physical salute to the fantastic *possibilities* of life in this country—but only for those with true grit. And we were chock full of that. (p. 18)

Later, we hear him describe the scene at the Circus Circus, where the "Forty Flying Carazito Brothers" are doing a trapeze act with "four muzzled Wolverines and the Six Nymphet Sisters from San Diego," a scene which he sums up with "this madness goes on and on, but nobody seems to notice" (p. 46). Perhaps they do not notice because they, too, are in search of the "American Dream, that vision of the Big Winner somehow emerging from the last-minute pre-dawn chaos of a stale Vegas casino" (p. 57). In Las Vegas, Thompson says, "there was madness in any direction, at any hour" (p. 67) in a city where "everybody's guilty" and the "only crime is getting caught" (p. 72); he adds that "psychedelics are almost irrelevant in a town where you can wander into a casino any time of the day or night and witness the crucifixion of a gorilla" (p. 190). Eventually, not only do we realize that no one really notices the frankly unbelievable things Thompson and his lawyer are doing, but when they finally end up at the Drug Convention in chapters 6 and 7, we actually start to think of our anti-heroes as the sensible ones in the room. We agree that it was probably "easy enough to sit there with a head full of mescaline and listen to hour after hour of irrelevant gibberish" since the officers in attendance "didn't know mescaline from macaroni" (p. 143).

What Thompson makes us do, if we are paying attention, is consider who is right, who is thinking clearly and who is mad, and what America is. Is America something to be defended against the likes of Thompson, or is it something to be protected from the idiots in the Drug Convention? What about the gamblers outside the Drug Convention, understanding America as the Great Land of Get-Rich-Quick—after all, is the coin-in-the-slot short cut to happiness really that different from the pill-in-the-mouth method? Or could it be that the good people who stay away from Las Vegas altogether are the true Americans? Who has it right? The answer, of course, is all of the above. Baudelaire says in *On Wine and Hashish* (1851/2002) that "sobriety diminishes, discriminates, and says no; drunkenness expands, unites, says yes" (p. xiv), but America says both.

Romanticism

In Xanadu did Kubla Khan
A stately pleasure dome decree:
Where Alph, the sacred river, ran
Through caverns measureless to man
Down to a sunless sea.

—Coleridge, "Kubla Khan," 1816

One example of the blurry line between sobriety and drunkenness in America is our Romanticism. The birth of our country only slightly predates the Romantic movement in England and western Europe inspired in large part by the French Revolution, and many of our early, formative documents carry elements of that same spirit. Our own Transcendental movement would follow soon after the highpoint of Romanticism in Europe, and would pick up many of its major themes and ideas from its Old World cousin. And while the United States would soon after be divided by war and then swept into the industrial age and other ways of looking at the world and how to live in it, many aspects of Romanticism seem to have been tangled into the root structure of the American consciousness.

Of course, Romanticism in Europe also meant the flourishing of a drug culture and the literature that would openly discuss it for the first time, and this aspect of the movement seems to have made its way across the ocean as well. As Boon (2002) reports, much of England at this time took opium as a medicine, but also as "one whose nonmedical effects might also be enjoyed" (p. 31). This seems especially true of the most prominent Romantic poets—William Blake excepted (p. 12). In fact, Coleridge seems in many ways to be a sort of linchpin in a movement that did not use drugs more than the rest of the populace, but did speak "much more lyrically" (p. 31) about their experiences with drugs. It is important to note that many of these writers, Coleridge and De Quincey for example, often at least claimed "medical reasons for their first use of drugs" (p. 32) rather than the kind of decadence we associate with writers and artists on drugs today. However, what we often see in their work is less a simple health regimen than something more like a passionate love affair with drugs, full of pains and joys not found elsewhere. In De Quincey's landmark *Confessions* (1821/2003), the author calls opium "a panacea [...] for all human woes," and wonders that "happiness might now be bought for a penny, and carried in the waistcoat pocket" (p. 44). Baudelaire describes the experience with hashish a little later (1851/2002) in even more glowing terms, saying that under its spell "all philosophical problems are solved," that "all contradiction has become unity," and that "man has qualified as God" (p. 23)—and he says that he likes wine even better.

Both writers also go on to detail the great pains their drug addictions cause them, and do not gloss over the ugly effects of drug use, but none of this is anything worth repeating here. It may have been news then, but it certainly is not today. Everyone knows that drug users claim great ecstasies and horrible torments in their experiences; we have heard these stories countless times by now. What is still interesting, though, is the intellectual side of drug use, the promise it seems to offer of something that has not been experienced, of life that has not been lived. A century after Baudelaire, Aldous Huxley (1954) was still following the Romantic quest for *something more*, even borrowing a title from Blake for his *Doors of Perception*, which recounts his experience with mescaline. He says that he hoped through drugs to "change [his] ordinary mode of consciousness" in order to be able to know "what the visionary, the medium, even the mystic were talking about" (p. 14). He wanted what he thought Blake and van Gogh had; he wanted to see "what the artist is congenitally equipped to see all the time" (p. 33).

However, the curious cases of Blake and van Gogh aside, many of our greatest artists also thought they might not have access to Huxley's place where "all things are perceived as infinite and holy" (p. 43) without the help of drugs. Coleridge is a perfect example. A brilliant thinker and talented writer whose work has been both enduring and influential, even Coleridge thought that there were realms beyond his reach, or at least while he was sober, as the legend surrounding his poem "Kubla Khan" (1816) shows us. The poem is nearly unintelligible, full of contrary images that frustrate all attempts to reconcile them and characters and events that spring from nowhere and disappear just as quickly. But the poem, in this case, may not be the point. Published with it was the famous explanation that he had composed no less than "from two to three hundred lines" (p. 729), the whole poem entire, in the throes of a deep opium dream. However, so the story goes, he was interrupted by "a person on business from Porlock" (p. 729), and lost all but a few fragments that amounted to the final, published 54 lines.

This is where America comes in. The story with Coleridge, and the United States, is not about what is, or what was, or even what will be—it is about what *could* be. This is a country founded on possibilities that might never be actualized, on the idea of what we might accomplish if only we could get beyond our million little men from Porlock, those pesky realities so hard to match up to the Romantic ideals we find in our dreams. We are all familiar with the paradox of our earliest days, full of ecstatic, Romantic pronouncements that "all men are created equal" and are endowed "with inherent and inalienable rights" (Jefferson, 1776, p. 37) made by men who owned slaves. We have heard Walt Whitman proclaim in 1855 that "Americans of all nations at any time upon the earth have probably the fullest poetical nature," and call America a "teeming nation of nations" in which the President takes "off his hat" to the people "and not they to him" (p. 1001) a mere six years before much of America's ugliness was laid bare for the world to see. We wrote our country into existence founded on promises and ideals which no nation had yet brought to fruition, and which we still have not; we, not unlike Huxley, wondered if there might be *something more*, and are still hoping for it. Perhaps Americans have always been drawn to the Romantic possibilities that drugs offer for the same reasons that so many writers and artists have been drawn to them, and for the same reasons that Thompson set his search for America in Las Vegas; we have always been, as Boon (2002) says De Quincey's drug tale is, a "fabrication that inhabits a no man's land between fiction and reality" (p. 62). We are a country birthed in the Romantic poetry of freedom, and equality, and *possibility*, even though we have always known that "the poet puts truth in abeyance and leaves it hanging there" (Plant, 1999, p. 23). In short, we have always been a country on drugs, even when we were not on drugs.

The Cult of the Maverick

First of all I wan' thank my connect
The most important person with all due respect
Thanks for the duffle bag, the brown paper bag
The Nike shoe box for holding all this cash

—Jay-Z, "Roc Boys (And the Winner Is)," 2007

The kind of "drug story" writing pioneered by De Quincey, Coleridge, Baudelaire and many others (notably Robert Louis Stevenson's 1886 *Strange Case of Dr. Jekyll and Mr. Hyde*) has never died off, and has perhaps become its own literary industry in America, flourishing with the Beats and continuing through today. Writers like Salant and Wurtzel are following in the footsteps of people like Thompson, who are in turn following people like Kerouac, Ginsberg, and Burroughs. In addition to our Romanticism, perhaps this kind of writing is so successful in America because of our love for the maverick, the outlaw, the law-breaker who is not quite a criminal; the man who lives by his own code because he knows that code is right and does not care what anyone else says about it. Though not all mavericks use drugs, drug users fit so easily into these roles because of drugs' complicated place in legal history; drug crimes are often seen as "victimless" crimes, at least when it comes to possession or even distribution in some cases, and so they can overlap with the maverick individualism on which we Americans so often pride ourselves.

Most high school students are proof of this love of the maverick. The "cool" guy in class is stereotypically rebellious, disrespectful to "the Man," "different," and he often uses drugs, or is at least rumored to. Students also love the mavericks we read about, and come alive to the vicarious thrills of people who dared, drugs or no drugs, to do what they cannot, or do not even want to do themselves; I had a student one year who refused to read anything I assigned, but could not be torn away from a book about crank he picked out himself. My seniors often hate *Beowulf* unless I play up the trash-talking standoff between Unferth and the hero (2000, lines 499-606), and emphasize Beowulf's ridiculous choice to face Grendel bare-handed. And all of my students, without fail, perk up when any biographical information in textbooks mention drug use (Coleridge is a favorite). Teachers are not immune, either; who knows how many students have been taught by now that Robert Frost's "The Road Not Taken" (1992) can be paraphrased to be a maverick manifesto, to say something like "go your own way in life if you want to be successful," completely ignoring Frost's subtle clues that the narrator is just lying to cover up his own confusion about how things worked out the way they did.

For literary mavericks on drugs, we have no shortage of examples like Dean Moriarty's wild-eyed, untameable enthusiasm and energy in *On The Road* (1955), Burroughs's shoulder-shrugging callousness towards the whole bleak ugliness of the drug culture in *Junky* (1953/2003), and Salant's comment in *Leaving Dirty Jersey* on his first drug arrest that "I was being toughened, and I wanted more" (2007, p. 22). But we do not have to go anywhere near books to find evidence of our love for the maverick in America. Popular music, for example, is virtually held up as an industry by it. Hip hop, rock, and country music, three of our most dominant genres, meet at a crossroads marked as much by the maverick as by the blues—and come to think of it, was there a blues singer who was not also a maverick?

The maverick is just as present in our popular film industry as well, and not just as Tom Cruise's character nickname in *Top Gun* (1986). The quote from Jay-Z above is not only representative of well-worn hip hop trends, but it is also notable because it is part of a song called "Roc Boys (And the Winner Is)" on an album inspired by the film *American Gangster* (2007), about a drug dealer's rise and fall. This film is one of countless maverick stories in American film history about mob bosses, blunt-force action heroes out for revenge, impossibly clever and lovable thieves of all sorts, and lone-wolf tough-guy cowboys, and a quick glance at any major movie star's resume on the Internet Movie Database will reveal this formula for Hollywood success. Mel Gibson, for example, made his career playing mavericks in films like *What Women Want* (2000), *The Patriot* (2000), *Payback* (1999), the *Lethal Weapon* series (1987, 1989, 1992, 1998), *Conspiracy Theory* (1997), *Braveheart* (1995), and the *Mad Max* series (1979, 1981, 1985). He was even in a film called *Maverick* (1994). And John Wayne, maybe our Greatest American Hero of our Greatest American Genre, is a Western maverick example almost too obvious to describe, especially in his famous role as Rooster Cogburn in *True Grit* (Wallis & Hathaway, 1969). Mattie is a young woman out to avenge her father's death, and LeBeouf might be a vaunted Texas Ranger, but everyone knows that that story belongs to Rooster Cogburn, the alcoholic mess of a U.S. Marshal barely more law-abiding than the men he hunts so viciously. Not only do we love Wayne's Rooster Cogburn, but we remade the film in 2010 (Coen & Coen), with Jeff Bridges in the Rooster role, and lavished it with even more critical and popular acclaim.

The maverick has been no strange figure in our politics, either, though it could perhaps be argued that Donald Trump has taken this personality characteristic farther than most have dared, especially in such a high office. Indeed, our first act as a country was an announcement of rebellion, written and signed by mavericks who would go on to frame a new country run by mavericks. For example, William Carlos Williams (1925) paints George Washington as a take-on-all-comers, classic tough guy, setting the mold for the Great American Leader: "Here was a man of tremendous vitality buried in a massive frame and under a rather stolid and untractable exterior which the ladies somewhat feared, I fancy" (p. 140). He even explains Washington's reputation for truth-telling by saying that "it was a good scratching to him to take it on and see himself through. He knew he would come through" (p. 141). Another politician, Huey Long, had a maverick story we loved to hear so much that its fictionally enhanced version became Robert Penn Warren's Pulitzer Prize-winning *All the King's Men* (1946), and we have even paid to see a film version of it—more than once. It is perhaps no wonder, then, that Susan Faludi comments in *The Terror Dream* (2007) that our leadership atmosphere after the 9/11 attacks became a "Wild West stage set" (p. 5). It is also maybe a little clearer, in considering our love of the maverick, why many people voted for George W. Bush rather than John Kerry in 2004 (mavericks do not windsurf, for one). And also, maybe, why a country that legally disapproves of certain drugs still elects presidents who used to do them.

Modernism

I want a new drug
One that won't make me sick
One that won't make me crash my car
Or make me feel three feet thick

—Huey Lewis, "I Want a New Drug," 1983

In addition to Romanticism, and our love of the maverick, we cannot forget another crucial part of the American consciousness that strengthens our ties to drug culture, particularly in terms of production of new drugs: our tremendous, modernist pride. Why experiment with drugs, and continually develop new ones for further experimentation? Because we can. We are smart, we are brave, and we have the resources. And it could just be that producing new drugs and taking them will make us stronger, healthier, more focused, more productive Americans and a better country altogether. In fact, we can do all kinds of things people can hardly imagine until we pull them off. We built a free country from the ground up, defeated the Nazis, outlasted the Soviets, put a man on the moon, managed to dominate the world economy and its pop culture, and generally grew to think of ourselves as the unstoppable, undeniable "greatest country on Earth." We also think that as long as we keep our collective foot on the pedal, this position of ours will last into eternity. And we will accept no less; just think of the national shame when we do not "win" the medal count at the Olympic Games! To say that the stakes are high for us is an understatement; our national identity is lashed tightly to being bigger, faster, bolder, and richer, and if we need drugs, even sometimes illegal drugs, to stay that way, or if some of our new "wonder drugs" turn out to have pretty nasty side effects—well, we just might not talk about that. At best, we may make some half-hearted show of concern about our drug issues, like busting teenagers who smoke marijuana or harassing the professional athletes we demand impossible performances from. Like Thompson says, in America, the only crime is getting caught.

The recent technological advances that are both products and engines of our modernism are obvious everywhere we look in America (even if we certainly buy more than we build), with the rapid proliferation in recent years of smart-everything, computer-as-whatever-you-can-think-of, whole-world-in-my-pocket-right-now devices. All of these things, and many others, help us work faster and hopefully more efficiently—I am not writing this by hand, after all. Speed and efficiency, in fact, are acceptable reasons to do anything, especially with young people; our new wave communication and research practices may not be better for us in some ways than their "old wave" counterparts, but they are certainly faster. With a mobile phone, we do not have to wait until we get home to call someone (like the dark ages of twenty-five years ago), and we can quickly be found anywhere, or find anyone else; email and a million other "social media" apps cut the "snail mail" wait time from two or three days to an instant, GPS systems in our cars or phones call out directions to us while we drive—in short (pun intended), we keep moving faster, faster, faster. We may have lost some depth, patience, privacy, and sense of direction— and that's just in these examples—but we have certainly picked up speed. In the scientific and medical fields, we also insist that our new technologies help us work better and better, too. For example, we have imaging technology that sees better than our eyes do and conveniently translates that information into shapes and colors we can experience (Ihde, 2002, p. 47). Paul Churchland (1995) also says that "medical diagnosis is another domain where artificial networks are sure to do better than humans" (p. 303). Eugene Thacker (2005) even reports—notice the techno-speak— that scientists may soon be able to "*reprogram* the body on the cellular-molecular level to accomplish [cell and tissue] regeneration on its own" (p. 294, my italics).

In a world where are our technologies are quickly starting to exceed our natural abilities to keep up with their pace, we have often decided that drugs can be an answer. Even Baudelaire, writer of romantic prose that he is, claims some pretty modernist, productive reasons for his love of wine, asserting that it "elevates the will," it is "a physical aid," it is "hard-working"; as he sums up, "wine is for the ordinary people who work hard and deserve to drink it" (1851/2002, p. 27). And really, as Boon (2002) reminds us, drugs are just technologies as well, and so using them as a response to technological advances is fairly logical (p. 171). In conventional medicine, the drug answer is obvious and accepted, if often unconsidered critically. In the case of so many health conditions these days, we could make lifestyle changes, participate in physical rehabilitation or treatment programs, have surgery—or take pills, which are the fastest and easiest treatment of all, or at least seem that way, like the Google of the medical world. This attitude is not nearly as new as Google, though. While television may be flooded during nearly every commercial break with ads for supposedly new breakthroughs in medicine, we have been increasingly looking to drugs in the western world, especially in America, to cure what ails us for over a hundred years now. Each new "wonder drug" today has a predecessor we also pinned our medical hopes to; let us not forget that Freud used cocaine to help his patients at the turn of the twentieth century before he and Coca-Cola were convinced of its dangers, and people like Timothy Leary (Plant, 1999, p. 132) hoped to do the same with drugs like LSD in the 1960s.

Lest we think that these doctors are simply renegades, we should remember that interest in drugs for a variety of productive purposes is not limited to a small group of people, or even a type. In fact, Boon (2002) even says that "from the 1930s to the 1960s," one of the primary sections of the populace exploring psychedelics was "people of conservative or right-wing orientation" (p. 258), some of them in very powerful positions. For example, the CIA became interested in LSD and other new drugs for help in interrogation during the Cold War (Plant, 1999, p. 125), and they were not the only ones seeking a drug advantage on the world stage. Plant also tells us that soldiers "entangled with advanced technologies of war" (p. 122) from Britain, Germany, and Japan, particularly pilots, were given amphetamines to help them keep up with the new speed of their duties. Even world leaders like Hitler, Churchill, and Kennedy turned to speed to manage a quickly changing world (p. 123). In other words, Kerouac and Kennedy both worked on speed; the culture and counter-culture in America were both led by people fuelled by amphetamines. Even those of us on the metaphorical sidelines of this drug culture look down our noses at "speed freaks" while we load up on caffeine or "energy drinks" to get us through the day.

This pervasiveness of stimulants, for example, may actually be fitting, since as Plant says, "all the ups and downs, the highs and lows of drugs are highs and lows of speed" (p. 217). When we need to go faster, be more productive, we can use drugs; and if we fail to keep up, or feel overwhelmed, we can use drugs to slow down, too. What the industrial age did to drugs in America, primarily, is turn them into a tool like any other, a conception of drugs that has endured into the twenty-first century—legal and illegal alike. What is the difference, really, aside from the law, between fuelling Kerouac with amphetamines to increase his productivity and prescribing a child Ritalin to increase his, a practice whose ill effects inspired Dr. Peter Breggin to write an entire book in order to combat it, with *Talking Back to Ritalin* (2001)? Wurtzel brings home the paradox of our legal/illegal drug culture in *More, Now, Again: A Memoir of Addiction* (2002). The book begins with, "The first time I took Ritalin I had been clean for four months. It was prescribed because I had trouble focusing" (p. 15). By page 34, she is snorting it like the cocaine-cousin it is. We have problems, and we want drugs to fix them. Maybe a doctor prescribes them, and maybe he does not. Either way, like the song says, we want a new drug.

Capitalism

The best things in life are free
But you can give them to the birds and bees
I need money

—Barrett Strong, "I Want Money," 1959

Of these four aspects of the American consciousness that complicate our country's relationship with drugs, capitalism is by far the most obvious, the most pervasive, and likely the most dangerous. After all, there is a way to see a drug pusher as an entrepreneur of a different stripe, and it is no secret that much of the Kennedy fortune was made in bootlegging alcohol. Max Weber argued in *The Protestant Ethic and the Spirit of Capitalism* that our current attitude of "acquisition as the ultimate purpose in life" (1905, p. 53) can be traced to an interpretation of the protestant values that are at our roots, and capitalism today seems about as easy to extract from our country's identity as "In God We Trust" would be from the dollar bill. To delineate all of the ways capitalism affects our daily lives and our thinking as individuals and as a nation would take books, not pages, and would be largely unnecessary for anyone who lives here. It should suffice to say that everything is for sale in America, and everyone is buying.

This has been the case for quite a while, but we seem to find new ways to do business every day. We live in houses, not homes, and there are entire television networks now devoted to increasing the monetary value of the building in which we (temporarily) reside. Our educations, too, are largely a matter of exchange: when we are young we take tests in exchange for grades, which we then combine with a considerable sum of money and exchange for a college degree, which we will then exchange for the opportunity to make more money. When we get out of college and decide to move on from our "vintage" rock band t-shirts, we can sell them on eBay or Craigslist or create our own internet boutique. And if times really get tough, we can even sell body parts on the sly; Waldby and Mitchell (2006) tell us in their book *Tissue Economies* that a kidney today could bring as much as "$10,000 to $20,000" (p. 172). And let us be nice to those around us, just in case: the human body, if "dead for less than 15 hours," can be worth as much as "$50,000 on the open market" (Sharp, 2007, p. 43).

Today, we must be good businessmen to be good Americans, or at least buy a lot of things. As Reynolds (2003) puts it, "being a good citizen means being a good consumer" (p. 99). Our own President Bush solidified this when he urged us to spend our money to help prop up the economy after 9/11—to be American, buy American. And just in case buying new cars or clothes did not make us feel well enough, we could always buy drugs, which GlaxoSmithKline, among others, was happy to point out. Angell (2005) reports in *The Truth About Drug Companies* that after 9/11, "the company launched an ambitious campaign" promoting their drug Paxil for "generalized anxiety disorder" (p. 88). And here, right where consumer culture and drug culture combine in the form of the pharmaceutical industry, is where things get really messy.

Angell reminds us that the pharmaceutical industry "has been far and away the most profitable in the United States" for over two decades (p. xxiii), and also that it has a large and powerful lobby in Washington (p. 198), which means that it is likely to stay that way. But, given our already discussed love of Romanticism, the maverick, and modernism, this should be no surprise. After all, if we did not like the industry's product so much, it would not be nearly as successful. It is unclear, however, how thin the line is in this case between really, really liking a product so much we want to have it all the time, and being addicted to it. Add to that the pharmaceutical industry's possibly shady advertising practices (p. 117), ethically problematic relationships with doctors (p. 130), and "free samples" programs with patients (p. 262), and we may have some reason to be suspicious and worried. When people use drugs to fill their needs or solve their problems or simply to feel better, and they feel like the drugs work, they will come back. This seems to be true whether the "druggist" wears a white coat or stalks a street corner.

Ritalin is a prime example of why we might have some things to fear from this confluence of our interests. "Brand loyalty," according to Jenkins (2006) in *Convergence Culture*, is like the "holy grail" for corporations (p.

72), because it means a steady consumer base that is unlikely to go elsewhere or support conflicting products. In other words, if the brand loyalty is strong enough, a company can be almost guaranteed a certain level of safety and success. Jenkins points out that the logical place to establish this relationship is with children, and laments that "marketers have turned our children into walking billboards" (p. 138) who not only buy loyally, but actively encourage others to do so as well. This is pretty simple, and pretty logical, business strategy; but when we give our kids drugs like Ritalin, we might be doing much the same thing, with much worse consequences than kids overspending for jeans to get the right brand.

If Ritalin really were not addictive, really had no side effects, and really did help children succeed in school, even then we would still be teaching them that drugs were the answer to life's problems. What must it do to a child's self-image when we repeatedly insist that these drugs "only help him be more like himself," for example—that it is the drugs that make him acceptable, and likable, and successful? And with Ritalin, we are doing far more damage, because it "not only fails to improve learning and academic performance, it impairs mental function" (Breggin, 2001, p. 130), and it does have harmful side effects (p. 32). Parents worried about marijuana being a "gateway drug" should probably be more worried about Ritalin, which "encourages lifelong dependence" (p. 12). This is largely because, as Wurtzel discovered when she crushed it and snorted it, "the effects of methamphetamine, like those of cocaine, are largely indistinguishable from Ritalin" (p. 104). With maybe as many as "7–10% or more of America's school-age children" (p. 3) on drugs like Ritalin, it could be that there will never be such a thing as a "drug-free school zone," no matter how many signs we put up.

It sometimes seems, especially with our increased use of drugs like Ritalin, as if we are heading for the kind of society described in Huxley's *Brave New World* (1932); that if we are not careful and conscious when it comes to our reliance on and relationship with drugs, we could end up in a world in which people are "so conditioned" through drug use that "they practically can't help behaving as they ought to behave. And if anything should go wrong, there's *soma*" (p. 220). And as for our War on Drugs, it does not really seem to be a war we even want to win. That is not to say, however, that fighting it is not good for us in some ways; in fact, our current drug culture offers us a little of everything. Those who want to try to open the "doors of perception" can probably find what they need easy enough. For those who want to be mavericks instead of just watching them on the big screen, there are plenty of drugs just taboo enough to make a reputation, with a relatively small risk of serious punishment if people are clever and careful. For our modernist needs, we can load up on energy drinks, or Ritalin, or both, and never have so much as a scrape with the law. And there is certainly plenty of money to go around in serving all of these needs, including making authors wealthy who write about their drug experiences. Even the politicians and the straight-edge crowd, who publicly denounce all such drug use, have the law and "Say No to Drugs" campaigns to reassure them, and to make them feel better. And the wheels of America, the land of yes and no, the paradoxical land of everything, keep on turning.

It is no wonder that Phillip K. Dick marveled at the terrible, awe-inspiring, circular efficiency of it all in *A Scanner Darkly* (1977), in which the American everyman main character Arctor-Fred-Bruce (he's eventually not sure of his name, either) is all of these things in one life. It is a story of only victims; if the villains exist, they are faceless, and if the terrible tragedy can be thwarted, or even slowed, it is not at all clear where we should begin. When we are such complex parts of both problem and solution, hope is hard to find, and the puzzle that is the American relationship with drugs baffles—maybe there is a pill that could clear our heads? And so Dick's protagonist does the best things he can think of (though thinking of it gets increasingly hard), and in the process encapsulates in one life the gamut of drug experience: he is the high-seeking druggie, the successful dealer, the undercover narcotics agent, the tragic rehab patient, and finally the still-productive near-vegetable who we realize, slowly, will spend what is left of his days helping to cultivate the very drug that defined and wrecked his life; to help the people at "New-Path" in their efforts to build "their civilization within the chaos" (p. 265)—which is as good a description of America today as any. It is a story that ought to be sobering.

References

Angell, M. (2005). *The truth about drug companies.* New York, NY: Random House.
Baudelaire, C. (2002). *On wine and hashish* (A. Brown, Trans.). London, UK: Hesperus Press Limited. (Original work published 1851)
Beowulf (S. Heaney, Trans.). (2000). New York, NY: W. W. Norton & Company.
Boon, M. (2002). *The road of excess: A history of writers on drugs.* Cambridge, MA: Harvard University Press.
Burroughs, W. S. (2003). *Junky: 50th anniversary definitive edition.* New York, NY: Penguin Books. (Original work published 1953)
Breggin, P. R. (2001). *Talking back to Ritalin: What doctors aren't telling you about stimulants and ADHD.* Cambridge, MA: Perseus Publishing.

Churchland, P. M. (1995). *The engine of reason, the seat of the soul: A philosophical journey into the brain*. Cambridge, MA: The MIT Press.

Coen, E., & Coen, J. (Producers and Directors). (2010). *True Grit* [Motion Picture]. United States: Paramount Pictures.

Coleridge, S. T. (1816). Kubla khan. In A. K. Mellor & R. E. Matlak, (Eds.), *British literature 1780-1830* (p. 729). Fort Worth, TX: Harcourt Brace College Publishers.

De Quincey, T. (2003). *Confessions of an English opium-eater*. New York, NY: Penguin Books. (Original work published 1821)

Dick, P. K. (1977). *A scanner darkly*. New York, NY: Vintage Books.

Earle, S. (1996). CCKMP. On *I feel alright* [CD]. Burbank, CA: Warners Bros.

Faludi, S. (2007). *The terror dream: Fear and fantasy in post-9/11 America*. New York, NY: Metropolitan Books.

Frost, R. (1992). *Selected poems*. New York, NY: Gramercy Books.

Gordy, B., & Bradford, J. (1959). I want money [Recorded by Barrett Strong]. Detroit, MI: Anna Records.

Harrison Narcotics Tax Act, 1914.
    https://www.naabt.org/documents/Harrison_Narcotics_Tax_Act_1914.pdf

Hayes, C. & Lewis, H. (1983). I want a new drug [Recorded by Huey Lewis and the News]. On *Sports* [CD]. London, UK: Chrysalis.

Hughes, L. (1932). *The panther and the lash*. New York, NY: Vintage Classics.

Huxley, A. (1932). *Brave new world*. New York, NY: HarperCollins Publishers, Inc.Ihde, D. (2002). *Bodies in technology*. Minneapolis, MN: The University of Minnesota Press.

IMDb. (2019). Mel Gibson. Retrieved 16 March, 2019, from http://www.imdb.com/name/nm0000154/

IMDb. (2019). Steve Earle. Retrieved 16 March, 2019, from http://www.imdb.com/name/nm 0247351/

Jay-Z. (2007). Roc boys (and the winner is…). On *American gangster* [CD]. New York, NY: Roc-A-Fella

Jefferson, T. (1776). A declaration by the representatives of the United States of America, in general congress assembled. In W. L. Andrews (Ed.), *The literature of the American south: A Norton anthology* (pp. 37-41). New York, NY: W. W. Norton & Company.

Jenkins, H. (2006). *Convergence culture: Where old and new media collide*. New York, NY: New York University Press.

Kerouac, J. (1955). *On the road*. New York, NY: Penguin Books.

Plant, S. (1999). *Writing on drugs*. New York, NY: Picador USA.

Reynolds, W. M. (2003). *Curriculum: A river runs through it*. New York, NY: Peter Lang.

Salant, J. (2007). *Leaving dirty Jersey: A crystal meth memoir*. New York, NY: Simon Spotlight Entertainment.

Scott, R., Grazer, B., Whitaker, J., Zaillian, S., & Pileggi, N. (Producers), & Scott, R. (Director). (2007). *American gangster* [Motion picture]. United States: Universal Pictures.

Sharp, L. (2007). *Bodies, commodities, & biotechnologies: Death, mourning, & scientific desire in the realm of human organ transfer*. New York, NY: Columbia University Press.

Simpson, D., & Bruckheimer, J. (Producers), & Scott, T. (Director). (1986). *Top gun* [Motion picture]. United States: Paramount Pictures.

Stevenson, R. L. (1886). *Strange case of Dr. Jekyll and Mr. Hyde*. Oxford, UK: Oxford University Press.

Thacker, E. (2005). *The global genome: Biotechnology, politics, and culture*. Cambridge, MA: The MIT Press.

Thompson, H. S. (1971). *Fear and loathing in Las Vegas*. New York, NY: Modern Library.

Waldby, C., & Mitchell, R. (2006). *Tissue economies: Blood, organs, and cell lines in late capitalism*. Durham, NC: Duke University Press.

Wallis, H. B. (Producer), & Hathaway, H. (Director). (1969). *True Grit* [Motion Picture]. United States: Paramount Pictures.

Warren, R. P. (1946). *All the king's men*. Orlando, FL: Harcourt, Inc.

Weber, M. (1958). *The protestant ethic and the spirit of capitalism* (T. Parsons, Trans.).
Mineola, NY: Dover Publications, Inc.

Whitman, W. (1855). Preface. In D. McQuade (Ed.), *The Harper American literature* (pp. 1001-1014).
New York, NY: Harper & Row, Publishers.

Williams, W. C. (1925). *In the American grain*. New York, NY: New Directions.

Wurtzel, E. (2002). *More, now, again: A memoir of addiction*. New York, NY: Simon & Schuster.

Chapter 10

I'm Not Here, This Isn't Happening

The Not/There, Headlessness, and the Ghastly Being of the Teacher-Scholar

James Grant

Introduction

One of my favorite ghost stories goes something like as follows. A young girl is at a party where she hears a story about how standing on graves will incite the person resting inside to reach up, grab the trespasser, and drag them under. The girl boasts about not being scared of graveyards, and especially not of being pulled into some dead person's grave; it's all foolish superstition, right? Some of the other kids at the party call her bluff, challenging her to go to a nearby cemetery all alone. To prove that she has truly done the deed, she must take the knife that one of the partygoers gives her and plunge it into the grave she has stood upon, marking the spot as one she has definitely visited. Between the darkness of the night and the mysteries that creep along through the shadows, the closer she gets to the grave she will stand on, the more worked-up and anxious she finds herself, but she manages to make it to a plot with her wits still mostly about her and stab the knife into the spot. When she goes to leave, however, she finds that something has, in fact, grabbed hold of her. She struggles to get away, but finds it has gripped her firmly; she cannot flee. Later, when enough time has passed that the others at the party begin to worry, they go to look for her, finding her dead body splayed out over a grave. In her haste, it turns out, she drove the knife into her own dress, sticking herself to the spot, and ultimately dying of fright.

The great thing about this "ghost" story is that it doesn't actually need any ghosts at all. It doesn't even require the ever-present monster of humanity that tends to lurk in the background of so many tales of terror. There are *no* bad guys outside of the ones the sole victim's own mind creates, and we don't even get to *meet* those ones. Not even the people who dare the main character to go into the graveyard do so out of any

David P. Owen, Jr (ed.), Field Theory: Curriculum Studies at Work, 189–207.

identifiable malice, and when she comes up missing, they care enough to go looking for her. And yet, even without these seemingly necessary hallmarks of Horror[v]: real darkness; real terror; real death. What the story requires, and what it presents to us about our potential as wilful actors, is a sense of what I like to call the *not/there*, a strange and paradoxical situation wherein a being is both present and absent at the same time. This very paradox—much like being a headless body, or bodiless head, each of which points in its own way to a sort of completion, despite being incomplete—is part of what allows so many works of Horror to "work their magic" in generating a sense of dread in their audiences, and can be a powerful tool for contemplating the potentially fractured being of the teacher-scholar.

The Not/There

Let me begin with what I do *not* mean by the not/there. While there is a similarity, what I am not talking about is Derrida's (1967/1997; 1973) notion of the *trace*. Derrida's *trace*, (perhaps over-) simplified, is a presence that is understood *through* a thing's absence. With *trace*, *because of* a thing's noticeable absence, it becomes present to us. The catch, though, is that the moment it *becomes* present, it is *actually* present, and so the *trace* as a *trace*, disappears, writes itself off. Any present is the result of a no-longer-present past, which is the result of a different no-longer-here past, all of which point toward a not-quite-here-yet future; all of these no-longers and not-quites form the trace of a present moment. *Trace*, then, is an expression of postmodern ontology, always fractured between referents. The not/there, however, while grounded in the ontological, is also aesthetic, experiential, and exists all-at-once *in* a present moment.

The not/there, while possible with other genres of fiction, is a phenomenon most particular to the Horror genre in its capacity to instill a sense of dread in its audience, whether that dread exists in the moment or (and perhaps especially so) if it is something that lingers or comes on after we have digested a work or let it percolate in our minds for a while. For concision, I will use Hill & Carpenter's (1978) *Halloween* (with a few other titles, as well) to illustrate through the entirety of this piece, making the assumption that my audience is at least somewhat familiar with the characters Michael Myers and Laurie Strode that this film introduced to the world.

There is a scene toward the end of the film wherein Laurie, having just fended off the murderous and masked Michael (and this mask is an issue that will carry a not insignificant weight in the discussion below) and potentially incapacitated him for good, rests by a door with Michael lain out on a bed in the shot behind her. Because the tension built to such a great degree only moments before, and because Laurie is a character that we want to like, we grant her this brief reprieve; we understand. For these very same reasons, however, when Michael sits up on that bed, revealing once more the threat that he is—regardless of the fact that Laurie is completely unaware—*we fear for her*, and with the internalization of that fear *for her*, we simply *fear*. While many moments in Horror texts depend on a *shared* sense of fear, with characters shaping our emotions for us through their screams and gasps, this scene and others like it complicate this sense of dread within works of Horror and the empathy from which they seem to stem. If empathy "makes the experiences of others salient and important—your pain becomes my pain, your thirst becomes my thirst, and so I rescue you" (Bloom, 2016, p.21), the extended internalization that results in our fear allows us not only to *feel with* characters, but to *become* them, psychically, however momentarily. Yet, the distance between our lives, our health and safety, and the perils of on-screen or in-book victims could not be more vast or obvious. We sit comfortably in our living rooms or in a theater amongst leagues of other audience members; they run screaming through deserted houses and rain-soaked forests. Thus, while empathy may be a starting point, it is a point that audiences that respond with any relevant terror transcend. While Winter (2017) argues that the "more substantial, successful, groundbreaking horror films," (amongst which, I must note, while generating a list of examples, he claims *Halloween* has no place, despite its consistent note as *the* game-changing slasher film) "all have one thing in common, which is the emotional bond viewers feel with their characters," the horror that the monsters of these works engender *aside from* any empathy we may feel for the brutalized victims and Final Girls (cf. Clover (1992, 1996)) comes from the monsters themselves, and our own dealing with the threat that they present for our own lives. Empathy starts with an Other, however similar they may seem to us (another factor that may determine the degree of empathy for them which we are capable of achieving (Bloom, 2016)) moves to ourselves through internalization, and is returned to that Other. In the case of Horror texts, the internalization remains, takes precedent.

The fear that we experience, then, in these moments of dread, is a fear of something not/there. The image is very much present, and it is contextualized as an image of something that should be menacing by the narrative of the story in which it exists, and yet it is absolutely *not* present as anything beyond an image on a screen. It poses no real-world threat, yet results in an indubitable real-world anxiety over its being. Through our buying-in to the narrative that the story provides, we make it present, despite its absolute remove; we place ourselves into the world that is presented to us, though we are simultaneously aware of its being a projected world. When we return home from the theater, or turn off our televisions, and still feel a need to look over our shoulders, we've carried with us a fear of something that never was; that making-present of the never-was *is* the not/there. We make the object of our fear present, yet it is nowhere to be seen, only experienced in our direction toward the world.

The Not/There as Horrific Ground

While *trace* has its philosophical roots in the fractious worldview of postmodernism, the not/there as a *concept* is grounded more in Object-Oriented Ontology, and most particularly Harman's (2005, 2011) work and ideas concerning sensuality. For Harman, objects ultimately have two sets of properties, the real and the sensual. Objects' sensual properties are those things that we experience directly, with sensuality being constructed of those "gaseous qualities that *are* present, in which objects do take form and become manifest" (Harman, 2005, p. 44); all the sights, sounds, smells, tastes, and textures that we use to approach objects and understand them. These qualities are quite different from the real, toward which we may only point or reach, and never grasp. Once we begin to believe we have a thing pinned down, it has escaped us, changed, become more or different than we thought, like Proteus making his way through the sea. The reality of a thing can never fully be realized, and this is where the not/there comes into play, because it continuously straddles the line between the sensual and the real, never allowing us to determine whether it is graspable or not in its present unpresence, and concretizing the notion that, beyond our moment-to-moment experience, there *is* something else that informs that experience.

This is not the end. Let's try an experiment. For each of the following images, allow it to come to full bloom in your imagination. Linger on it. Expand outward and let the world solidify around it in your mind. Here we go. Imagine a Spanish doubloon at the bottom of a Martian crater. Imagine the handle of a screwdriver on an Alaskan mountain peak. Imagine the shell of a Buick Skylark in the bottom of a barely surfaced, dead volcano, shrouded by shrubbery in East Central Georgia. What happens here, when we really allow these images manifest, is that—through imagining objects outside of their everyday contexts and keeping them on an equal plane of importance and being to those that still exist within their range of access to our thought—we challenge our anthropocentrism through decentering our stake in being the central grounding force of objects. That is, we take seriously the idea that objects do not need to exist within our minds and perception to be real. Trees that fall in forests really do make sounds, regardless of who is around to hear them. The world-for-us becomes a strange concept. We go further: if the world is not for-us, what does that mean for how we have grounded ourselves ontologically? What is the being of the keyboard that I am typing on right now if it is not being-for-me? Does it have being beyond my use for it? The keyboard *itself* escapes me, becomes troublesome.

Harman often (2005; 2011; 2016, for instance) writes of the inaccessibility of objects, noting that we only really have access to the qualities of the objects, and that this can lead to a reductionism of sorts, consistently making objects *objects-for-us*. Although we may never be able to grasp objects-in-themselves, he argues, philosophy is the *love* of wisdom, not wisdom itself, and so seeking into what will constantly slip away can still be illuminating. On this apprehension of images and not of things themselves, writing about the concept of love in Dante's *Divine Comedy*, Harman (2016) notes that

> things are shown only through their effects, not directly. For this reason, it may seem that love itself is capable only of enjoying images, not of desiring the real substantial forms that lie behind any thing's outward effects. Yet [...] love is a pathway beyond such mere imagery and effect-mongering. Awakened by the image, the soul can turn steadfastly towards the object with love, and then the nature of the object unites with the soul *through beauty*. In short, love and beauty offer a path to the real that does not fall short, as does perception or knowledge, or the inner substantial form of things. Aesthetics is elevated to first philosophy. (p. 147)

Aside from the outcome-based intentions of an artist, what is important in an aesthetic moment is intentionality on the part of the individual experiencing that moment. To what do we turn our attention? What elements of *this* moment, of *this* experience come together to create a whole that set it apart from the flow of other moments? What about this instant organizes the chaos of the everyday in a way that makes sense? Love and beauty (and keep in mind, we are not discussing beauty as described by replicated societal norms, but as experienced in any given moment by an individual) are pre-reflective, yet provide an access to things that no amount of ink spilled in reflection could ever organize. This does not mean that such ink-spilling is not worthwhile, but rather places the greater concern on *experience*.

Just as love and beauty are pre-reflective and provide a means through which we may organize our respective worlds, mid- and post-reflective fear and *ugliness* throw those same worlds into chaos, destabilizing the ego- and anthropo-centrality of our will and sense of organization that we have cast onto the world. *I don't like this world. I don't want it to be like this. Wait, it isn't like this. It's only like this for me. My fear is my fear, regardless of whether I want it. The object of my fear only exists as an object at all for me. It exists somewhere beyond my ability to bring it forth or dismiss it. What power do I have? Am I what I thought? Am I anything at all?* If we take some time to consider aesthetics as the philosophy from which all other philosophical modes spring forth, the not/there becomes the ground for horror through its tenacious making-weird of the ground we thought we could stand on.

The Not/There, Potential, and Dread

In making present what would not be present to anyone but the observer, the not/there reveals the world that *does* have its observer as its ground as one of infinite possibility, of unthinkable potential, and thus—since it comes out of a sense of hauntedness and anxiety—of indefatigable dread. Along with the not/there, that is, comes the realization of the potential for things to be other than they are, to be more or less than they are as they currently present themselves, to be even more beyond our control than we may have previously imagined. The headless body upon which we can imagine a head *becomes* simultaneously headless and fully cephalized. At the same time, the bodiless head *wants* a body in our imagination; immediate experience supplies the parts, and the constant need for uniformity and organization demands that we supply a whole. Displacement of this sort unsettles us, disturbs our senses of space and essence. Every thing that is out of place becomes a thing and a no-thing, an uncanny phenomenon that may disturb and upturn our sense of aesthetic wholeness, making the world a place of unacceptable, unlivable horror.

Thus, with every decision we make comes the dread of losing its opposite, of living with the life that becomes closed to us in the act of decision-making. The existential dread of going forth into the world and carving a path, leaving all other paths behind in so doing is not a new concept. Kierkegaard's (1843/2004) pitting of the aesthetic life against the ethical life is a fine enough example. Yet, for all that *Either/or* now exists as one whole work, it is rather telling that the first half, focusing on the aesthetic life, and the "Seducer's Diary" which close the section not are not only sold as standalone texts, but also outsell the work as a combined entity. It would appear in the either/or decision between contemplating the aesthetic life, the ethical life, and the potential marriage of the two, we have been effectively seduced by the pleasures of the aesthetic. Does this suggest that the fear of missing out on those aesthetic pleasures through pursuing the ethical is strong enough to drive us in that direction? After all, as we are thrown into a world in which time is a limiting factor, we must prioritize our pursuits. Thus, I have no good reason to answer "no."

With every decision we make that affects us in a way that demands we contemplate it, then, and consider its final effects as significant to who and what we are, the not/there is lurking right behind the scenes, subtly promoting that sense of dread. The choice between this and that necessarily binds up this and that, and in the moment of decision, however much the thing we decide against disappears as a possibility, it still has a claim to reality, ghostly though it may be. Harman (2010) notes that the mechanics of this sort of *allure* "can be found in many places, but especially so in the case of ghosts: instead of the normal relation between a withdrawn real thing and its sensual surface traits, a ghost suggests a certain ungraspable spirit lying beyond all access" (p. 63). This is no different for the ghosts of possibilities past. While they lie beyond access, existing only as could-have-beens, they still call out to us, beckon us forward to consider them, and alter our worlds in the process.

Headlessness

As an extension of the concept of the not/there developed above, I would like to take some time to explore the uncanniness of headlessness—both human and nonhuman, but with a focus more on the human—as both a reality and as a metaphor. Not only has the very strangeness of this particular *part minus whole* equation been a significant source of terror and wonder in folklore, religious texts, war stories, and works of Horror for thousands of years, the images of headless bodies and bodiless heads are also symbolically rich in political, social, aesthetic, and ethical implications.

As a brief introduction, let us start with the story of Miracle Mike. The short version of Miracle Mike's tale goes like this: in 1945, an American farmer named Lloyd Olsen decapitated one of his chickens and discovered soon after doing so that the chicken was still alive. This was not just a "chicken with its head off" nervous reaction that would eventually wear down once the tissue decayed: the chicken was just alive. Olsen and his wife kept it that way for roughly eighteen months by feeding it with a dropper and clearing mucus from its neck with a syringe. While the head had been completely severed from the body, much—not all!—of the brain, which for chickens lies further to the back of the head than in mammalian brains, was still intact (Stoel-Walker, 2015). This does not say much for how bright chickens are—and never mind that, after learning of the money the Olsens went on to make through showing off Mike at sideshows, exactly zero of the farmers and university scientists who, for money and fame or scientific progress and understanding, tried to make a Mike of their own were successful—and it gives a whole new insight into what it means to be a bird brain! Beyond what Mike's story has given to galliform disregard and idiomatic expression, it has also provided us an interesting insight into the inexhaustible human curiosity for the freakish and uncanny. As I just mentioned, the Olsens made quite a bit of money— the modern equivalent of nearly $50,000 per month (Pettman, 2014)— over the course of a sideshow stint.

Bogdan (1988) and Hartzman (2006) each make clear that sideshows and Freakshows were largely built on exploitation, however much an individual performer might have been involved in the process. The work of these two historians reveals that it is easily the case that most often, so-called Freakshows and sideshow acts are driven by a sort of schadenfreude and mimetic projection. People pay their nickels to laugh and gawk at the freaks to cast their own awfulness onto something or someone else, or at least as a distraction and palliative for the misery in their own lives. Mike suggests something different, though. Not different in a way that turns that understanding on its ear, but in a way that at least provides for a spectrum of interpretations. The living headless chicken is easily enough something to thrill at; there is a horror to it, for sure, as the uncanny reality that this thing that ought to be dead *really is alive* stretches the chicken across two categories that ought to be mutually exclusive, decentering the steady ground of reality. The I-dare-you-to-look/I-dared-to-look potential can be expected to have driven a significant portion of entry fees. Still, Mike's freakishness is founded on *survival*. While pointing and snickering is a well-identified response to the sideshow freak, it seems that what we have in Mike's case is *wonder*. As terrible as it might have been, there is reason enough to believe that whatever emotions Mike stirred in his audiences were founded not on a sense of or need for superiority, but out of an unshakable sense of awe.

The Headless Horseman, a perhaps more well-known example of famous headless individuals in American history, is another thing altogether. The awe and wonder that Mike may have inspired are nowhere to be seen here, and little is left beyond terror. While Washington Irving's (1820/2009) tale may be the definitive text regarding the decephalized Hessian, and Ruder, Schroder, and Burton's (1999) version provides interesting character studies of Ichabod Crane and Katrina Van Tassel, as well as a horrific vision of the Horseman, I prefer, for its sheer simplicity and development of visual tension, the Disney, Geronimi, and Kinney (1949) telling of the tale. In this version, not only are we eventually met with a terrifying vision of the Horseman (and never have a head suggested beyond the flaming pumpkin that he carries), but Ichabod's ensuing terror as he rides home on his final fateful night, imagining and bringing to life the Horseman before he ever appears on screen is a perfect example of the allure of the not/there. I shall take this up in the section immediately below on the headless body.

Just as uncanny and rife with metaphoric potential as the animated body without a head is the image of the head divorced from the body. While it is the head, that great symbol of intellect and organization that drives the body and gives it purpose, the head without the body becomes a strangely useless thing. Trigg (2014) notes that "we tend to impose a unity on the body, which forces parts of the body to cohere in relation to the whole. Remove a body part, and what remains is an organ, as alien as the other side of the cosmos" (pp. 136-137). The head being the "organ" *sine qua non*, the idea of it existing without a body to guide becomes almost doubly alien. On the one hand, we have a thing removed from its context. On the other, that removed thing is what generally *provides* the context for the thing from which it is missing. Along with it, we can imagine a world of ideas floating about in space that will never come to any sort of fruition. *Theory is fine, I guess*, the bodiless head tells us, *but who cares if you are not able to act on any of it.*

Bodiless heads appear in all sorts of literary contexts, from the ancient tales from *The Mabinogion* that feature the talking head of Bran the Blessed, which entertains the survivors of a monstrous battle for seven years (trans. 2007) to the *at least* four severed heads that appear on stage across the span of Shakespeare's (Bevington, c.1589/1997) *Henry VI*, to the nearly uncountable lone crania that have flashed across film screens since at least D.W. Griffith's *Intolerance* (1916), which provides audiences not only decapitations, but also heads floating by on the ends of sticks. While Horror films provide a wide variety of corpseless crowns upon which to meditate, I would like to spend some time below with the ant-ridden, sun-baked head of Charlie, from Frakes, Knudsen, Patrick, and Aster's (2018) *Hereditary*. It is not only the distanced, slant-yet-focused view of this head that the film provides viewers that will be important here, but also the contextual relevance of the head to the film's plot. All things considered, Charlie's head, *as* an emblem of motionless theory, gives us one of this decade's most powerful meditative images for exploring the concept of frustrated theoretic potential.

The Headless Body

The horror of the body without a head functions on several different levels, and I would explore just two of them here. I should note that, for the sake of timeliness, these explorations are a mere toe-dip into that pool. The two areas where I would like to focus our attention are on the head as the center for reason, and the head as the central image for *human life*, and thus, as extensions of these, headless bodies as bodies devoid of reason, and life devoid of humanity. I will return at the end of this segment to the idea of the not/there to ground these discussions.

As I mentioned above, Disney's (Disney, Geronimi, and Kinney, 1949) telling of the tale of the Headless Horseman is, if not the *most* entertaining version of the story, at least the most potentially instructive for my purposes here. About halfway through the film, once Brom Bones— Ichabod Crane's key antagonist aside from the Horseman—discovers that Ichabod is deathly afraid of spooks and specters, he tells the story of the Headless Horseman through song. Tellingly, the refrain of the song that Bones sings repeats the line "don't try to figure out a plan / you can't reason with a headless man," an idea at which Bataille (1936/1985) would have cried "Hooray! Bring on the headless one and the absence of human reason." Such was his desire: to imagine a world free from the anthropomorphism that human reason brings along with it, casting all things in our image. The absence of the Horseman's reasoning that would have come along with his headlessness would have seemingly erased any human-centric designs he had toward mastery over the world, thus making his ends those of pure body, of—if you will—immediate gut reactions and need.

The problem with such an understanding of the Horseman's headlessness, though, is that it falls apart rather quickly. When he first appears onscreen, the Horseman laughs, and continues to do so throughout the extensive chase scene with Ichabod. While he carries the flaming head of a pumpkin with him, it is not through this head that he laughs, but from some unknown place, residing deep in the cavity of his chest. In one instance, Ichabod flies from his horse, landing on the body of the Horseman, and the two are face to...not so much of a face. Ichabod looks into the cavern where the Horseman's neck would be, and withdraws, shaking uncontrollably as the deep, echoing laugh emerges from that pit. This laughter, all things considered, is a *knowing* laughter. He *knows* he has a victim, he *knows* he will win out, he *knows* he will have a new head (Ichabod's) to rest upon his shoulders. This is not a knowing that can emerge without reason, and that reason writes onto the body of the ghastly and strange the complete and unified body of the human. It is a knowing that seeks to normalize what is weird. While it may be a knee-jerk impulse for a body to want to replace a head, that impulse would seem to come from a *need* for centrality and organization, i.e., a need for the guidance of reason. The Horseman's reasonless reason, then, comes from some deep-seated desire for just that.

Enter the horror of the not/there. If what the Headless Horseman wants is a head (hint: it is), then even though he does not have the complete capacity for reason, there is a reasonability even in the absence of that capacity. This is uncanny. This is *weird*. The horror, though, arises for Ichabod in the extension of that weird not/there that allows him to imagine his own body as the one that is headless, as his *own* head will rest atop the body of the Headless Horseman. This reality, for Ichabod, is not/there. His head, while present on his body momentarily, is also fully realized as completing the form of the Not-So-Headless-Anymore Horseman. What's more than this, of course, is that we get to imagine Ichabod headless along the way, as the Horseman chops at him, and his entire head dips into the collar of his shirt. The not/there does not exist for Ichabod alone. We, as an engaged audience, supply the images of both a headless Ichabod and a Headed Horseman as the drama ensues. We share Ichabod's horror, and extend its uncanniness into our own experience.

One last thing to consider about this story is that we never know of Ichabod's actual demise. We only have his empty hat and a shattered pumpkin from which to draw conclusions. It is rumored, we learn, that he took up residence in a nearby county where he settled down comfortably. This, though, is marked pointedly as mere rumor. Interestingly, that final image of a hat without a head to fill it, in knowing from whence it came, has a similar effect as imagining Ichabod's body without a head. Both are the signifiers of what we want to imagine as ineffable wholes, only to have that imagining burst to so many bits, fracturing our sense of reality just that much more.

For as much as Bataille (1936/1985) railed against the notion of the human head as the grounding metaphor for human life and the very reason for the universe, as much as he may have celebrated escaping the head, those railings and celebrations end up flat. Just as we cannot truly imagine our own deaths—our own *being* dead—we cannot truly escape our heads. The object-oriented ontology on which I have drawn throughout this piece, for all of its aims in displacing the anthropos in anthropocentric understandings of the world, still understands its limits, recognizing that the reality of thing-being is always beyond our grasp. While Harman (2010, 2011) enumerates four tensions (time, space, eidos, and essence) between objects and their real and aesthetic qualities, and successfully argues that the objects do not need human interlocutors to validate themselves or their reality in the midst of many of these tensions, those individuals who are of sound mind still exist *in this world of tensions and relations*, and so are constantly "in our own heads" as we navigate our way through the world. Such a reality is inescapable. Regardless of where we go, then, we always come back to the head.

Of course, as Thacker (2014) clarifies, with regard to Bataille, the removal of the head is metaphorical of both the head of the body politic and the anthropomorphism, which "hides the already-existent state of the human being turning itself inside-out" (p. 15). This anthropomorphic turning inside out is both a constant remaking of the world *in our own image*, and the habit of seeing ourselves *in* the entire world. When the head becomes synonymous with human *being* itself (as it so often does—consider what we really mean when we say to our friends, "don't lose your head!") the metaphoric extension that comes along with the thought of being a body without that head is horrific indeed. Instead of having an organizing unit that seeks to take in the world and organize it—if Trigg's (2014) notions of alienness, thinghood, and our need to see things as wholes hold true—human being gets reduced to stomach-being, which would take in the world to *consume* it. As this relates to the body politic, consider this: what if, per Thacker (2014) through Bataille, the head of the body politic has nothing to do with heads of nations and sovereign reign. When we put rulers aside, as it happens, we replace them immediately. This is Burroughs's (1959/1990) algebra: take out the top, it always gets replaced, and by something that ends up looking more or less the same. The image of headlessness loses its potential for terror when the metaphor stops there. The head becomes something *other*, a symbol of power, and power that we really do not possess ourselves, regardless of our views on representative democracy, and it is just fine if there is no head because we do not see ourselves *in* that head or *as* that all-consuming gut. We are the arms, the legs, the things that do the work. We would not even really *want* to imagine ourselves as the heads, because then the evils that come along with the power we would displace emerge from our own doings. The catch is that the metaphor does not, in fact, end there. If, though, anthropomorphism—or really anthropocentrism—is the issue (hint: it is) it becomes striking again. The metaphor becomes less…metaphorical. It hits home differently. While the notion of being headless has its own reasons for bringing about a sense of dread, the thing is, reflectively, *we are always the disembodied head that we take in* when we view a disembodied head. The body without us becomes the *world* without us, *life* without us, and this is unimaginable, because here we are. This is the horror of the not/there of our being not here.

The Bodiless Head

He just kept going. Peter did. After the accident. He just kept going, got out of the car, went into the house, and went to bed. It was not until the next morning that anyone knew what happened. And it is at this point, after the seemingly infinite screams of her mother where we get to see it, miles away from the body to which it ought to be attached, lying, ripped, rotting, and ant-ridden by the roadside: Charlie's head. As I mentioned above, the film *Hereditary* (Frakes, Knudsen, Patrick, & Aster, 2018) provides modern viewers one of the richest images of a bodiless head that the medium of film has ever offered. Although the head in question does appear in a Horror film, and is quite jolting, even upon subsequent viewings, the significance of this particular head lies far beyond its shock value. While only minutes before, the head belonged to the girl who was *supposed* to be the face of this film, here it lies in the dirt, by the roadside, becoming more alien—and, ironically, through Trigg's (2014) argumentation above, more human, more *us* in the viewer's need to supply a whole to this ever-so-recognizable part—the longer we reflect upon it, and with every new detail. It is not just that the skin of the face is mangled, though this is a beginning. A troop of ants make their way across the face. The wind off of the ground and arising from distant traffic blows by uncaringly. We remember how, before the accident, Peter looked into the rearview mirror, seeing only Charlie's head floating there in the darkness, and the foreshadowing is painful, Charlie's head isolated in the mirror becoming, in our memories, a decapitation all its own. The very starkness of all of the imagery and extensive sensual detail that come along with Charlie's bodiless head, then, through an object-oriented approach, allows us a different take on the not/there and its capacity for horror.

At the bottom of it, Charlie's head is just that. It is nothing more than a thing on the side of the road. There is no Charlie there anymore. The ants make this clear. The uncaring sun blaring down and the pitiless wind do the same. The whole world comes together to deny any humanity to this not-Charlie, and yet, we cannot help but supply the rest of her. She is right there, and this ability, this incessant *allure* toward filling in what is missing changes the world for us. While Harman's (2010) above idea about allure related to ghostliness, I argue here that, in the case of Charlie's head, no ghost is necessary, the ghost is supplied by the specter that is Charlie's disembodied, out of place head. We want to imagine the rest of her filling out that picture, completing an identifiable whole, but both the horror of believing that this *thing* could possibly be human again (a belief that we cannot seem to outstrip) and the thought that the humanity that this thing *ought* to represent could be so distant from any other signs of human being combine to create an experience of the not/there that is hard to walk away from.

A similar, yet remarkably different, way that some Horror films focus an audience's attention on the head is through the inclusion of masks. I mentioned above that the mask that Michael Myers wears in Hill & Carpenter's (1978) *Halloween* would be important for our discussion. Before discussing this work, though, I would like to briefly go into major plot point of *Halloween III* (Carpenter, Hill, & Wallace, 1982), which, I should note, does not feature Myers at all. In this film, the villain's ultimate plan is to ensure that a mass of children wear a set of masks on Halloween that are rigged to merge with the wearer when exposed to a special signal, eventually resurrecting the ancient rites of the pagan holiday Samhain. On this, Thacker (2014) notes that the masks mutate "the head of the wearer into a goopey, bloody mass. Here the mask overlaps with the head, sometimes resulting in a paradoxical decapitation of the mask, and the unmasking of the head" (p. 28). What is most significant here are the notions of merging and the decapitation of masks. In *The Curriculum of Horror* (Grant, 2019) I noted that when there is struggle in works of Horror, the audience's attention is drawn to the site of the source of the struggle—the knife, the chainsaw, what have you—and that those sources, aside from being extensions of the characters' souls (per Serres (1985/2016), who argues that the soul is the point of focus when the attention is drawn from one place to the next, and those places are proclaimed by a subject's *I* as a whole) become the shared soul of audience members as well. With regard to masks, it is not so different: when a killer is wearing one, it takes precedent, often even over the implements of murder that they wield. The fact that Michael is going to kill someone is one thing; the fact that he's doing *while wearing a mask* is another thing altogether. When cephalization is a metaphor for centralization, the mask "makes the man," as it were; the mask *becomes* the head of the killer, and ultimately becomes the killer *himself*. While the knife or chainsaw or whatever tool becomes an extension of the hand (Heidegger, 1926/1962), the hand is a further extension of the mind, the only avenue into which we have is the mask; the mask is all possible things. Thus, the masked villain becomes a sort of bodied head, a new iteration of the not/there, wherein all elements are actually present, but still grounded in the being of the mask, and so not necessarily present on their own terms. As the mask becomes the reality, we understand that the very being of this reality is a thing that has been *manufactured*. The killer is very much present in this case, and yet is little more than the extension of a piece of plastic, that plastic being a stand-in for the head that it covers. What we find, then, is that in this instance where we would see nothing but a head, the falseness of that head points toward decapitation. The masked head does not become the bodiless head. Instead, when the mask is all there is, we have a whole new case of the headless body.

How To Disappear Completely

Many readers will be disappointed by this point. It's all just been philosophizing and Horror stuff. Even when he does decide to talk about education a little, it's just theorizing about it. What's any of this got to do with actually teaching? The down-and-dirty, in-the-trenches stuff? I mean, I get that this whole text is supposed to be about blurring the lines between practitioners and theorists, but there doesn't seem to be much of a blur here; it's all just theory. Even if he were to start applying this to teaching, it'd sort of just be tacked-on, wouldn't it? Jeez, what a longwinded poser. It's a fair enough complaint, but this is the down-and-dirty so often. I get an idea, I theorize about its implications and usefulness, I test it out, and I start over. The worlds of theory and action, in my experience, do not cross over so much as they remain perpetually on each other's borders. The question is not so much one of uncanny hybridity as it is of being any one thing at any one time. While werewolves are always werewolves, in terms of particular instances, they are only ever extroverted as wolves, men, or some transitional thing that is not quite any of it, eternally holding whatever other binary end may be the one in question as an inevitable potential. It is this potential that is really the issue here, particularly with regard to the classroom.

For the teacher/theorist, the potential to be one or the other of these things in any given moment is always present when we are being the other over it. The other thing is always not/there, and in moments of doubt or perceived failure, that not/there is the ghost of the actor we could have been. If what I needed last Tuesday when my fourth-period AP Language students seemed to be overwhelmed at what I was throwing out at them was to *theorize* along with them *with* what I was throwing at them, they may have been more receptive, and now that moment has passed, that ship has sailed, and is hoisting a ghostly Jolly Roger somewhere along the high seas. Too much of being any one thing disallows the potential human flourishing of my students, and this is a horrible, horrifying thought, and my constant dilemma. At the same time, having too much of *my own being* tied up in one passing identity or another necessarily limits my ability and capacity to be more than I am for my students.

I teach English, and in my experience, we English teachers like to imagine ourselves as purveyors (do not read: gatekeepers) of culture, as people who promote the growth of the *human* as well as the development of skills. The problem, though, is that however much students, parents, and even in-house administrators may be on board with this mindset in any individual schoolhouse, human-ness is not exactly a thing that can be defined (cf. Harman, 2010, 2016; Heidegger, 1926/1962; Trigg, 2014), and so cannot be reliably tested by state governments, and so cannot be supplementally funded by federal governments, and so perpetually sits on the back burners of educational systems while whatever shiny new research-based *practical* (read: personhood ignoring) *system* of educating du jour becomes a mandate in our classrooms. This is lamentable, but creates an unnecessary binary in the question of whether we should educate toward the human or toward testable skills. After all, if my students cannot produce decent thesis statements after a year with me, but do leave my room more empathetic toward other humans and more willing to consider the humanity underlying anyone's problems, I should count that as a win, right? Shouldn't I also be able to count it a win, though, if a student gains no recognizable *human* growth but *is* able to clearly state their own ideas and elaborate on the arguments behind those ideas? It does not sound as pretty, but, as Morris (2016) has stated, aesthetics is not always about beauty, but about how we organize our worlds.

The false questions that educators are faced with daily is whether we are to produce headless bodies or bodiless heads, whether we are to *be* headless bodies or bodiless heads, because, oddly, the joining of the two is what begins to seem uncanny once we get into the removed sphere of state-level testing, concerned with measurability and quantifiable products, despite the lip service of "whole child" educational manifestos. No longer is it the head that is detached from the body in what feels like an alien atmosphere the thing that draws the horror of the not/there, it is the whole person in a world that is not set up for whole people that does.

This is only appearance, though. The reality behind those appearances is that choosing either one over the other invites the constant horror of the not/there. When I allow the measurable results of state testing to define how I conduct my classroom, I stop thinking for myself (or at least put on blinders as to what my options are, preferring the illusion of choice over expanding the walls of possible choices), I stop thinking for my students, I limit the prospects of education to pre-defined dimensions, and this limitation cannot be outstripped or hidden from. My head becomes irrelevant, slips into the cavity of a body that is expected to move about puppet-like, and the world stops being a world to be known, only to be consumed. If we are to educate away from the consumerism that Weaver (2010) warns us underscores so much of the modern American education system, we must invite the head to join the body. Of course, the danger here is in becoming like the Headless Horseman, blindly seeking out any old head that happens to bobble along, devoid of any theory about the world or our places in it. And theory, as Harman (2010) notes, "is what disrupts the usual dull bond between the sensual object and its real hidden traits" (p. 63). Theory, that is, allows us to move beyond the humdrum, taken-for-granted world that is handed to us, that we are supposed to believe exists as it has been presented, and see *mystery* in it once more.

If, conversely, I deny the validity of measurable results, seeking only to guide toward my self-defined idea of humanity, I necessarily deny my students the opportunity to master skills that others their age are developing, a fact that will, in the long run, end up producing a limited set of opportunities, and undoing much of the human flourishing that I sought to empower. If theory is what disrupts a taken-for-granted understanding of the world, it stands to reason that a purely theoretical stance toward the world disallows a world-at-hand. Where theory needs a tension between objects and their effects to address, to deny either the objects *or* their effects is to deny the unity of the thing. The world becomes unreal, untethered, nothing but pure mind. Here we have students mirroring the reality of Charlie's head, rotting on the roadside and being consumed by the alien world around them because they lack the capacity for movement within that world.

One of the primary horrific realities of teaching is that we write onto the bodies of our developing students the complete and unified body of the complete human, a person fully formed, and it is strange to look at them and see this missing. The even weirder thing is that we *know* they are still in formation. Yet, what we do not see—what we *cannot* see— moment-to-moment, is a person developing. We see a person fully formed to this point. And then the absence comes. And we see it. It was not/there the whole time. What other presences have we written, we wonder. How many other heads are simply placed by our imaginations? How many heads that we imagine missing have been there the whole time?

One of the most interesting things about that ghost story I mentioned at the start is the very acephalic nature of it. The girl, boasting the power of reason (most particularly her own reason) over superstition, places the head at the seat of power, yet immediately upon taking her friends' dare usurps that throne. Reason disappears into ego. *Projecting an image of reasonability*—a head with little need for a body save to move it around— becomes the most important thing; promoting the value of head, she loses her head, becomes little more than a body moved by its own passions, disappears into the idea of a self she would never again get to be. As long as the conversation around education remains a war of head against body, those who would run around being and creating either bodies or heads will do little more than populate the world with monstrosity.

References

Bataille, G. (1985). The sacred conspiracy. In A. Stoekel (Ed., Trans.), C.R. Lovitt, & D.M.

Leslie, Jr. (Trans.). *Visions of excess: Selected writings 1927-1939* (pp. 178-181). Minneapolis, MN: University of Minnesota Press.

Bevington, D. (Ed.). (1997). *The complete works of William Shakespeare* (4th Ed.). New York, NY: Longman. (Original work published c.1589)

Bloom, P. (2016). *Against empathy: The case for rational compassion.* New York, NY: HarperCollins Publishers.

Bogdan, R. (1988). *Freak show: Presenting human oddities for amusement and profit.* Chicago, IL: The University of Chicago Press.

Burroughs, W.S. (1990). *Naked lunch.* New York, NY: Grove Press. (Original work published 1959)

Carpenter, J., Hill, D. (producers), and Wallace, T.L. (director) (1982). *Halloween III: Season of the witch* [Motion Picture]. USA: Dino De Laurentiis Company.

Clover, C. (1992). *Men, women, and chainsaws: Gender in the modern horror film.* Princeton, NJ: Princeton University Press.

Clover, C. (1996). Her body, himself: Gender in the slasher film. In B.K. Grant (Ed.), *The dread of difference* (pp. 66-113). Austin, TX: The University of Texas Press.

Derrida, J. (1973). *Speech and phenomena: And other essays on Husserl's theory of signs.* (D. Allison, Trans.). Evanston, IL: Northwestern University Press.

Derrida, J. (1997). *Of grammatology.* (G.C. Spivak, Trans.). Baltimore, MD: The Johns Hopkins University Press. (Original work published 1967)

Disney, W. (producer), Geronimi, C., & Kinney, J. (directors). (1949). *The legend of Sleepy Hollow* [Motion Picture]. USA: Walt Disney Productions.

Frakes, K.S., Knudsen, L., Patrick, B. (Producers) & Aster, A. (Director). (2018). *Hereditary* [Motion Picture]. USA: PalmStar Media.

Grant, J. (2019). *The curriculum of horror: Or, the pedagogies of monsters, madmen, and the misanthropic.* New York, NY: Peter Lang.

Griffith, D.W. (Producer & Director). (1916). *Intolerance: Love's struggle throughout the ages* [Motion Picture]. USA: Triangle Film Corporation.

Harman, G. (2005). *Guerilla metaphysics: Phenomenology and the carpentry of things.* Chicago, IL: Open Court.

Harman, G. (2010). *Circus philosophicus.* Hants, UK: O Books.

Harman, G. (2011). *The quadruple object.* Alresford, Hants, UK: Zero Books.

Harman, G. (2016). *Dante's broken hammer.* London, UK: Repeater Books.

Hartzman, M. (2006). *American sideshow: An encyclopedia of history's most wondrous and curiously strange performers.* New York, NY: The Penguin Group.

Heidegger, M. (1962). *Being and time.* J. Macquarrie & E. Robinson (Trans.). San Francisco,CA: HarperSanFrancisco. (Original work published 1926)

Hill, D. (producer) & Carpenter, J. (director). (1978). *Halloween* [Motion Picture]. USA: Compass International Pictures

Irving, W. (2009). *The legend of Sleepy Hollow: And other stories.* New York, NY: The Modern Library. (Original work published 1820)

Kierkegaard, S. (2004). *Either/or: A fragment of life.* (A. Hannay, Trans.). New York, NY: Penguin Classics.

Morris, M. (2016). *Curriculum studies guidebooks* (Vol. 2). New York, NY: Peter Lang.

Pettman, D. (2014). What came first, the chicken or the head? In [No eds] *And They Were Two in One and One in Two.* No City, UK: Schism Press. Pp. 7-9

Rudin, S., Schroeder, A. (producers) & Burton, T. (director). (1999). *Sleepy Hollow* [Motion Picture]. USA: Paramount Pictures.

Serres, M. (2016). *The five senses: A philosophy of mingled bodies* [Kindle version]. (M. Sankey & P. Cowley, Trans.). New York, NY: Bloomsbury Revelations. Retrieved from www.amazon.com. (Original work published 1985)

Stoel-Walker, C. (2015, September 10). *The chicken that lived for 18 months without a head.* Retrieved from https://www.bbc.com/news/magazine-34198390

Thacker, E. (2014). Thing and no-thing. In [No eds] *And They Were Two in One and One in Two.* No city, UK: Schism Press. Pp. 11-30.

Trigg, D. (2014). *The thing: A phenomenology of horror.* Alresford, Hants, UK: Zero Books.

Weaver, J. A. (2010). *Educating the posthuman: Biosciences, fiction, and curriculum studies.* Boston, MA: Sense Publishers.

Winter, M. (2017, November 15). *Watch: How to build empathy in a horror film (and why it's so important).* Retrieved from https://nofilmschool.com/2017/11/watch-how-build-empathy-horror-film

notes

[v] Herein, I have capitalized Horror to distinguish between naming the genre as such and the feeling that the genre is intended to create in its audience.

Chapter 11

"To Make Some Sense Out of This Mess"

Popular Art and Wilco

David P. Owen, Jr.

**A note before you begin reading: This chapter was written with a soundtrack in mind. The songs have been marked with superscript, and the whole list can be found in the appendix. Take a few minutes, if you can, to listen to them as you go, whether you put together a playlist before you begin or look them up one at a time; it might take longer to read, but it also might be more fun.

*　　*　　*

We'll find a way regardless
To make some sense out of this mess
Well it's a test but I believe
A kiss is all we need

—Wilco, "Nothing'severgonnastandinmyway(again)," 1999[1]

What's the World Got in Store for You Now?[2]

These lyrics from Wilco's 1999 album *Summerteeth* seem to be about love, not popular art or media—but these things today are no less messy, and Wilco should know. The world of popular arts is certainly a mess, but it is also a glorious mess full of possibilities and new avenues for expression and audience experience, and there are few more fascinating activities today for scholars and fans alike than to follow the various ways working popular artists, like the band Wilco, navigate their way through the

David P. Owen, Jr (ed.), *Field Theory: Curriculum Studies at Work*, 209–231.

proliferation of forces and media technologies that characterize our current popular culture environment in the United States. And if we are going to heed the countless calls of scholars like Kilbourne (1999) to help our students use the "tools of media education that enable us to understand, analyze, interpret" (p. 305) and otherwise empower ourselves in a new media world, perhaps more case studies like this one are needed.

The primary cause of this glorious mess of new media is the digitization of nearly everything. In many aspects of our lives in the 21st century, digitization means greater ease of storage, filing, retrieval, transmission, translation, and transaction, among other things, of almost all of the information we need to conduct our everyday lives and businesses. It also means we can do all of these things faster, and many of them more independently than ever before. In the popular arts, though, the changes brought about by digitization are especially interesting; as M. B. N. Hansen (2004) notes, digitized information "can just as easily be rendered as a sound file, a static image, a video clip, or an immersive, interactive world, not to mention a number of forms that do not correlate so neatly with our sensory capacities" (p. 22). As audience members, we have a lot of faculties to use; as popular artists, we have a lot of decisions to make. We do not have to look around much before we find evidence of new, digitally-born media creatures everywhere; our students can probably make a longer list than we can. And because most of these "rendering" options M. B. N. Hansen mentions can not only be experienced, but also produced, with personal computers or other widely available technologies, for perhaps the first time people all across the United States, at least, have financial and technological access to the resources that help create and distribute the popular arts.

For example, I myself have written, performed, recorded, pressed, and sold my own albums[3] of original music. I wrote my songs, found some friends with talent, knowledge, and equipment, and got to work in basements and borrowed spaces full of our own instruments and a tangle of cables—no outside "industry" help needed. My wife even designed the album art. These types of projects can also be accomplished in other media; I had a high school student one year who wrote, filmed, and edited with her own equipment a pilot for an original sitcom starring her friends for a school project, and every time I teach Film Studies I have groups of students produce their own original short films with their own equipment. In short, the popular arts are more "popular," in the sense of *of the people*, than ever before. However, not everything is made easier by digitization, or the new freedoms and choices that come along with it. First of all, while a popular artist today *can* wear many hats, as the saying goes, from the first kernel of imagination all the way to marketing decisions with the finished creation, it also seems like he *must*; these new resources and opportunities don't matter much if he doesn't know what to do with them. Secondly, despite our access to many of the same resources, what my students and I have done, and what Wilco does, are still in some ways two very different things. If this were little league sports, my students and I would get "participation" ribbons; the big trophy, or "success" in the new media mess, is more complicated. In fact, it is not at all clear what "success" even means now, or if it means the same thing for everybody. Is the finished creative work enough? Or, is it:

1.   Making a lot of money? (How much?)
2.   Loyal, devoted fans? (How many?)
3.   Critical acclaim? (From whom?)

These and many other questions must be asked of anyone interested in pursuing the popular arts, because the answers will significantly determine how he will be able to "find a way" in the mess of new media. In addition, popular artists like Wilco today are pushed and pulled by many, often competing, forces and interests; they must struggle with issues like "popular" vs. "fine" arts, aesthetic interests vs. business interests, and authenticity vs. artificiality. And if they do comfortably locate themselves in all of those discussions, they can then get down to making the millions of media technology decisions that wait.

He Takes All His Words From the Books That You Don't Read Anyway[4]

These issues have likely been around in some form as long as the popular arts have been around, or at least as long as they have been "popular" in both senses of the word—both *of the people* and *experienced, appreciated, and liked by a lot of the people*. These arts have long been contrasted with what we have called "fine" arts, and any attempt to distinguish between "popular" arts and "fine" arts is immediately messy. Most people call theater, opera, and "classical" music "fine" arts, and sketch comedy, Broadway musicals, and hip hop "popular" arts. But examined closely, the differences between these forms are not so easy to discern, and are mostly a matter of accredited training and tradition. When pop music singer/songwriter Damien Rice closes his album *O* (2003)[5] accompanied by an opera singer, what do we call that? Are the musicians in Wilco "fine" artists when they use violins and "popular" artists when they use fiddles?

Hall (1996) says that "popular culture always has its base in the experiences, the pleasures, the memories, the traditions of the people" (p. 469); however, at the risk of sounding like a smart aleck, what other kind of culture is there? Are some of us "the people" and some of us not? And how "un-popular" can something be, and still be considered part of our "culture"? What Hall and others clearly understand is that the distinction between "fine" arts and "popular" arts is primarily one of condescension, made by men, women, and organizations interested in distinguishing among classes and matters of taste rather than forms of expression. In fact, today the "fine" label seems to be applied to those arts that are not *experienced, appreciated, and liked by a lot of the people*—in short, most of us don't like them much. In defense against extinction, advocates for these arts have shunned the *of the people* aspect of "popularity" as well, finding refuge in elitism.

Seldes (1924/2001) made this case long ago, arguing that "there is a vast snobbery of the intellect which repays the deadly hours of boredom" we spend with "fine" arts, and calling us "the inheritors of a tradition that what is worth while must be dull" (p. 311). He begins the list of "propositions" that sum up his book by saying that aside from snobbery, "there is no opposition between the great [fine] and the lively [popular] arts" (p. 349, my brackets), and argues in fact that we need both if we want "to live fully" (p. 346). Panofsky (1997) also comes to the defense of the popular arts and their "liveliness" by saying that "films are not only 'art'" but also, with a few exceptions, "the only visual art entirely alive" (p. 94). English professor Pichaske (1999) makes a similar case for popular music, asserting that "rock songs do virtually everything that traditional, or 'linear,' poetry does—with the possible exception of making a shape on the page" (p. 96). However, this claim of "snobbery" can also be a trap for popular artists. Panofsky (1997) argues that film must avoid "literary ambitions" (p. 96) and says its dialogue "had better not be poetry" (p. 100). Seldes (1924/2001) also warns against a "pretentiousness, a base desire to be above the crowd and yet to please [...] the crowd" (p. 78), but these statements certainly do not clear up the mess. Is Damien Rice "pretentious" for using an opera singer? If so, it is unclear where the lines must be drawn, and what kinds of instrumentation, knowledge, training, and intellectual sophistication, not to mention wealth and/or "breeding," are to be allowed in the "popular" arts.

Some Strange Purse Stuffed Nervous With Gold[6]

Another aspect of the popular arts in which it seems a delicate balance must be maintained concerns issues of aesthetic pursuits and commodification. If Damien Rice decides to include an opera singer in all of his songs for purely artistic reasons, he will not likely be considered a "fine" artist, but he will likely suffer a decrease in record sales—he will be less "popular." Conversely, if Yo-Yo Ma records an album of Led Zeppelin covers on cello, he will likely lose respect as a "fine" artist, but make more money from record sales and gain "popularity." The economic relationship between artist and audience has always been messy, and is particularly so in the popular arts. If such an artist appears too calculated in his efforts to please his audience with his work, he is branded a "sellout" and risks attacks from critics and fans alike. However, if he challenges his audience too much artistically, he risks being branded "inaccessible" or "pretentious"—or being ignored, which is even worse. Sell too much, and be ridiculed, and maybe abandoned; sell too little, and disappear.

As The Project on Disney reminds us in *Inside the Mouse* (1995), there is perhaps no better example than Disney World of how pervasive the practices and trappings of commodification are today. The whole world, it seems, at all times occupies one position or the other in the buyer/seller relationship; in EPCOT, this is almost literally true, as all of the "participating" countries are "signified by culturally specific, generally clichéd, but usually marketable attributes" (Kuenz, p. 77). Those of us who do not wish to buy or sell anything literally do not exist in EPCOT's version of the world—a small world indeed. Kilbourne says the problem extends far beyond Disney's considerable walls, and finds in *Can't Buy My Love* (1999), her study of advertising and its effects on us, that "everything in the world—nature, animals, people—is just so much stuff to be consumed or to be used to sell us something" (p. 77). This is true, she says, even of MTV—once the mass-media gateway for popular musicians—which "presents itself publicly as a place for rebels and nonconformists" (p. 40) but really serves up its audience as a captive demographic for its advertisers. Perhaps if we are shocked by the nearly inescapable capitalism, especially in our media, it is only because we have not been paying attention; Williams (1974/2003) reminds us that in American television "the first development was commercial and a public-service element was later added, in the margin or as palliative" (p. 31). M. Hansen (1991) discovers a similar history for film, pointing out that many "artistic" developments, like the feature film, came about as an appeal to "audiences who could afford higher admission fees, who had more leisure time and longer attention spans" (p. 62).

You Look Honest When You're Telling a Lie[7]

The bottom line, like it or not, is that a popular artist today must sell something, or go the "hobby" route and get another job. In fact, full-time artists of all kinds have always had to choose between commercial appeal and patronage, which are both kinds of selling; only the methods of selling have changed over the centuries. But today, a popular artist must not only make art that does not seem like art (pretentious!) and sell it to us without seeming like he is selling it to us (sellout!); he must often also do these things while maintaining his "authenticity" (phony!), which is equally difficult and mysterious, or at least elusive. For example, Bettie (1995) finds that people love the TV show *Roseanne* "because it is so 'real'" (p. 31), meaning that the characters seem like real people with real lives, and real problems and joys. I know what they mean—I quit watching it when Roseanne won the lottery and started having convoluted dream sequences.

Of course, none of those beliefs about the show were ever true, and we all, really, know that the show is *a show*—scripted, appropriately-lit, carefully-cast, and, like everything else, exhaustively market-researched. Cavicchi (1998) likewise finds that fans of another successful popular artist, Bruce Springsteen, like him and his music partially because he "has always been someone who has been associated with a certain authenticity" (p. 64); in other words, they feel that the man who writes the songs and sings them onstage is basically the man they might meet on the street. Of course, there is almost no evidence that this is true, either, since few of us really know *that* Springsteen, or ever will, and one can hardly make judgments about someone's character based on interviews, chance encounters on the street, or the kind of meet-and-greet sessions popular artists often construct to interact directly with fans. Besides, we have to admit that we don't even really *want* them to be real, or like us; we want them to be like us, but better, or funnier, or if-we-could-sing-like-that. We already know regular, *real* people, and if they were so entertaining, we wouldn't need television or records nearly so much.

This authentic/artificial, real/unreal line seems especially hard to draw these days, and our new media technologies aren't helping us make the distinction any easier. Benjamin's (1968) remark that "any man today can lay claim to being filmed" (p. 231) seems truer all the time, and the truer it becomes, the less we seem to be sure about what "true" or "real" is. "Reality" television is the most obvious example of this difficulty, with documentary film and literary "memoirs" close behind. The scandals about such popular arts being disingenuously scripted or otherwise manipulated are familiar and numerous, and besides, as my wife always says, "even if those people were real before the show started, after a season or two they aren't anymore." We used to have "actors" and well, the rest of us; now we have a seemingly endless supply of "television personalities." In some ways, we seem to have arrived at "the borderline between art and life," the popular arts as perpetual carnival, in the sense that "carnival does not know footlights," since "it does not acknowledge any distinction between actors and spectators" (Bakhtin, 1968/1984, p. 7). And when we consider the popular arts' license to openly flaunt the subversion of, disregard for, or outright rebellion against the moral and social codes of our time, the popular arts-as-carnival idea does seem fitting.

In fact, at first this carnivalesque property of popular arts today seems like a good thing. After all, we could all probably use the "temporary liberation from the prevailing truth and from the established order" (Bakhtin, 1968/1984, p. 10) that carnival provides, and Bakhtin promises too that it "offers the chance to have a new outlook on the world, to realize the relative nature of all that exists, and to enter a completely new order of things" (p. 34). However, Bakhtin extolls the virtues of carnival as he knew it: the scheduled, temporary disruption of everyday life; Bakhtin's carnival ridicules and elevates whatever it wants to, but for a limited time only. And as confusing as that carnival can be, mixing and sullying—"messying"—all that we know or thought we did, at least we know when it starts and ends. It is not so clear with the carnival that is popular arts, especially as digitization and the Internet have seemingly made those arts exist everywhere all the time. If cameras follow a family constantly, is it still a family, or is it a TV show? What if that family is the Obamas, or the Trumps?

All of My Maps Have Been Overthrown[8]

Our lives are so technologically mediated now, as well, that is hard to know what we are seeing or listening to, despite our demands for "authenticity." Some have even begun to wonder if we are "posthuman," thinking of our countless technological and media dependencies as relationships that make us not quite human, or maybe *more than* human, not sure if we are "handicapped" or early-stage cyborgs. And I must confess that Bluetooth, smartphones, and that guy with two prosthetic legs who almost made the Olympic track team have made me wonder. However, Sobchack (2004), who has a prosthetic leg, disagrees with this assessment, or at least insists that our prosthetics, whatever form they may take, are secondary (p. 205), and she urges us not to get "carried away" (p. 170). In fact, she argues that we must remember the "embodied and radically material nature of human existence" (p. 1). M. B. N. Hansen (2004) agrees, and asserts that the relative formlessness digitization has brought to new media makes the body—the authentic, real body—more important than ever: "simply put, as media lose their material specificity, the body takes on a more prominent function as a selective processor of information" (p. 22). Whereas the medium used to primarily determine how popular arts were experienced by the body, now the body can determine the medium through which the popular arts are manifested. To M. B. N. Hansen, "a bodily processing of the action" is what makes it "'real' for the participant" (p. 41). In other words, in this "'hallucinatory' dimension" (p. 41) that comprises so many of our media experiences today, *Roseanne* is "real" if it looks and sounds real to us, and Springsteen is "authentic" if our ears and eyes say he is.

So, to sum up the mess so far, a popular artist today must be "talented" but not "artsy," a "seller" but not a "sellout," and "real"—to us, whatever we decide that is (but not too real). And then, if he is still on his feet, he must express himself by correctly choosing from among a variety of digital media. And this step is no small feat, either. Just getting someone to see or hear a work in the popular arts is trickier than it used to be; in the old days, pleasing one of the well-funded and resourced gatekeepers was the biggest challenge. Pre-digitization, if the network or film production company or record label or supportive investor, etc., gave an artist the proverbial go-ahead, a large audience was often within reach. Now, the rules have changed as the media have digitized; new media have "made the classical spectator an object of nostalgic contemplation" (M. Hansen, 1991, p. 3). Or, to use Benjamin's words, "the cathedral leaves its locale" (1968, p. 221), and the works often seem to rush around chasing an audience who won't sit still. The popular arts have gained new legs, but now they must surely use them.

I Survived—That's Good Enough For Now[9]

Indeed, digitization has apparently made the life of the audience easier and that of the full-time popular artist more difficult for two reasons: choice and "potential for viewer mobility" (M. B. N. Hansen, 2004, p. 36). If an audience is loyal to a popular artist (or willing to be caught, as it were), choosing a media format (or multiple formats) can be a heaven of free creativity; for an artist without such an audience, it is surely a hell of indecision and frustrating trial and error. If he limits himself too much to one form, he risks being lost in the popular arts crowd, but if he makes himself too available, he risks sensory overload and interest saturation. And there is always the chance he never catches anyone long enough to even be rejected.

This highly competitive atmosphere for the arts has in fact been developing for some time, before widespread digitization, and it is only getting harder and harder to survive after it. Williams (1974/2003) has noticed that for media forms like newspapers and television, "the level of viability, the scale-mark of independent survival, rises continuously, and at times dramatically, as the general market is extended" (p. 38). Benjamin (1968) has pointed out, as well, that as arts have experienced more and more "emancipation" from particular times and places, those that travel well have gained in popularity and importance, since "it is easier to exhibit a portrait bust" than it is "the statue of a divinity that has its fixed place in the interior of a temple" (p. 225).

While Benjamin (1968) has argued that arts removed from their roots in a time and place would have to sacrifice the "aura of the work of art" (p. 221), some like Goodwin (1988/1990) have argued that digitization has changed the way we should even think about "aura," at least in music; for him, since there is "no discernible difference" between the sounds created in the studio and those captured and played back digitally, what we have is more like "mass production of the aura" (p. 259). This way of thinking about "aura" is problematic for some art forms (architecture being an obvious example), but it is interesting for others, like film, television, and photography. I would add, inspired by M. B. N. Hansen (2004), that it is perhaps our own personal experience of a digital work that gives it its "aura" in a new media world; for architecture, I still need to go there, but for many other art forms, digitization brings them to me, "aura" intact. Maybe that "aura" has to do with the time and place I first experience the film, or piece of music; maybe the sights and sounds and smells and memories I most associate with the digital work of art give it its "aura." And maybe, today Benjamin might say that those arts that are "emancipated" from *analog* roots have a better chance than those who cannot be adequately experienced digitally. Regardless, what is clear is that for better or worse, the arts are on the move and changing, both at various speeds, and it could be that some artists and art forms are not going to be able to keep up.

Indeed, and especially with the increased "emancipation" brought about by digitization, it seems that the world of popular arts has become increasingly (or maybe just more obviously) Darwinian; perhaps what looks like a mess in the popular arts is really just natural selection getting ready to do its work. To borrow from the biological sciences and Bob Dylan simultaneously, the times are a-changin' in the new media world of popular arts, and they who adapt best win. Without the gatekeeper system to all but guarantee safety or oblivion, the popular artists who best figure out how to connect through digital media with an audience receptive and loyal to their artistic expressions will be the most "successful"; those who make too many wrong moves or lack important skills at some stage in the new creation and distribution processes will, at least metaphorically, die off. Like any organism, those who want to live and prosper all over the world will have to be the most adaptive, while those who want local or niche success will need to connect most specifically and symbiotically with their respective audiences. In fact, perhaps even the digitization of information is evidence that "evolution is real and wondrous, and that the idea of natural selection has survived and succeeded because it fits the observable facts" (Quammen, 2006, p. 231). And perhaps the smallest of details will mean life or death in the popular arts, too, just as it has in our biological existence: Miller (2008) reminds us that the "key molecules of life" are constructed from just a few atoms, and if the chemical properties of these atoms "differed in a significant way, life would be quite different—or might even fail to exist at all" (p. 119).

I'm the Man Who Loves You[10]

Before examining what kind of popular arts organism Wilco is, or forecasting its chances for survival in its chosen ecosystem, I have a confession to make in the interests of disclosure: I am a Wilco fan. I have, on occasion, called them "the best band in America." I have also called them "the American Beatles" (not for the fame, obviously—for the artistry, and the mixture of melody and bold experimentation). In fact, Wilco is one of the few musical artists I don't know personally whose logo-emblazoned t-shirts I will proudly wear in public, and my 8-year-old son has been able to name members of the band for years now. On the other hand, I am not a president-of-the-fan-club type, nor do I even belong to a Wilco fan club. I don't like every song they've recorded, or every show they've played, and I don't think I would be awed in the least if I encountered any of the band's members in person. Long story short, I just generally really like what they do.

All of this is just to admit that I enter this discussion with a bit of bias tagging along. Lucky for me, such a study by a fan is not unprecedented, and other studies like this one have perhaps shown better than an "outsider" could that necessary symbiotic relationship between the popular arts and fans of them. For example, Penley (1997) writes NASA/TREK as a fan of both the space agency and the television show, and calls the fan-link between them "a collectively elaborated story that weaves together science and science fiction to help write, think, and launch us into space" (p. 9)—perhaps both figuratively and literally. Cavicchi (1998) also openly admits his appreciation for Bruce Springsteen in Tramps Like Us. In fact, he is proud to be a fan of "Bruce" and other musical acts, saying that his fandom has "gotten [him] through many tough times over the years and has been the source of many friendships, including [his] relationship with [his] wife" (p. 8). Cavicchi even devotes a whole section of his book to "becoming-a-fan-stories" (p. 86), and it is perhaps fitting that I begin my discussion of Wilco specifically with my own.

After a chance, premature experience with Wilco, I came to be a fan of the band much later, in the way that I imagine most people discover them: through word of mouth and testimony from musicians. My first experience with Wilco was also my first real rock concert, in the summer of 1995, not long after the band was formed from the ashes of alternative country legend Uncle Tupelo[11]. They performed as the opening act[12] of a traveling festival, the Horde Tour, headlined by Ziggy Marley[13], The Black Crowes[14], and Blues Traveler[15]. However, in 1995 those other bands were the ticket-sellers; if anyone came just to hear Wilco, I didn't see them. In fact, I was pretty underwhelmed by their set, and wrote them off. Years later, though, my little brother convinced me to give them another listen, and he gave me copies of two Wilco albums he was suddenly obsessed with: Summerteeth (1999) and Yankee Hotel Foxtrot (2002). This time around, I was much more interested and liked them even more than my brother, though it still took a while before I would call myself a "fan." But when I started my own band, met scores of musicians, and learned to hear differently, I was hooked, I think, for good.

You Can't Hear 'Em on the Radio[16]

Wilco is the kind of band that would have likely died out years ago, under the old models, but actually seems to be thriving under the new ones. If they get radio play, it's not near anywhere I've ever been. If they have had any "hit singles," I don't remember them. Nor do I recall any music videos—they have made a few, but mostly fan videos and concert footage show up on YouTube. They do, however, get pretty consistent coverage from music magazines and experience acclaim from music critics. They also have a loyal, "in-the-know" fan base. Most of these fans also know, and don't seem to mind, that Wilco is not really a very "marketable" band: they are too weird, have had a seemingly ever-changing lineup and sound, do not even try very hard to be photogenic, and by now are mostly in their forties and fifties. The attitude, from band and fans alike, seems to be that you either get Wilco, or you don't. But if you do "get" Wilco, finding another fan is truly a communal, relationship-building experience, and seeing them live inspires feelings of belonging, in which "the individual feels that he is an indissoluable part of the collectivity, a member of the people's mass body" (Bakhtin, 1968/1984, p. 255). And perhaps in the way Wilco interacts with the collective body that is their fans, there are clues to their continued success in the mess of new media popular arts.

Every Song is a Comeback

What you once were isn't what you want to be any more

—Wilco, "A Shot in the Arm," 1999[17]

Wilco have published ten full-length albums since the band's inception, not including two collaborative albums with artist Billy Bragg, some live recordings, the greatest-hits-type re-release project *What's Your 20?* (2014), or the decades-spanning collection of rarities and "B-sides" called *Alpha Mike Foxtrot* (2014). They have also participated in numerous "side" recording and performing projects in various solo and combo permutations with a number of other artists. Each one of these recordings is significantly and sometimes strikingly different, and very few fans agree on what their "best" album, or lineup, is. Sometimes fan websites and interview features even resort to graphs and charts just to explain their recording history (which is actually pretty helpful for new fans). They have also employed a variety of formats for their recorded work, from vinyl to CD to digital download, and many combinations thereof; their solution to the new media formatting wars seems to be to offer everything in almost every way imaginable, and let the fans decide. And speaking of offering everything, they sell many live recordings (available in a variety of downloadable formats) of their shows from their website (wilcoworld.net) in a section they call "roadcase."

However, they also seem to be very conscious and careful about formatting and design choices; they have won a Grammy award for their album packaging for *A Ghost is Born* (2004), and once, in a moment that would make Kilbourne (1999) proud, they decided to turn a planned live DVD into an audio-only CD because in shots of the crowd, "everywhere you looked, there were logos" (Moon, 2005, p. 105). Also, they tend to reward purchases of one format with a free (or nearly free) gift of their music in another. For example, *A Ghost is Born* (2004) came "enhanced" with a QuickTime file that contained a live performance, and *Sky Blue Sky* (2007) came with a link which allowed fans to download five more songs in mp3 format (three new ones and two live versions of songs on the album)[18]. My copy of the strangely self-titled 2009 seventh album, *Wilco (The Album)*, pre-ordered from their website, arrived in the mail on the release date in 180-gram "audiophile" vinyl format, accompanied by the CD version—all for $20, or roughly $2 more than a big box store would sell me the CD alone. When I ordered it, Wilco immediately let me download one of the album's songs for free[19]. I bought their eighth album, *The Whole Love* (2011)[20] much the same way, but I didn't buy the album after that at all—at least not at first. My appreciation for their music didn't change, but I actually didn't know the album was coming, and then suddenly discovered that they had released the inexplicably (absurdly?) titled project *Star Wars* (2015)[21] for free online. This was no tossed-off, second-rate collection, though—it is actually one of my favorites—and I eventually bought the CD from them anyway (I wanted the better sound as well as the packaging and liner notes). This album was also quickly followed by *Schmilco* (2016)[22], a very different-sounding album from *Star Wars* despite their close release dates, and when my copy arrived in the mail it was accompanied by an officially endorsed, Wilco-logo-and-artwork-emblazoned fake-chewing-gum-hand-shock toy. Yes, just like that one you thought was hilarious when you were ten years old.

If their lineup, format, and distribution choices are varied and often surprising, the actual music they produce is equally difficult to pin down. Critic Geoffrey Hines, in a review of *Sky Blue Sky* (2007), says that the melodies "consistently draw us in, but the songs never allow us to get comfortable" (2007, p. 64), a comment that could be applied almost anywhere in Wilco's catalog. So could his claim that "the great thing about pop music is the way it provides a license to grab from anything and everything to make a good song," which could almost serve as Wilco's motto. In their musical history, few musical genres have been left unturned, few instruments have failed to make an appearance somewhere, and really no kitchen utensil or hubcap or answering machine message seems out of the question as a musical resource. Even the lyrical content varies, from simple rock sing-alongs to sentimental love ballads to dark and disturbing imagist works to what almost seems like serious-minded, fine-arts-style poetry on songs like "Hummingbird"[23] from *A Ghost is Born* (2004). Tweedy apparently means it when he says, in a review of an Albert Ayler DVD, that an artist achieves "everything [Tweedy] find[s] virtuous in free music" when he "can play anything he wants" and "he's freed up his mind to the point where he can play like a little kid finger-paints" (Moon, 2005, p. 106, my brackets).

The music of Wilco has been described as both "roots music" and "experimental" and is, quite frankly, pretty hard to categorize: it changes often from album to album, but always somehow sounds like Wilco, and each time there is both something familiar and alien about it. "Avant-garde roots rock"? "Art-damaged Americana"? I never know quite what to tell people about it. Its roots stretch far enough back to claim strong influence from Woody Guthrie (the *Mermaid Avenue* projects with Billy Bragg[24] are full of songs built from old Guthrie lyrics), and its vision looks far enough into the future that Wilco's new albums often have to grow on their fans a while first, too; we have to catch up. In fact, Wilco seems to move and change as fast as the new media does, which is perhaps one of the keys to the band's success so far. The best way to explain the music of Wilco might be to quote two people who, so far as I know, don't even listen to them: David Brackett and Gilbert Seldes (pretty sure about the last one). Brackett (1995/2000) tells us that "frequently there is no single origin for the popular music text; and what is perceived by the audience as the emotional focal point of the song (the lead vocalist) may or may not be responsible for other aspects of the song's production" (p. 14). This is especially true in Wilco's case; people are drawn to different aspects of the band, varying even from song to song: maybe here it's the lyrics, there it's the guitar duel, over there it's the inventive bass line, or even the feedback-laden, programmed loop. Some think of Jeff Tweedy, the lead songwriter and singer, as a dictatorial-mastermind-poet figure, while others find whatever he is doing on each song to be the least important part. In addition, it is hard to even tell which musician is playing which part from song to song, or even what kind of instruments are making the sounds recorded on their albums. Live footage sometimes clears this up—

sometimes. Long story short, popular music in Wilco's hands seems to have few rules and very blurry edges. This is perhaps best exemplified by "Art of Almost,"[25] a seven-minute, often-abrasive blast of strangely interwoven melodies and rhythms from *The Whole Love* (2011) that seems like it can't decide if it wants to invite you in or kick you out. It's an unusual choice, perhaps, for an album-opening song, seemingly as much warning as welcome mat, but it is also a quintessential "Wilco" song.

However, interestingly enough, Seldes (1924/2001) gives us the impression that what Wilco does meets precisely his idea of popular music, saying that "the popular song is so varied, so full of interest, that for a moment at least one can pretend that it isn't vulgar, detestable, the ruin of musical taste, and a symptom of degeneracy" (p. 57). And perhaps "so full of interest" is the one quality that links Wilco's musical creations together, and keeps their fans eager to see what they sound like next time around.

I Need a Kamera

I need a camera
To my eye
To my eye, reminding
Which lies have I been hiding
Which echoes belong

—Wilco, "Kamera," 2002[26]

Aside from their lineup and sound changes and numerous side projects, Wilco is also different from many other bands today in their use of film as a way to express themselves artistically and entertain their fans. Music critics often half-jokingly call them the "most documented band in the world" mostly because they somehow manage, with little or no radio play, relatively small record sales numbers (only a few albums certified gold), and varying levels of label support, to stay both in the public ears *and* eyes. And, just as is the case with their music recordings, the films involving Wilco also vary widely, in content, format, and distribution, evident in three notable examples: *I Am Trying to Break Your Heart* (2003), *Shake it Off* (2007), and *Ashes of American Flags* (2009).

In the realm of visual media, it is unclear whether Wilco's members have chosen film over television, or whether the current media environment has chosen for them; as Williams (1974/2003) notes, "for many years yet, central programming and networking authorities are going to continue" (p. 153) to control television broadcasting, and until those organizations embrace Wilco, television, like radio, is not particularly feasible as a medium for their expression and connection with their audience. Film, especially since the DVD age, and even more so now in the streaming age, is much more accessible for the popular artists in the *of the people* sense. Not only is a film rendered on DVD or streamed online a lot cheaper and easier to both make and distribute than a film was pre-digitization, but since most people end up watching these films on their television screens or phones or tablets, the effect is as *popular* as television, but circumvents the networks' power to control what is broadcast.

Circumventing this corporate power is even one of the primary themes of the first film, *I Am Trying to Break Your Heart* (2003)[27], a theater release on 35-mm film that was later converted to a DVD version that features an additional 70 minutes of music and interview footage. Music critic David Fricke says in the substantial booklet that accompanies the DVD version that the film began as an attempt to capture "the soul of *Yankee Hotel Foxtrot*," Wilco's most famous/infamous album to date, and that the group was an interesting subject because of its "critical acclaim, audience devotion, and creative nerve." However, though Director Sam Jones began with the idea "to make a film that chronicled the making of a record from start to finish," the end result is a film that means a variety of things to a variety of people. Longtime fans get to see Wilco in the midst of the creative process, and get to watch them fight, and defeat, the record label executives who dislike the album's experimental sound so much that they fire Wilco upon the album's completion—only to have a sister label under the same corporate umbrella buy it back at multiple times the original cost. Aesthetes get to see devoted artists following their muse, no matter the obstacles or pressures. Musicians get to see some of the methods behind the magic, and also insight into complicated and combustible band dynamics (one member was fired just before the recording sessions; another just after their completion).

In many ways, *Shake it Off* (2007)[28] feels like a response, or counter, to the chaos and flux of *I Am Trying to Break Your Heart* (2003). The film comes as a DVD companion in a specially packaged version of the *Sky Blue Sky* (2007) album for only a few dollars more, and paints a much different picture of Wilco's inner workings—maybe to show balance, maybe to show growth or artistic maturity. In any case, the film is simple in content and execution, a strategy outlined from the beginning in Tweedy's remarks that "the world is so mysterious and so scary and kind of terrifying right now...I just want somebody to sing me a song." And that is what Wilco does, performing "live" in their loft many of the tracks on *Sky Blue Sky* (2007), interspersed with commentary about the songs' origins or development and peaceful footage of the band playing, shopping for instruments, or interacting like a happy family of artists. In contrast to the passive-aggressive hell that seemed to engulf the band during the recording of *Yankee Hotel Foxtrot* (2002), Wilco would have us see them now as a sort of idyllic, idealistic musical collective, comfortable in its skin and with the direction in which it is headed artistically. Despite confessing to the pressures of being Wilco's CEO-figure as well as "having people say they like you, say that they want you to keep being something that they can like and believe in," Tweedy insists that this version of Wilco is just "a band that feels really comfortable with the notion of just sitting down and playing some songs together."

Finally, *Ashes of American Flags* (2009)[29] is a film portrait of the band on the road, released exclusively on DVD, but featuring a link when loaded into a computer that allows fans to download directly from Wilco's website audio mp3s of all of the songs featured on the DVD—all for the price of a normal album ($15-$20). This time around, Wilco, comfortable in the relative stability of a few years with the same lineup, is interested in articulating an artistic position and showcasing its prowess as a live band in front of audiences around the country. For example, the DVD was timed to be released on "National Record Store Day" only at small record stores, with big box stores having to wait two more weeks. In fact, the anti-corporate theme carries throughout the film, from member Pat Sansone's interests in Polaroid photography ("capturing these little pieces of a fading America with a fading technology") to bassist John Stirratt's testimony against the "Walmartization of Southern towns." Tweedy also takes the opportunity to defend the virtues of "representational art" and his interests in the musical version of it, and also warns against over-thinking popular music by saying that those who "rationalize and philosophize about it" are ultimately "just trying to catch the wind."

The properties specific to this new media are used to great effect by Wilco, and are perhaps a model for other popular artists; these films are primarily documentaries of a sort, offering glimpses of and information about Wilco unavailable through other means. For example, the "televisual spectator" of Wilco "can see things from places—and hence, from perspectives and points of view (and it is not trivial that these are often more than one)—where his or her body is not (and often never can be) situated" (Weber, 1996, p. 116). In other words, fans watching Wilco's films have far more access to the band, onstage and off, than is available through their audio recordings. On the other hand, though "television *overcomes* distance and separation," it "can do so only because it also *becomes* separation" (p. 116); we can get closer to the band in some ways, but we are ultimately not backstage, even if the camera is. Because of this separation, films are always "creating something," and the camera serves just as much "as an instrument of distortion as of reproduction" (Seldes, 1924/2001, p. 339).

This distance and separation can actually be a positive aspect of film in the hands of popular artists like Wilco; a band that is so meticulous about the details of albums and packaging can use the film "screen" to make carefully articulated statements about its identity and artistic purposes. Panofsky (1997) says that the "problem is to shoot unstylized reality in such a way that the result has style" (p. 123), and this is exactly what Wilco seems to have done. These films often seem to be aiming for a new media version of the "onstage film lecturer" (M. Hansen, 1991, p. 96) popular in the early 1900's. They have, through film, joined images of the band making and performing its music with discussions of both, as well as sometimes award-winning cinematography (*Ashes of American Flags*) that lets the band musically, verbally, and visually say exactly what it wants to.

Words Without a Song[30]

We've got solid-state technology,
Tapes on the floor,
Some songs we can't afford to play

—Wilco, "Red Eyed and Blue"[31]

These lines are part of a song from the 1996 album *Being There*, but they could actually serve as a preface to what is perhaps Wilco's most interesting artistic venture to date, *The Wilco Book* (2004). Though at first glance a hardcover codex hardly seems to belong in a discussion about how a band succeeds in the new media world of popular arts, *The Wilco Book* is no ordinary book, to say the least. It is a quirky, surprising collection of various things Wilco, and also includes a number of things that are best described as "peripheral," in the way that footnotes are both part of the standard text and also not part of it. This book, in fact, is like a book of *only* footnotes; it has no plot, little in the way of linear structure, a confusing authorship (to put it mildly), and has no discernible aim or purpose, except that it is "about" Wilco and assumedly for people who like them. Rather than one text, the book is more like many texts of various kinds, loosely connected by little more than some association with Wilco and the two thick covers at the front and back. Between those two covers can be found some sample of almost every part of a popular musical artist's world: stories, poetry, interviews, essays, pages from notebooks, discussions of popular aesthetics, visual art, photo journalism, art photography, diagrams of stage setups, pictures of instruments, a CD of alternate takes and sound experiments, and a host of other things that don't fit easily into any category already established.

Before the book is even opened, it is theoretically and philosophically interesting. Weber (1996) says that in television, "far and near are no longer mutually exclusive but rather converge and overlap" (p. 125); as if to show him that his scope is too limited, the cover of the book frustrates the clarity of the giant letters announcing the title on the spine by showing a picture of what is presumably the band in their dressing room. I say presumably because no band member's face can be seen. The camera angle (a shot of a mirror reflection, no less) is such that a flier, vanity mirror lights, and the edge of the cover obscure the band members' faces, as if to foreground the idea that we will be both let in and kept out of that inner sanctum. In fact, maybe even digitization is too narrow a way to delineate new media possibilities, since *The Wilco Book* (2004) is a great example of how analog and digital, old and new, can interact in interesting ways.

In addition to the near/far issues, the artists responsible for this work seem to have listened closely to Barthes (1977), who says "to give a text an Author is to impose a limit on that text, to furnish it with a final signified, to close the writing" (p. 147). *The Wilco Book* (2004) bears the stamp of no author on its cover or spine, and is attributed vaguely in a few places only to "Wilco and PictureBox, Inc." (p. 17). Instead, the book opens with a blue and white graphic image, followed by what we only find out later is a notebook-scribbling exercise designed to stave off Tweedy's panic attacks, followed by 15 pages of selections from a work called *Found Poetry* by Bern Porter. When we finally find the "Contents" section of the book, we discover that the "Bern Porter" part was chapter one, chapter two will be devoted to "The Loft" where Wilco write and record, chapter three will be all about their instruments (mostly pictures), and chapter six will be about "Time." All told, there are nine "chapters," seven appendices, and an "Interlude" which features writing by Henry Miller and graphic art by Fred Tomaselli. This "Contents" section is followed by a two-page photo of the power lines that serve as the supply for "The Loft," and then one featuring the band's suitcases.

Was I lost the first time I tried to read *The Wilco Book* (2004)? Yes. However, I also eventually decided that it was the best book about any band I had seen, as it somehow captured more of what I wanted to know about Wilco than any band biography or interview could. And though it does not directly subvert mainstream culture or level any political hierarchies, I found in this book something like what Bakhtin says about carnival, that "the boundaries between the play and life are intentionally erased. Life is itself on stage" (1968/1984, p. 258). What is usually prominent about Wilco (released albums, biographies, etc.) is here ignored, and what is usually ignored or kept hidden is now on display. I realized that what I really want to do is go to the Loft, look at their instruments, hear snippets of their philosophies about music, see some of their influences firsthand, read what an expert says about them, talk to their sound engineers, flip through their notebooks. Even see what kind of suitcases they use. And if I still don't feel, after "reading" the whole book, that I understand everything about Wilco that they have to say, I find out that's okay; Tweedy is there, on page 109, to remind us that he's "really suspect of the idea that there's ever been a fully realized piece of art," and that we should be, too.

Ultimately, *The Wilco Book* (2004) causes what Benjamin might call a "deepening of apperception"; to steal directly from him his comments about another book, "this book isolated and made analyzable things which had heretofore floated along unnoticed in the broad stream of perception" (1968, p. 235). The work is also Darwinian in that it is (r)evolutionary as a media form and also exhibits the interests of the scientist himself, being "enamored, as ever, with the beautiful significance of tiny details and the big truth of interconnectedness" (Quammen, 2006, p. 240). It is an artistic masterstroke from a band that has so far been a successful adaptor in the new media world of popular arts because it has been able to wed the best of the old and new in a time of media flux; it has been able to "make some sense out of this mess." *The Wilco Book* is evidence, surely, that in the popular arts, too, we "live in a universe that is simply brimming with evolutionary possibilities" (Miller, 2008, p. 134).

Theologians, They Don't Know Nothing About My Soul[32]

The lesson we learn in studying Wilco is much the same lesson Cavicchi (1998) says we learn from studying Bruce Springsteen: it is generally assumed that "ordinary people should learn about the world from the intellectual theories of academics," but it is also true that "academics, in turn, can learn much about the world from the folk explanations of ordinary people" (p. 10); to do so these scholars must "start being more relevant, start engaging the ideas of the people about whom they write" (p. 189). What we need today, if we are to help our students "find a way" in the mess of new media, is a theologian with soul, or Gramsci's "organic intellectual" (Hall, 1996, p. 268). This kind of academic lives both inside and outside the academy, responsible for not only being "at the very forefront of intellectual theoretical work," but also for "transmitting those ideas, that knowledge, through the intellectual function, to those who do not belong, professionally, in the intellectual class" (p. 268). He must be the academic who remembers that there is life worth living on both sides of the academy walls. He must be the one who remembers, as well, that there are still doors and windows joining those two worlds, and he must live in those "liminal" spaces (Owen, 2011, p. 2), literally and figuratively on the *threshold*, making sure that those "evolutionary possibilities" (Miller, 2008, p. 134) do not go unrecognized.

Coda

The "organic intellectual" Gramsci describes, the "liminal scholar" I've written about—they're not much different than the "teacher-theorist" to which this book has been devoted. *Of course* the world needs specialists, and we benefit immensely from the talented, focused, deep-divers among us who go where few of us can, or want to, follow. But we also need more people-between, intermediaries, translators in the literal and metaphorical sense, who help us talk to each other and remind us how blurry the edges are between fields the world over, whether those fields be physical or academic. I owe a great deal to the theorists in my education who wanted to be even more, and I hope there will be plenty of teachers to follow who want to do the same. As Frost (1992) noted, "something there is that doesn't love a wall," and I hope we won't continue to build more of them than we need. Maybe "good fences make good neighbors" (1992), but I bet a good conversation—a thoughtful one that lasts, full of substance, and understanding, and goodwill—I bet that works even better.

References

Bakhtin, M. (1984). *Rabelais and his world* (H. Iswolsky, Trans.). Bloomington, IN: Indiana University Press. (Original work published 1968)

Barthes, R. (1977). *Images, music, text.* New York, NY: Hill and Wang.

Benjamin, W. (1968). The work of art in the age of mechanical reproduction (H. Zohn, Trans.). In H. Arendt (Ed.), *Illuminations* (pp. 217-51). New York, NY: Schocken Books.

Berger, A., Winton, B., Winton, C., Hustwit, G., & Vanco, J. (Producers), & Jones, S. (Director). (2003). *I am trying to break your heart* [Motion picture]. United States: Plexifilm.

Bettie, J. (1995). Roseanne and the changing face of working-class iconography. *Social Text, 45*(14), 125-149. Durham, NC: Duke University Press.

Billy Bragg and Wilco. (1998). "California Stars." *Mermaid avenue* [CD]. New York, NY: Elektra.

Brackett, D. (2000). *Interpreting popular music*. Berkeley, CA: University of California Press. (Original work published 1995)

Canty, B. (Producer/Director), & Green, C. (Producer/Director). (2007). *Shake it off* [Motion picture]. United States: Nonesuch.

Canty, B. (Producer/Director), & Green, C. (Producer/Director). (2009). *Ashes of American flags* [Motion picture]. United States: Nonesuch.

Cavicchi, D. (1998). *Tramps like us: Music and meaning among Springsteen fans*. New York, NY: Oxford University Press.

Frost, R. (1992). Mending wall. In *Robert Frost: Selected poems*. New York, NY: Gramercy Books.

Goodwin, A. (1990). Sample and hold: Pop music in the digital age of reproduction. In S. Frith & A. Goodwin (Eds.), *On record: Rock, pop, & the written word* (pp. 258-273). London, UK: Routledge. (Original work published 1988)

Hall, S., Morley, D., & Chen, K.-H. (1996). Stuart Hall: *Critical dialogues in cultural studies*. London, UK: Routledge.

Hansen, M. (1991). *Babel and Babylon: Spectatorship in American silent film*. Cambridge, MA: Harvard University Press.

Hansen, M. B. N. (2004). *New philosophy for new media*. Cambridge, MA: The MIT Press.

Himes, G. (2007, June). Speak what you feel. *Paste, 32*, 64.

Kilbourne, J. (1999). *Can't buy my love: How advertising changes the way we think and feel*. New York, NY: Touchstone.

Kuenz, J. (1995). It's a small world after all. In The Project on Disney (Ed.), *Inside the mouse; Work and play at Disney World* (pp. 54-78). Durham, NC: Duke University Press.

Miller, K. R. (2008). *Only a theory: Evolution and the battle for America's soul*. New York, NY: Viking.

Moon, T. (2005, December). Live and kicking: Wilco's Jeff Tweedy picks his most essential live albums of all time. *HARP*, 104-109.

Owen, Jr., D. P. (2011). *The need for revision: Curriculum, literature, and the 21st century*. Rotterdam, NL: Sense Publishers.

Panofsky, E. (1997). Style and medium in the motion pictures. In I. Lavin (Ed.), *Three essays on style* (pp. 93-123). Cambridge, MA: The MIT Press.

Penley, C. (1997). *NASA/TREK: Popular science and sex in America*. London, UK: Verso.

Pichaske, D. R. (1999). Poetry, pedagogy, and popular music: Renegade reflections. *Popular Music and Society, 23*(4), 83-104.

Quammen, D. (2006). *The reluctant Mr. Darwin*. New York, NY: Atlas Books.

Rice, D. (2003). *O* [CD]. New York, NY: Vector Recordings.

Seldes, G. (2001). *The 7 lively arts*. Mineola, NY: Dover Publications, Inc. (Original work published 1924)

Sobchack, V. (2004). *Carnal thoughts: Embodiment and moving image culture*. Berkeley, CA: University of California Press.

Weber, S. (1996). Television: Set and screen. In A. Cholodenko (Ed.), *Mass mediauras: Form, technics, media* (pp. 108-128). Stanford, CA: Stanford University Press.

Wilco. (1995). *A.M.* [CD]. New York, NY: Sire/Reprise.

Wilco. (1996). *Being there* [CD]. New York, NY: Sire/Reprise.

Wilco. (1999). *Summerteeth* [CD]. Burbank, CA: Warner Bros.

Wilco. (2002). *Yankee Hotel Foxtrot* [CD]. New York, NY: Nonesuch.

Wilco. (2004). *a ghost is born* [CD]. New York, NY: Nonesuch.

Wilco. (2007). *Sky blue sky* [CD]. New York, NY: Nonesuch.

Wilco. (2009). *Wilco (The Album)* [CD]. New York, NY: Nonesuch.

Wilco. (2011). *The Whole Love* [CD]. Easthampton, MA: dBpm.

Wilco. (2014). *What's Your 20?* [CD]. Easthampton, MA: dBpm.

Wilco. (2014). *Alpha Mike Foxtrot* [CD]. Easthampton, MA: dBpm.

Wilco. (2015). *Star Wars* [CD]. Easthampton, MA: dBpm.

Wilco. (2016). *Schmilco* [CD]. Easthampton, MA: dBpm.

Wilco and Picture Box, Inc. (2004). *The Wilco book.* New York, NY: Picture Box, Inc.

Williams, R. (2003). *Television.* London, UK: Routledge. (Original work published 1974)

Appendix to Chapter 11

1. Wilco. (1999). "Nothing'severgonnastandinmyway (again)." Summerteeth. Burbank, CA: Warner Bros.
2. Wilco. (1996). "What's the world got in store?" Being there. New York, NY: Sire/Reprise.
3. Owen, D. (2004). "Cold Savannah blues." Once out loud.
4. Wilco. (2002). "Poor places." Yankee Hotel Foxtrot. New York, NY: Nonesuch.
5. Rice, D. (2003). "Eskimo." O. New York, NY: Vector Recordings.
6. Wilco. (1999). "When you wake up feeling old." Summerteeth. Burbank, CA: Warner Bros.
7. Wilco. (1996). "misunderstood." Being there. New York, NY: Sire/Reprise.
8. Wilco. (2007). "You are my face." Sky blue sky. New York, NY: Nonesuch.
9. Wilco. (2007). "Sky blue sky." Sky blue sky. New York, NY: Nonesuch.
10. Wilco. (2002). "I'm the man who loves you." Yankee Hotel Foxtrot. New York, NY: Nonesuch.
11. Uncle Tupelo. (2002). "Graveyard Shift." 89/93: An anthology. New York, NY: Sony Legacy.
12. Wilco. (1995). "I must be high." A.M. New York, NY: Sire/Reprise.
13. Marley, Z. (1988). "Tomorrow People." Conscious party. London, UK: Virgin.
14. Black Crowes, The. (1990). "Hard to Handle." Shake Your Money Maker. Los Angeles, CA: Def American.
15. Blues Traveler. (1994). "Run-Around." Four. Santa Monica, CA: A&M.
16. Wilco. (2004). "The Late Greats." a ghost is born. New York, NY: Nonesuch.
17. Wilco. (1999). "A shot in the arm." Summerteeth. Burbank, CA: Warner Bros.
18. Wilco. (2007). "The Thanks I Get." Sky blue sky (extra track). New York, NY: Nonesuch.
19. Wilco. (2009). "You Never Know." Wilco (The Album). New York, NY: Nonesuch.

20. Wilco. (2011). "Born Alone." The Whole Love. Easthampton, MA: dBpm.
21. Wilco. (2015). "Random Name Generator." Star Wars. Easthampton, MA: dBpm
22. Wilco. (2016). "Someone to Lose." Schmilco. Easthampton, MA: dBpm.
23. Wilco. (2004). "Hummingbird." a ghost is born. New York, NY: Nonesuch.
24. Billy Bragg and Wilco. (1998). "California Stars." Mermaid Avenue. New York, NY: Elektra.
25. Wilco. (2011). "Art of Almost." The Whole Love. Easthampton, MA: dBpm.
26. Wilco. (2002). "Kamera." Yankee Hotel Foxtrot. New York, NY: Nonesuch.
27. Wilco. (2002). "I am trying to break your heart." Yankee Hotel Foxtrot. New York, NY: Nonesuch.
28. Wilco. (2007). "Shake it Off." Sky blue sky. New York, NY: Nonesuch.
29. Wilco. (2009). "Ashes of American Flags." On Canty, B. (Producer/Director), & Green, C. (Producer/Director), Ashes of American flags [Motion picture]. United States: Nonesuch.
30. Wilco. (2002). "Pot kettle black." Yankee Hotel Foxtrot. New York, NY: Nonesuch.
31. Wilco. (1996). "red-eyed and blue." Being there. New York, NY: Sire/Reprise.
32. Wilco. (2004). "Theologians." A ghost is born. New York, NY: Nonesuch.

About the Authors

Stacey T. Brown is the Coordinator for the International Baccalaureate Diploma Programme for a school district near Augusta, Georgia, where she has been teaching high school English since 2002. She has a doctorate in Curriculum Studies from Georgia Southern University. Her research and writing focus on solitude and isolation of the individual, commodification, standardization, and monoculture in education, and the private-and-public intellectual.

John Cato holds a doctorate in Curriculum Studies from Georgia Southern University. He has been an educator since 1997, teaching mathematics and physics. His research interests include expertise, acquisition of knowledge, systems of logic, and identity. He has previously published "Mindset Matters" (The Physics Teacher, 2011).

James Grant is a recent doctoral graduate of Georgia Southern University's Curriculum Studies program. His primary interests are cultural and media studies within the context of curriculum, with a focus on how the monstrous emerges across those categories, or rather, how the aesthetics of works of Horror translate to an understanding of the twenty-first century classroom, be that classroom in a school building or in the broader sense of culture. He has been an educator since 2009, and has worked at the middle and high school levels in private and public institutions, teaching classes in English, debate, and film.

Dana Compton McCullough has taught middle school science and language arts, 5th grade science, math, and language arts, and various high school science classes for 26 years near Augusta, Georgia. She holds a doctorate in Curriculum Studies from Georgia Southern University. She currently teaches Advanced Placement Biology and Forensic Science, and hosts a school wide event known as Wear Red to Honor Henrietta Lacks with her students. The event emphasizes the connections between science instruction, literature, and social justice.

David P. Owen, Jr., teaches and writes in a variety of fields in Augusta, Georgia. He is a liminal scholar whose research interests include literature, popular music, cultural curriculum studies, film and television studies, Southern studies, complexity theory, aesthetics, technology, and philosophy. His works include *Fireflies: Memory, Identity, and Poetry* (Brill | Sense Publishers, 2017), *The Need for Revision: Curriculum, Literature, and the 21st Century* (Sense Publishers, 2011), *Once Out Loud* (2004), and *William Blake's "The Everlasting Gospel": A Hypertext Edition* (University of Georgia, 2001).

CPSIA information can be obtained
at www.ICGtesting.com
Printed in the USA
LVHW031558130522
718729LV00012B/773

9 781645 040224